D0455691

The Future of Terrorism

The Future of Terrorism

ISIS, AL-QAEDA, AND THE ALT-RIGHT

WALTER LAQUEUR

AND

CHRISTOPHER WALL

THOMAS DUNNE BOOKS
ST. MARTIN'S PRESS
NEW YORK

THOMAS DUNNE BOOKS.
An imprint of St. Martin's Press.

THE FUTURE OF TERRORISM. Copyright © 2018 by Walter Laqueur and Christopher
Wall. All rights reserved. Printed in the United States of America. For information,
address St. Martin's Press, 175 Fifth Avenue, New York, N.Y. 10010.

www.thomasdunnebooks.com
www.stmartins.com

Design by Meryl Sussman Levavi

Library of Congress Cataloging-in-Publication Data

Names: Laqueur, Walter, 1921– author. | Wall, Christopher, 1989– author.
Title: The future of terrorism : ISIS, Al-Qaeda, and the alt-right / Walter Laqueur
    and Christopher Wall.
Description: New York, N.Y. : Thomas Dunne Books, [2018] | Includes bibliographical
    references and index.
Identifiers: LCCN 2017059935| ISBN 9781250142511 (hardcover : alk. paper) |
    ISBN 9781250142528 (ebook : alk. paper)
Subjects: LCSH: Terrorism.
Classification: LCC HV6431 .L3476 2018 | DDC 363.325—dc23
LC record available at https://lccn.loc.gov/2017059935

Our books may be purchased in bulk for promotional, educational, or business
use. Please contact your local bookseller or the Macmillan Corporate and
Premium Sales Department at 1-800-221-7945, extension 5442, or by email at
MacmillanSpecialMarkets@macmillan.com.

First Edition: July 2018

10 9 8 7 6 5 4 3 2 1

CONTENTS

PART 2

CONTEMPORARY TERRORISM

PART 3

REFLECTIONS ON TERRORISM

The Future of Terrorism

INTRODUCTION:
TERRORISM AND ITS FUTURE

AFTER THE DEATH OF OSAMA BIN LADEN IN MAY 2011, PRESIDENT Obama declared that al-Qaeda no longer posed a threat to the United States and that the danger of terrorism was receding. Yet within three years, his words became hollow with the rise of Islamic State (IS; known as ISIS but referred to throughout this book as IS) and continued plotting by al-Qaeda. Since that fateful day in May, both IS and AQ have expanded their reach across North Africa, the Middle East, and South Asia, inspired thousands to travel to join their fight, and executed violent atrocities like the November 2015 Paris attacks, the March 2016 Brussels Airport bombing, and the August 2017 vehicle attacks in Barcelona. The public wants to know, of course, why this is happening and when it is likely to end. There has been a deluge of literature published in the past decade that has tried to answer these two questions, but much of it is incomplete in its analysis, fails to explore the structure of terrorism, or approaches the topic with specifics that are too technical for a general audience.

The fact is that terrorism is a phenomenon rife with inconsistencies, conspiracies, mixed ideologies, and the ability to generate immense fear, which is exploited by both politicians and terrorists alike. This has made giving an objective accounting of the subject nigh impossible largely because in the public sphere, there is no common ground in terms of a definition, modality, or strategic purpose. All that people understand is that seemingly chaotic events conspire to bring about tragedies and death, and that victims and perpetrators launch accusations and counteraccusations about responsibility and guilt. Little effort is made to help the public understand what distinguishes terrorism from other forms of political violence waged by nonstate actors, such as guerrilla warfare or insurgency, especially when terrorists often obfuscate the distinctions in their propaganda and their justifications for violence. Adding to this confusion is the way terrorism portrays itself. Until recently, few terrorist groups ever identified as such, and even fewer would argue that their violence was not justified either from a humanitarian perspective or from a strictly moral view. In addition, for most of the time it has been in use as a tactic, terrorism has seen groups emerge from all over the ideological spectrum: the violent left-wing intellectuals of Europe, the brutal fascists in Germany and Italy prior to World War II, and various groups from all the world's major religions. Not surprisingly, given its persistence and variability in structure and ideology, the use of the word *terrorism* often degenerates into an ad hominem used by political rivals to sully their opponents and their policies.

Today, terrorism has the ability, more than ever, to upend the global political order. IS's advance across northern Iraq not only left thousands dead through horrific acts of violence but also sought to challenge the very concept of the nation-state by erasing the borders between Iraq and Syria and establishing a pan-Islamic political entity that claimed sovereignty over the world's entire Muslim population. In the West, brazen plots by IS and al-Qaeda helped usher in populists in both Europe and North America with decidedly Islamophobic messages. In the United States and the United Kingdom, politicians offered extreme and radical solutions to the problem of terrorism that threatened to upend their liberal-democratic political charters. In both instances, these individuals were elected. Claiming terrorism is a violent act inextricably linked to a particular religion or part of the world is not enough. One needs to learn its historical background to understand what terrorism actually is and how to define it. Only then can we contextualize modern terrorism, because we will have a paradigm for evaluating brazen new acts committed by any future terrorist entity. Aside from history, there is a critical need for explorations and explanations of the actors as well as the jargon associated with the modern terrorist threat. This includes terms like *lone-wolf terrorism*, the idea of the caliphate, propaganda of the deed, the various branches of both IS and al-Qaeda, and even the terrorist groups unassociated with these movements. Finally, it is imperative to understand the rationale and reasoning for terrorism. The scary truth, despite what the media suggests, is that terrorism is not the product of psychosis or irrationality; if anything, it is an extremely logical and reasonable form of political violence that produces results. Yet despite this and the way terrorists portray themselves to the world, in the final analysis, they are nonstate actors that commit violence against non-military targets outside of war zones to fuel an emotional response that will affect the politics of a group, society, nation, or even continent. This, by every extant legal convention, is both illegal and without justification.

As one of the authors of this present effort, I, Walter Laqueur, first wrote of terrorism more than forty years ago, when the field was quite in-choate and few had bothered to give a systematic accounting of the phe-nomenon. In my book *Terrorism*, I noted that terrorism was one of the most widely discussed issues of the time but also one of the least understood. In the years that have passed, interest has not waned but rather has grown exponentially as other great dangers seem to have receded. More than a quarter century after the Cold War's conclusion, with new risks of conflict between world powers and permanent ecological disaster on the horizon, is the enormous amount of publicity for terrorism justified, or is its impor-tance and prevalence exaggerated? We shall return to this question later.

Recent manifestations of terrorism have been described in countless books, monographs, articles, plays, novels, and movies, with varying de-grees of sophistication. Terror has fascinated metaphysicians and popular novelists alike. The causes of terrorism, its financial sources, the distinc-tion between terrorism and guerrilla warfare—these and many other issues have been debated and commented upon in many quarters and in various languages. It is perhaps noteworthy that there is little about this subject written in Arabic (other than publications created by IS and other such organizations) or in Russian, even though it can be taken for granted that the phenomenon has not escaped the attention of the Russian policy mak-ers and secret services. But what could be the reason for the neglect of terrorism in Arab literature?

What has been very seldom discussed with the general public is the ef-ficacy of terrorism in changing the very structure of government. An example would be 9/11. Historians, political scientists, and others have written at length in their technical journals about how it shaped the political character of the United States, its allies, and other countries—giving voice to hawkish leaders and restrictive legislation—but rarely is the public fully briefed on domestic or international structural changes. The attacks on New York and Washington had an enormous impact on public opinion and on policy makers, especially in the United States, but also in other countries. The attacks led to the establishment of the Department of Homeland Security, and according to *The Washington Post*, the employment of "about 200,000 contractors and about 188,000 federal employees," not including "uniformed members of the Coast Guard."* This is a larger staff than most other U.S. government agencies. Following the attacks, NATO activated Article V of its charter in a show of solidarity with the United States, enmeshing member states into the prolonged conflict that is Afghanistan. But in what way have the events of 9/11 changed the international balance of power? This is hard to measure. Since that morning, the United States has prioritized conflicts in the Middle East and has diverted resources it would have used to counter or, at the very least, accommodate the rise of China in the western Pacific. This focus on the Middle East has meant that would-be terrorist leaders have been in the United States' crosshairs, undoubtedly hastening their deaths. Indeed, given how skilled the United States has become at killing terrorists, there was a joke for a while that the surest way to die was to become al-Qaeda's third in command, given how frequently American drone strikes targeted them. Not surprisingly, this gave space for China to assert itself and work toward asserting hegemony in the Pacific, knowing that the United States was too immersed in conflicts of choice to bother responding. It is doubtful that this was al-Qaeda's objective. China both opposes the group's long-term ambitions of a caliphate that rules the world and represses its Uighur population, a minority Muslim sect in the western part of the country.

To what extent have those attacks and their aftermath promoted the aims of those who initiated and carried them out? It precipitated the wars in Iraq and the subsequent rise of IS, but it is debatable to what extent the war was the result of al-Qaeda's brilliance or miscalculations on the part

---

* See Ed O'Keefe, "At Homeland Security, Contractors Outnumber Federal Workers," *Washington Post*, February 25, 2010, accessed November 17, 2017, http://www.washingtonpost.com/wp-dyn /content/article/2010/02/24/AR2010022405433.html.

of the governments of the United States and Iraq. For all the influence of these terror groups, they cannot outmaneuver an organized and well-formed government capable of enacting reform to deprive terrorist groups of further victories and, with them, new recruits. This seems to be the reason why, in the seventeen years since 9/11, no operation of similar magnitude has been carried out, despite the worldwide networks of al-Qaeda and IS. This is not to predict that similar attacks will not happen in the future but only to say that it seems unlikely.

Indeed, the most recent indications are that IS's push to establish a new caliphate has been a failure. By trying to "liberate" territory, IS exposed itself to counterattacks by superior forces and was driven from many of the regions it had previously captured. This happened despite the fact that those in the fight to counter IS never used their full strength en masse when seeking to uproot it. The battle for Aleppo started in July 2012 and ended in December 2016. If there had been a truly determined effort to dislodge the conquerors, it could have ended in a matter of months, if not weeks. Aleppo was fought by the corrupt and weakened Assad regime, facing serious defections and other international constraints, and it still managed to withstand the pressure. If anything, Assad held back because an overwhelming attack killing even more civilians would truly bring the wrath of the international community, which, unlike IS, is capable of removing him from power. If Assad can hold off a protracted terrorist insurgency waged by multiple actors and claim victory, can al-Qaeda and IS really pose a threat to strong and stable Western governments?

Regardless, the world's leading terrorist organizations are bound to continue. The parts of the world hardly touched by the impact of terrorism in the last fifteen years will likely become targets in the near future. Militants are mobilizing in Southeast Asia. Attacks there were common shortly after 9/11, but slowed down following a concerted counterterrorism policy by the various countries in the region. This appears to be a temporary lull, as militants in the Philippines are emerging once more, undoubtedly inspired by successes experienced by terrorist groups in other parts of the world. Above all else, though, the United States and Europe are experiencing greater threats by terrorists than before. In these latter two theaters, the fighters are often returning from the battlefields of the Middle East, but local supporters who have been radicalized in recent years will soon join the action as well. The sheer multiplicity of threats has left security services in Europe overwhelmed and the United States seeking new measures to monitor the challenge posed by latent militants.

The issue of winning over new supporters through radicalization is an interesting and important one, and it has not yet been studied sufficiently. In the public discourse, the tendency has been to impute a more deterministic role to religion or to poverty, without taking into account the full universe of terrorist operations throughout time. Moreover, it highlights two relatively new features of terrorist operations: the lone-wolf phenomenon and internet indoctrination. The First Amendment of the United States Constitution protects freedom of speech, but should those protections be extended to include advocacy for and the dissemination of terrorist propaganda? These freedoms are not as protected in Europe and other parts of the world, making the United States a curious case study. There is a similar problem with the mobilization of recruits for any terrorist operation. While Europe has taken steps to criminalize this behavior, in the United States, the right to assembly gives a degree of protection, as long as the goal is not the commission of a crime. What differentiates between student groups exercising their freedom of speech and individuals organizing to further the actions of a terrorist group? One need look no further than the various American organizations that provided aid to the Irish Republican Army during "the Troubles," which the American government failed to criminalize and prosecute.

Maintaining this temporal awareness is necessary. It is far too easy to imbue the current era with a brand of uniqueness that it does not possess or, in the other extreme, turning it into a skeleton key for understanding all terrorism throughout history. In fact, a just chronology of terrorism begins in antiquity and most likely dates back further into prehistory. It precedes the political structures and institutions that animate this form of political violence. Even looking solely at modern terrorism, which dates back to the eighteenth century, there are stark generational differences that make it hard to generalize about terrorism. Professor David Rapoport, the retired UCLA political scientist, popularized the idea of modern terrorism occurring in waves. To the current moment, he has divided these waves into four distinct periods. The first covers the time before the First World War. He claims that it began in Russia in the 1880s, with the anarchists, before spreading elsewhere. There were a great many terrorist attacks, primarily in Europe, many of which were carried out by those drawing inspiration from the Russian example, targeting kings, prime ministers, generals, and other important figures. The second wave followed the signing of the Treaty of Versailles and was marked by a push for decolonization waged by nationalist movements around the world. This lasted until shortly before the start of the Vietnam War. The third wave emerged from those taking cues from the Vietcong and its ability to stymie the American war machine in Indochina. As such, it comprises mostly left-wing terrorism in Europe and elsewhere, including the Palestine Liberation Organization (PLO). This wave is commonly referred to as the New Left. The fourth and current period covers the attacks carried out by radical Islamists and other religious groups. It began during the 1970s in several Arab countries, with the deposition of the shah in Iran as the pivotal moment. In the beginning, it centered mainly on the Arab-Israeli conflict. In later years, terrible conflicts in a variety of Muslim countries came to the fore. The four-wave categorization is neither neat nor discrete. There certainly was overlap between decolonization movements and the emergence of the New Left. In fact, the third wave in many ways continued well into the early years of the current millennium, as the Tamil Tigers were not defeated until 2009. There is utility, nonetheless, in this ordinal classification, as it helps isolate the gradual evolutionary process that makes terrorism deadly.

THE CHANGES WROUGHT BY THE FOURTH WAVE

The fourth wave identified by Professor Rapoport continues unabatedly to the present day, and the concept has been widely accepted. It has been rightly remarked that a terrorist wave seems to last for about one generation, which suggests first and foremost that further research into the generational issue is necessary. Why were certain generations radicalized while others were not? These questions have been neglected perhaps because most of the research in modern terrorism has been conducted in English-speaking countries, and America and Britain were largely spared violent youth revolts. The attacks on 9/11 energized a surge of American and British scholars to consider terrorism from a modern perspective, which of course meant focusing on the Middle East. This created an academic environment in which many young scholars were driven to deduce universal explanations for a problem while studying cultures with which they were not intimately familiar. Their conclusions were marked by myopia, bound as they were by time, place, and their own cultural biases.

This is not to discredit their research. It nevertheless raises a question. Are we inhabiting a parallel historical situation to those who wrote the volume of scientific literature about the geocentric model of the universe, only for Copernicus to come along? Is it possible that even now terrorism is one of the least understood phenomena of our time? The number of articles and studies has now grown a hundredfold since the idea of the fourth wave was first postulated, and included in this body of work have been many contributions that greatly add to our collective knowledge. However, as mentioned earlier, some central issues for one reason or another have not been the subject of research and comment. Yet it is also true that in this immense collection of literature, there is much that is obviously untrue, and nonspecialist readers will experience considerable difficulty finding their way through the maze of claims and counterclaims. Above all, terrorism tends to change and, quite often, change beyond recognition.

For perspective, consider the introduction to my book *Terrorism*, dated April 1977. At that time, Anwar Sadat was still in power in Egypt, as was the shah in Iran. The Middle East was relatively quiet but for the Palestinian-Israeli conflict, which had been going on for thirty years. The "recent manifestations" of terrorism were scattered all over the globe; in Latin America, for instance, but most prominently in Europe. The Basque ETA figured prominently in the media, and so did the Italian Red Brigades and the German terrorist groups of the extreme left. The Soviet Union still existed. In brief, it was a very different world from that of the year 2001, let alone that of today.

The introduction to *The New Terrorism*, a follow-up volume written in the last year of the previous century, begins as follows:

> Four hundred twelve men, women, and children were hacked to death by terrorists on the night of December 29, 1997, in three isolated villages in Algeria's Elizane region. Four hundred perished when a group of the Shah's opponents burned a cinema in Abadan during the last phase of the monarchy in Iran. There were 328 victims when an Air India aircraft was exploded by Sikh terrorists in 1985, and 278 were killed in the Lockerbie disaster in Scotland in 1988 which was commissioned by Libya's Colonel Khadafi and car-

ried out by terrorists. Two hundred forty-one U.S. marines lost their lives when their barracks were attacked by suicide bombers in Beirut in 1983; 171 were killed when Libyan emissaries put a bomb on a French UTA plane in 1985. The largest toll in human life on American soil was paid when 169 men, women, and children died in the bombing of the Alfred P. Murrah Federal Building in Oklahoma City in 1995.

The world's situation has changed since 2000, and the Middle East has transformed even more dramatically. Colonel Qaddafi (then transliterated as Khadafi) is dead, but the danger of terrorism in Libya has by no means vanished. The experts at the turn of the century mentioned the possibility of Libya becoming a new Syria, the danger of southern Libya becoming the focus of a new attack, and the fears of a new terrorist drive from the south of this country toward the north.

These facts and figures of the last year of the last century, most of them forgotten today, seem less alarming when compared with the happenings since. Many more people perished in the attack on the World Trade Center than in all the events just mentioned. True, *The New Terrorism* included a chapter entitled, "Terrorist Motives: Marx, Muhammad, and Armageddon," and also sections that discussed the far right and exotic terrorism, but it was not yet clear that the age of jihadism had already dawned. The terrorist movements that preoccupied politicians and the media alike (such as Baader-Meinhof, the Red Brigades, and ETA) had either disappeared or were on the way out. It was an interregnum for terror worldwide. Having invaded Afghanistan in 1979, the Soviet Union withdrew its armed forces a decade later. American forces would not enter the country until late 2001.

Everything seems to be different today because it truly is different. Not only has the geography of terrorism changed, but in most ways its character has too, along with its aims and the way it manifests itself. Most of the terrorist groups of the past no longer exist or they have gone dormant; and the different terrorist groups that are more prominent now did not even exist two decades ago or were insignificant. The Middle East, and the Muslim world in general, has never been entirely free of terrorism, but its prevalence there now when compared to other regions is staggering. To mention this fact has been deemed inappropriate or tactless, and why this should be the case will be discussed further on in some detail. The differences between terrorism in ancient times and now, or even between the nineteenth century and now, are so profound that a number of basic questions arise.

How can the study of the past help us forecast the future of terrorism? When terrorist groups of the past claimed to be enacting struggles against tyranny, were they justified in a way that today's groups would not be if they made such claims? The prophets of the new caliphate seem to have nothing in common with the age of Ali Baba and Harun al-Rashid. The leaders of the new terrorism, including self-appointed caliphs, do not belong to the camp of freedom fighters in the contemporary world, but the word *terrorism* implies a lineage between them and Gerry Adams, Renato Curcio, or, going further back, the idealist youths in the Narodnaya Volya. An attempt to provide answers to these and similar questions will be undertaken in the present study.

Likewise, the majority of the literature on terrorism from the 1970s is correct, but this is because it refers almost entirely to descriptive accounts of individual terrorist movements such as the Irish Republican Army (IRA). A group that dates back to the late eighteenth century in various forms, the IRA is an offshoot of the Irish movement for national independence. This motivation for terrorism is unique to Ireland, although it shares similarities with other separatist groups in Europe that found themselves enthralled with the notion of nationhood following the French Revolution. How applicable is this to cases where such fervent nationalism is not at stake? When this form of terrorism abounded, there was very little scholarship on the topic, nor was there for many years after. Even if the acts of terrorism remained outside the bounds of scholarly research, were the causes of terrorism the subject of research? Have historians investigated why it occurred in some countries, during certain periods, and not others? There have been a multitude of theories on these lines, but none of them satisfactory. Why was there terrorism in Uruguay, one of the most developed countries of Latin America, in the 1970s, but none in Honduras, one of the poorest? The connection between economic trouble and terrorism was commonly cited, but subsequent (and more meticulous) research has shown that such a connection did not exist and still does not exist.

With greater justification, one could point to a connection between failed states and the spread of terrorism. Terrorism has occurred during the last two decades quite frequently in Africa, but not always in the very poorest nations. When nation-states fail, the reasons are usually manifold. Terrorism is unlikely to be the sole, or even the primary, cause. Years of inept governance, corruption, and other forms of political violence are much more likely culprits. There is a correlation between failed states and terrorism, but it seems to be a post hoc situation where terror groups take advantage of the de facto sanctuary offered by ungoverned spaces. Again, though, this follows after a state has collapsed and not before, as was the case in Somalia.

Another theory places the blame for the rise of terrorism on the occupation of sovereign territory by foreign countries. This was certainly the case in Afghanistan and some other highly publicized cases, but this theory does not apply to most. Few theories are entirely wrong (usually a few examples can be found to confirm just about any theory), but this idea has been discredited by the tendency to stretch the meaning of occupation. In the universe of terrorist campaigns, the association between occupation and terrorist violence is of such limited scope that it is questionable this idea has much purchase outside of narrow academic circles.

Psychopathology has been presented as a crucial factor in some particularly outrageous instances of contemporary terrorism, especially with regard to sadistic actions, including throat cutting, rape, the abduction of young girls for purposes of prostitution, burning people alive, and slavery. Atrocities of this and other kinds were not uncommon in Europe in antiquity and during the Middle Ages. It was also common throughout the conquest of the Americas and much of the early modern period, until the Enlightenment and its elevation of widespread legal constraints proscribed such cruelty. Such practices have occurred more recently; mainly in Africa, but also in other continents. Recent outbursts of violence seem to be a continuation of these practices and the undying idea that one's enemies should not only be eliminated but must also suffer grievous bodily harm in the process. In this sense, this problem is not unique to al-Qaeda or members of Islamic State. Psychopathology may well be involved in various manifestations of contemporary terrorism. Nonetheless, the cause for such brutality must have different justifications. The *how, why,* and *when* must be further investigated in connection with IS and like-minded groups. They seem to believe in methods of torture, not altogether dissimilar from the Spanish Inquisition and other European institutions that focused on religious outsiders, "witches," and other scapegoats. In Europe, torture devices such as the breaking wheel apparatus and breast rippers were mainly used for extracting confessions or information. In contrast, the torture practices of the so-called Islamic State are used primarily for punishment and spreading fear. Yet the effect seems to be the same and perversely mirrors the governments these organizations wish to destroy, such as the brutal Assad regime.

From psychopathology emerges a neglected area of inquiry on which we must focus: the nature and ecology of evil. Julia Kristeva, a French psychoanalyst of Bulgarian origin, became interested in this subject and remains one of few scholars who deals with it in her writing. Few have used her lens to explore terrorism. The peculiarities of terrorist movements in the Middle East, Africa, and Central Asia have been examined in many studies and need not be reiterated. Only the important differences between this kind of terrorism and earlier traditional kinds will be briefly noted. One question avails over and over: for all their idealism and their desire to advance the cause of their movement, why commit such violent acts that scream of inhumanity? Ignored, meanwhile, is the reason why some terrorist groups seem to exercise restraint, even when killing, and others engage in wanton bloodshed aimed at dehumanizing and obliterating victims through mutilation, decapitation, immolation, and other depredations.

Given the terrorist violence seen over the last decade, more important than examining the causes of terrorism is the question of what the future of terrorism holds. The most pressing question: How long will the present fourth wave last? The members of terrorist groups are not just radicals but fanatics. This is of particular importance when trying to understand the fourth wave. Yet again the phenomenon of fanaticism has hardly been studied, even at a time when acts of terrorism by suicide have become quite frequent (though not unique to the present, as evidenced by the kamikaze pilots in World War II and examples from other regions and periods). The most attention paid to the fanaticism phenomenon came from psychoanalysts. They concerned themselves with explaining Europe under Adolf Hitler and Communism, as well as what motivated people to rationalize and accept vile acts. This literature is dated, though, and the fanaticism associated with Nazism and Communism was quite different from that of terrorist movements, and even more specifically with that associated with IS. Whether its suicide attacks, rape, and pillage contextualized with religious meaning, the acceptance of brutality by its followers is start-ling. This continues even after its atrocities have been publicized and its failures become evident. Its fanatics remain convinced of the superiority of their cause. There is a potent degree of denial among the most radical ter-rorists. They pick and choose embellished facts that point to impending victory when, on the whole, the number of casualties for their movement are high and unsustainable. They are unable to cope with the concentrated on-slaught of nation-states. As will be explored later, the majority of terrorist movements fail, and yet fanatics have made an art of auguring some victo-rious outcome, which serves to inspire new terror groups as they "learn from the past" and try new approaches and strategies.

While most terrorist movements are doomed to fail, some have achieved marginal success, sometimes by modulating their violence, some-times through their enemies' mistakes, and frequently with self-inflicted wounds. Normally what happens is that they achieve some short-term tac-tical success that cannot result in sustained dominance or change. Terror-ist tactics like the hijacking of planes, for example, do not result in any ultimate control. Originally common in the 1970s, hijackings produced results until more effective controls on airports prevailed, along with the growing unwillingness of governments around the world to permit the landing of hijacked planes. These governments did not want to manifest sympathy or solidarity with hijackers. But above all, there was an absence of significant gains from these early hijackings—until the strategy evolved to include significant landmarks as crash points. This was the intention of the 1994 Air France hijackers who intended to attack the Eiffel Tower. They failed, but al-Qaeda consummated this approach in September 2001.

Another important change in the strategy and tactics of the terrorism associated with Salafist jihadist groups, particularly in the Middle East, has been the emphasis on the liberation (or domination) of territory, rather than attacks against individuals. This is curious for a few reasons. Success in conventional conflict is measured by the amount of space conquered in the shortest amount of time possible. Furthermore, this emphasis on con-quest brings them closer in operational design with the traditional guer-rilla groups of the twentieth century. The "liberation" of territories created obvious targets for counterterrorist forces that had not existed before. The advantage of the classical terrorist was the absence of territory, which made it easier to fade away and disperse after an attack. Counterterrorists were forced to allocate resources to gathering intelligence, tracking terrorists, and eliminating them. The problem for the terrorist group that considers geographic dominion a victory is that their continued legitimacy is based on being able to hold and administer the conquered territories, which is quite difficult for violent ideologues who know nothing about governing. Holding territory also means that terrorists must operate out in the open, making them easy targets for the modern air forces of most developed countries.

Among the "national liberation movements," several organizations stand out for their success using terrorist methods—the Mau Mau in Kenya, for instance, but also the Vietminh in Vietnam, the National Liberation Front (FLN) in Algeria, and Fidel Castro's movement in Cuba. However, terrorism itself was not the reason these movements prevailed. From a purely military point of view, for example, the French were successful in Algeria: they managed to stamp out the rebellion. But in the end, France was no longer strong enough to hold on to Algeria. Their victory, while complete, involved the use of torture, which helped mobilize the largely neutral Arab public, swelling the ranks of the FLN. Meanwhile, metropolitan France found itself disgusted by the wanton abuse of power by the French paratroopers, which went against the very values of French republicanism. It is worth remembering that in the 1950s, France did not view Algeria as a colony but rather as a "department" of the country, meaning this violence was meted out against French citizens, greatly delegitimizing the government, its methods, and its policy in Algeria. Ultimately, the FLN succeeded because the French public no longer supported the war effort. Disentangling the cause and effect of this conflict is impossible, but attributing success exclusively to the FLN's adoption of terrorism is impossible. One could realistically argue things might have been different had France not been so heavy-handed in its treatment of Algeria's Arab population, and even with the FLN's violence, Algeria would still form part of France.

In this context, it is worth considering what IS accomplished in 2014. The liberation of territories and the proclamation of a new caliphate generated an aura of great power, almost invincibility. But these impressions were (as the setbacks of the IS movement in 2016/2017 were to show) exaggerated and at times misleading. These so-called liberated territories were sparsely populated or unpopulated. Nor has it ever been clear to what extent these territories were under the control and governance of their "liberators." A common trope justifying this position was the supposed wealth IS had because of its control of oil fields and the advantages this conferred the organization in terms of maintaining its war-fighting capabilities. Those taking such a maximalist stance misunderstood the nature of terrorist groups. IS had engineers in its ranks, but few knew how to run oil fields. Any potential wealth would quickly dissipate due to the lack of a bureaucracy capable of extracting oil and selling it on the open market. This was even before the United States and its allies began targeting IS directly, which would only drain this wealth further. Indeed, a recent paper by Princeton professor Jacob Shapiro and a team of researchers from the World Bank demonstrates this.* Using satellite imagery, these scholars measured IS's oil production, detailing how most analysts overestimated the amount of oil sold and how unsustainable the group's oil-funded strategy of conquest was.

Most recently, IS has attempted to reframe its evident military defeats as temporary setbacks, claiming that the "caliphate" will continue in a virtual form despite desertions and loss of prestige. It will continue plotting and inspiring plots across the Middle East and Europe. Most likely, in the latter case, it will impel reforms and investments in the security sector that will blunt the long-term efficacy of these plots. That has been the tendency with terrorist movements in the past: to innovate, to succeed in the short term, and to find their lack of organizational capacity keeps them from achieving what they have in mind. Unless terrorist groups acquire nuclear weapons, this will likely continue to be the pattern, which should give readers cause for optimism. Terrorism's future depends more on how governments and societies react and learn to anticipate these challenges. If countries are proactive, if they calibrate their security and intelligence communities to these problems, the impact of terrorist activity will be blunted. Indeed, one can imagine an alternative universe where IS never emerged had the government in Iraq not been so capricious and so willing to alienate its Sunni population.

What about the geography of violence? In our time, terrorist operations are often based in Muslim countries or in countries where Muslims

---

* See Quy-Toan Do, Jacob N. Shapiro, Christopher D. Elvidge, Mohamed Abdel Jelil, Daniel P. Ahn, Kimberly Baugh, Jamie Hansen-Lewis, and Mikhail Zhizhin, "How Much Oil Is the Islamic State Group Producing?" (policy research working paper 8231, World Bank, Development Research Group, Poverty and Inequality Team, October 2017), accessed November 18, 2017, http://documents.worldbank.org/curated/en/239611509455488520/pdf/WPS8231.pdf.

constitute a significant part of the population. The question of why this should be the case has been discussed in great detail, but it is worth exploring. Does Islam preach violence to a greater extent than other religions? Appeals for violence can be found in the Old as well as the New Testament. The attitude of the Israelites toward the Philistines was not one of pacifism; and in Christianity (for instance, in the Gospel of Matthew), much can be found in the way of aggression and violence. The age of the Crusades constitutes another example. Meanwhile, the Qur'an (Sura al-Baqara) says, "No compulsion in religion." According to commentators, this statement referred to the faith of a girl in Medina who had been born Jewish, but raised Muslim, and eventually rejoined her tribe. Violence in the name of religion is not limited to Islam, and militant conversion is not a central tenet (and is, in fact, denounced) in Islamic scripture.

That said, appeals for a holy war in the present day are more numerous. There has been, in recent decades, a wave of religious fanaticism. Similar spikes have occurred in past centuries. The original expansion of Islam in the age of Muhammad came to a halt soon after the successful advance of its militants, who conquered North Africa and reached France by way of Spain, eventually halting at Tours and Poitiers in 732. The Franks were victorious, and the Arab forces had to retreat not only from their conquered French territories but also from most of Spain, excluding Al-Andalus, which remained in their hands for a long time thereafter. Some magnificent buildings in Granada and Cordoba bear witness to their presence. Later, the Turks reached Vienna twice—once in 1529 and again in 1683. This campaign was initiated by Suleiman the Magnificent, but his forces were defeated by an army of soldiers from a variety of countries. Popular songs like "Prinz Eugen, der edle Ritter" (Prince Eugene, the Noble Knight) are remembered to this day in connection with the "Turkish War," which lasted some fifteen years. But it is highly doubtful that these campaigns should be considered motivated by religion. They were wars between great powers, not primarily wars of religion, though it is worth reflecting on whether and how they have influenced the modern era. The present wave has, in all probability, to do with the weakened state of many Islamic countries. True again, the countries in which most Muslims live (such as Indonesia and India) have hardly been affected. Even in the countries in which most militant fighters and suicide terrorists have appeared, the overwhelming majority of the Muslim population wants a quiet life and often takes a dim view of the activities of the young militants who have been so prominent in the media. This should give readers pause when hearing the claims linking religion and terrorism, as the correlation from a historical perspective appears spurious.

Nevertheless, considering the predominance of explicit terrorist activity in Muslim countries, the source texts of Islam should be studied more deeply to determine their roles. Often, in public discourse, these texts become obfuscated or juxtaposed to the point that they are presented as one single, coherent whole, claiming to represent all of Islam. In teasing them apart, it is important to understand the modern Islamic terrorist mind-set. Many believe that Taqi ad-Din Ahmad ibn Taymiyyah (hereafter referred to as Ibn Taymiyyah), who lived from 1263 to 1328, was an important figure. He was a religious scholar, Damascus-educated, but frequently deviating from the then contemporary religious dogmas. This led to frequent incarcerations, during which he managed to produce influential works. In his writings, Ibn Taymiyyah sought the return of Sunni Islam to its early days and its early interpretations of the Qur'an. Seen in this light, he was a forerunner of progressive radical movements in Islam such as Salafism and Wahhabism. Ibn Taymiyyah is best remembered now as the godfather of jihad through his declaration of holy war against the Mongols. In his lifetime, a great expansion of Mongol power took place, and Damascus was twice occupied by the invaders. Such declarations had rarely taken place before (or were extremely infrequent) because in earlier centuries Islam had been the expanding power.

The origins of Wahhabism were in a then-remote part of the Arabian Peninsula. Wahhabi teachers (ulema) gained prominence in the region, which became the Kingdom of Saudi Arabia. The years of greatest influence of the Salafi movement began in the nineteenth century and continued up to the 1980s, declining thereafter. The founder of the movement, Muhammad ibn Abd al-Wahhab, was born around 1700, and he took a harsh stance on Muslims who attempted any innovation to the original concepts of Islam. He declared them, and anyone who disagreed with his stance, completely outside of Islam. However, the remoteness of the area in which these events took place caused the movement's influence outside Saudi Arabia to remain quite limited. That said, a strain of Wahhabism has always been important in Saudi domestic and foreign policy, and the movement gained a certain influence and some steadfast followers in far-away Egypt. To this day, all extremist Muslim groups are known as Wahhabi in Russia (particularly in the Caucasus), quite irrespective of their real character and inspiration.

Salafism is another distinct orthodox, revivalist movement in Islam. The name is derived from the word *salaf* (predecessor), role models of the past whose lives can be used as guides for followers in order to more closely observe the original admonitions and proscriptions of the Qur'an. Salafism appeared on the scene in the late nineteenth century in Egypt. Followers usually emphasized their closeness to the teachings of Ibn Taymiyyah. This movement was largely confined to Egypt. Since its decline, "Salafi burnout" has entered the language as a slang phrase to denote a surge of radicalism among the young generation followed by a quick disappearance. Today, Salafism is used interchangeably to describe Islamic terrorist groups by nonspecialist commentators. This is wrong. This book explores the concept in further detail later, but it is worth mentioning now that while there is a correlation between Salafism and terrorism, a Salafi follower is not necessarily a supporter of terrorism. One of the tasks this book hopes to accomplish is demystifying some of the commonly used vocabulary and bringing sense to a variety of movements that seem to share elements, but are inspired or caused by a varying array of phenomena.

The last two major changes concerning terrorism deal with the concept of so-called lone-wolf terrorists and, later, the concept of the caliphate. When the term *lone wolf* arose in the 1970s, the average American citizen would have sooner guessed it referred to a literal solitary beast than a human danger. Today, sadly, it is a household term that refers to a relatively new species of terrorism. Especially following the 2005 London bombings, there has been a desire to attribute great potential to the destructive power of these individuals over that of organizations like al-Qaeda. Some of the most highly regarded terrorism scholars forged a career from that moment, claiming that al-Qaeda was becoming irrelevant and the main terrorist threat was from radicalized individuals acting alone (but according to shared values and beliefs). Similar predictions were made by other highly placed scholars and government officials across the world. They were proven wrong both by al-Qaeda's continued plotting and its formation of franchises across the world, and later with the rise of IS. Of course, owing to the ambiguity of language and the desire to generalize with limited data, lone wolves are a highly debated concept. Firstly, lone wolves are not a totally new phenomenon. They have appeared time and time again in the history of terrorism, especially during the apogee of the anarchist movement. It reappeared in the United States when Timothy McVeigh bombed the Murrah Federal Building in Oklahoma City. Indeed, the phrase was first associated with Louis Beam, a notorious white supremacist who wrote a tract called *Leaderless Resistance* in 1962.

Secondly, and more controversially, it is questionable how much validity the concept has in explaining the current wave of terrorism. In the aforementioned London bombings, the initial belief was that the attacks were committed by homegrown radicals who learned to manufacture bombs from instructions found on the internet. Later it emerged that there was a nexus between the bombers and al-Qaeda. More recently, the same story line played out with the cargo truck driver who plowed into pedestrians in Nice, France. He had been in contact with a variety of Muslim radicals. While instances of homegrown radicals committing attacks do exist, a general trend is that some link to a terrorist organization usually emerges after the fact, undermining the explanatory power of the lone-wolf hypothesis.

Similarly, when the caliphate was mentioned fifty or sixty years ago, people would probably think of Harun al-Rashid as he strolled the streets of Baghdad at night, or of the beautiful Scheherazade telling her endless stories, or perhaps *Ali Baba and the Forty Thieves*. Alexander Orwin's recent essay, "In Search of the Vanished Caliphate," begins this investigation with drawing our attention to the Qur'anic origins of the caliphate:

Terse Qur'anic verses such as 2.30, 10.14, 10.73, and 38.26 already contain the general meaning of the term without explaining its specific implications. By means of a long and murky historical process that we cannot begin to explore here, the requirements of divinely ordained rule and succession expressed in the verses came to be embodied in a concrete institution. The 8th and 9th centuries, the Umayyad and Abbasid Caliphates ruled the entire Muslim world. Long after these mighty empires went the ways of all the powers of the earth, the sacred aura surrounding the Caliphate refused to dissipate. Deprived of all real political power by the 10th century, the Caliphate managed to subsist more or less continuously for another millennium, outliving countless empires and dynasties. It succumbed to the powers-that-be only in 1924, when Ataturk sought to usher in a new republican age by putting the old imperial Caliphate to rest. Its last figurehead, Abdulmecid II, was bundled ignominiously into a train bound for Europe.[*]

The contemporary idea and concept of the caliphate has mainly to do with the political program of IS. The caliphate concept goes back a very long time, even though it is not mentioned in the Qur'an or the Hadith. For a long time, it referred to the belief that Ottoman Sultan should be the protector and leader of all Muslims. It was disregarded for several centuries, but again became a factor of some prominence in the 1770s. It was again dismissed and eventually dropped altogether in the 1920s, when the last Sultan, his family, and his closest aides were exiled.

In World War I, the Turks made a half-hearted attempt to gain the support of Muslims in India through the invocation of the caliphate, but it was a total failure. There are allusions to this attempt in John Buchan's novel *Greenmantle*, a fine read but not at all reliable as a historical source. That the concept is again of great interest today has mainly to do with a changing political environment. Arab extremists do not want a Turkish sultan as their protector. The revival of the caliphate idea during the last decades of the twentieth century owed mainly to two political figures. The first was Abdülhamid II, who became the Turkish sultan in the 1870s. He was a poet, a wrestler, and an enthusiastic traveler, and he was fascinated by the caliphate idea. Abdülhamid II has entered Western popular culture as an almost magic and mystical figure. His sanity was doubted in a variety of books and even early silent movies. The other key figure was a major religious-political thinker named Rashid Rida. In a book published in 1922, Rida gave enthusiastic support to the caliphate idea. However, neither individual had a decisive impact on the subsequent fortunes of what we now call the caliphate. Such a support came only when IS, one of the most well-known terrorist groups of our time, absorbed the caliphate idea into the very center of its religious-political ideology and propagated it in a variety of manifestos, preaching the "old gospel" suitable for youths in the contemporary world. However, the activists who became the leaders of

---

[*] Alexander Orwin, "In Search of the Vanished Caliphate," *Current Trends in Islamic Ideology* 21 (March 2017): 5.

this movement were not figures of high caliber and magnetism and were not likely to be accepted by wider sections within Muslim communities. The self-appointed present caliph is Abu Bakr al-Baghdadi. The U.S. government has announced a reward of $25 million for his capture. This should have greatly added to his popularity among some radical segments in the Arab world, but he still has not been accepted as a major religious or political authority.

These are but a few examples of the great changes that have taken place in the discussions on the upsurge of Islamic terrorism. The extraordinarily intense public discourse on terrorism certainly centers on the fact that terrorism has been a top priority of the international political agenda for some time. Terrorism is as old as the trees. It predates, for obvious reasons, conventional warfare, but it never was a factor of such zealous interest until now.

Has this, perhaps, to do with the fact that there are more victims of terrorism than in the past? According to one well-known and respectable survey, approximately eighteen thousand people were killed in terrorist actions in 2013 (17,958 to be precise).* The great majority of terrorist attacks took place in five countries—namely, Iraq, Afghanistan, Pakistan, Nigeria, and Syria, in this order. But the number of those who died from heart disease that year was about forty times higher. Even the number of deaths from exotic diseases was exponentially higher than the number of terrorism victims. It is crucial to put our observance of and focus on terrorism in this way. However these figures are established, there is no doubt that terrorism is not the greatest peril facing mankind at the present time. This could change if, or when, terrorists acquire weapons of mass destruction. Thankfully, this has not happened yet, and our question concerning the reasons for the dominance of the terrorism debate in international discourse therefore remains unanswered.

Such statistics thirty or forty years ago would have presented a very different picture. European countries, Latin American countries, and of course countries at the center of the Arab-Israeli conflict would have figured on top of the list of countries affected by terrorism, and Nigeria would have probably not appeared at all. Furthermore, despite the necessity of

---

* Kathy Gilsinan, "The Geography of Terrorism," *Atlantic*, November 18, 2014, accessed November 18, 2017, https://www.theatlantic.com/international/archive/2014/11/the-geography-of-terrorism /382915/.

attempting to answer such questions, lists concerning individual countries are still not wholly reliable. If we do not have trustworthy figures for the German victims who perished during the last year of World War II (knowing how meticulous the Nazi Party was with record-keeping), we must pause before relying on figures from nations that lack the resources and systems to undertake such scrupulous research.

This brings up another important issue of debate, largely how terrorism is defined and discussed. Given the focus on the Middle East in recent years, this has opened terrorist scholars to accusations of Islamophobia and ignoring acts of violence perpetrated against civilians by nation-states. This type of argument is not unique. A few decades ago, some terrorism observers, mainly from the left, denounced the mainline experts in this field for ignoring what they called "state terrorism." It is, of course, beyond doubt that many more people have been killed throughout history as a result of wars and other forms of political violence, but terrorism in contemporary usage means something very specific. It has nothing to do with World War I or II. The attempt to disregard this fundamental truth usually stems from the wish to obfuscate differences for political reasons, or even to justify terrorist operations. Indeed, as early as 1977, we noted that finding a generally agreed-upon definition of terrorism would probably never succeed, and this has thus far proven to be correct. This is the case because terrorists, their victims, and their opponents will not agree on a common denominator, such as a mutually agreed-upon authority. Even inside these camps the most basic disagreements will not disappear. It is true that a clear definition of terrorism is highly desirable (not only because of the legal aspects it entails), but arriving at one still remains beyond our capacity. Perhaps the only observation that can be made without fear of contradiction is what has been said about pornography: you know it when you see it.

All the changes and discussion outlined so far have made their way into the public discourse and have become part of the political vocabulary in a very confused manner. With the rise to power of a new administration in 2017, terrorism remains very much at the top of the national agenda in the United States. President Trump promised that the terrorist movements would be obliterated, and he even mentioned the possibility that nuclear weapons would be used to that effect. Trump claimed that he knew more about terrorism and the ways to combat it than the generals, but there have been no striking successes in the war on terror during the first year of his administration. He dropped a massive bomb in Afghanistan, which had great psychological ramifications for those present, but he did so without a decision about his strategy for the country, preventing the United States from capitalizing on its impact. President Trump also promised to defeat the ideology of radical Islam, and he made certain promises concerning the illegal entry of refugees from Muslim countries. But this proved difficult. A sizable number of American citizens are Muslims, making it unclear how a travel ban could be carried out without violating the United States Constitution. Moreover, he seems to underplay the threat posed by right-wing terrorism. Given the cast of his administration, it is more likely that the language of terrorism is a rhetorical device used to mask some of the xenophobia he has adopted from such colorful characters as Steve Bannon and Stephen Miller, the latter being the author of the original executive order that sought to ban Muslims. In other words, President Trump has yet to articulate a counterterrorism strategy and seems reliant on the same ideas developed by President Obama.

In Europe, the issue has taken on a more palpable tone because of the larger number of attacks committed there. With attacks in Paris, London, Nice, Manchester, Barcelona, and elsewhere, the continent has suffered more terrorist violence compared to the United States. There too, much like the United States, terrorism has become politicized to mask obvious xenophobic tendencies, but it seems that the western part of the continent is more familiar with and resistant to those ideas than the United States. By the middle of 2017, both Marine Le Pen of France and Geert Wilders of the Netherlands had campaigned on staunchly racist platforms and lost their elections. Nonetheless, the specter of racist right-wing populism remains prominent, and becomes more so as nationalist parties obfuscate sober discussions on the challenge of terrorism by blaming citizens of their own countries. At the end of 2017, right-wing extremists held massive protests in Poland, resurrecting old fascist slogans, and in October, the extreme right came to power in the Czech Republic. At this point too, Viktor Orbán has been in power since 2010, making him at the time of this writing, the third-longest-serving prime minister in Hungary's history.

By confusing and mudding the conversation on terrorism, these politicians do a disservice to their citizens. As can be seen from this introduction, the study of terrorism is already one fraught with inconsistencies, mutable variables, and disagreements over the very meaning of the concept, and when biased individuals monopolize the media to speak untruths, the public suffers. It is no wonder that for many outsiders, understanding terrorism seems to require some sort of hermetic training to unravel the various threads informing it. With all these ideas introduced, it is worth outlining what comes next. The purpose of this book is to serve as a guide for nonspecialist readers wishing to make sense of terrorism. This book is not exhaustive in the topics it covers and cannot give a full taxonomy of what is and what is not to be considered terrorism, detail every terrorist movement in existence, or give robust leadership profiles. Instead, this book will endeavor to provide a general profile of modern terrorism for the lay reader.

As such, this book is divided into three sections. The first is a condensed history of terrorism, covering the earliest of such movements and showing its evolution over the centuries. Most of this material corresponds with the early history of terrorism, from the French Revolution through the end of World War II, and is intended to help answer some of the questions posed earlier in this introduction. The next section deals mainly with modern terrorism, exploring contemporary battlefields after 9/11, the ideologies that inform them, and how the phenomenon is studied. While this history is not exhaustive, it looks at the emergence of IS, its rivalry with al-Qaeda, different branches of al-Qaeda and IS throughout the world, and also the matter of terrorism in Europe and North America. The final section concerns reflections and general commentary on terrorism, from its culture to its origins, its evolution, and the future. Like any book seeking to make predictions, this section is at best speculative.

PART 1

History and the
Invention of Terrorism

1

THE HISTORY AND EMERGENCE
OF MODERN TERRORISM

ACCORDING TO AN OLD LATIN SAYING, "*HISTORIA MAGISTRA VITAE*," history is the teacher of life. Historians know that each historical situation is unique. Just because something happens in one instance it does not mean that it will happen again—circumstances are never quite the same. Historians do not believe in historic laws. They are no more qualified to predict the future than other mortals. History remains important in understanding and assessing current affairs but only with the awareness of its limits as an instrument of understanding these events. This applies as much to understanding terrorism as any other political or cultural developments.

The origins of terrorism go further back than organized warfare, but attacks by small bands of individuals on other groups, large or small, go back to times immemorial. Terrorism has arrested the attention of generations. Yet it remains a challenge to explain and elusive to define. Both the captivation it exerts and the challenge it imposes on interpretation come from the same source: a sudden, shocking, and ostentatious character. While even the outcome of war is shaped by agreed-upon rules and institutions, terrorism uniquely exploits and actively violates established norms, often by evading attribution through anonymity.

Terrorism has also catalyzed violent emotions throughout history. It conjures strikingly opposed figures: the age-old caricature of the musta-chioed menace with a snide smile, a fanatic without logic or reason; but also, on the flip side of the same coin, the freedom fighter compelled to play the reluctant hero. To many, the latter image is a wanton distortion. Yet, short of the unequivocal embrace of peaceful means, all political violence bares some hypocrisy.

Killing No Murder, observed Titus, Sexby, and Allen in 1657. Or put more simply, killing and murder are not the same. Similarly, the nature of combat does not predispose armed resistance to align with some gentle-man's code. As Friedrich Schiller's Wilhelm Tell declared, *"Nein, eine Grenze hat Tyrannenmacht":* no, tyranny does have a limit. Wilhelm Tell's refrain continues: "if the oppressed cannot anywhere find reprieve, as a last remedy, if nothing else, the sword." His chilling declaration has been em-ployed by many a freedom fighter, a justification to their resistant cause. Yet, many self-appointed Wilhelm Tells have impetuously invoked the sword, rhetorically clamoring for freedom from tyranny, but inwardly fanatical—they adorn their cause with the façade of self-defense while ea-gerly using the sword as though it were the answer to all problems of power.

For generations, many criminals have, as a last resort, attempted to advance their illicit activities by associating them with the ideal of patri-otism—an attempt not unlike that of modern terrorists who route funds through charitable organizations to launder (or cleanse) money of its illicit origins. Thus, the struggle for freedom has found itself obfuscated by those who, like horse thieves, avoid the hangman's noose by fabricating a back-story to blur the line between what is illegal and what is political. The study of terrorism and political violence has been further obstructed by the fact that the actors who use political violence to advance their interests are rarely ever either simple patriots in the vein of Wilhelm Tell or opportu-nistic horse-thief criminals, but both at once.

Edmund Burke's over-two-hundred-year-old *Letters on a Regicide Peace* (1796) was, by many accounts, responsible for introducing the word *terrorist* to the English language. Burke wrote, "Scratch any ideology and beneath it you will find a terrorist." Yet the relationship does not follow in the inverse—that is, simply scratching a terrorist will not always reveal an ideologue underneath.

Understanding terrorism remains a challenge for a variety of reasons. In the past hundred years alone, the character and purpose of terrorism itself has changed drastically. The actors who have elected to pursue terrorism, the means they have employed, the ends they have sought to achieve, have all in one way or another changed significantly over this period of time. Sofia Perovskaya and Emma Goldman are not as far removed from the likes of Ulrike Meinhof or Patty Hearst in years, but they could not be further apart when it comes to their moral and intellectual foundations. The difference in time serves us but little in anticipating and understanding the gulf in thinking. Another great challenge to understanding terrorism is structural. Terrorism is not an ideology like Marxism. Terrorism is a means. It is the instrument of the insurrectionist and the politician alike. Its employment is found across the political spectrum. Yet the employment of terrorism is not merely a tactic. Those who wield it have something in common. Whether they emerge from the extremes of the right or the left, whether they are nationalists or populists or even internationalists, they nonetheless have, as evidenced by their actions, reached the conclusion that, for them, an act of terror is the best idea they can think of to achieve their goals. Moreover, even if they have nothing else in common, terrorists are frequently more connected to other terrorists than they are willing or able to confess to themselves. Further, since terrorism and the decision to employ it can be conducted by anyone, its attraction supersedes the capacity of sovereign states to regulate thought, and thus transverses the borders of physical and political doctrines. It is, like Raymond Aron's "banal formula—the difference in quantity creates a difference in quality," a terrible ratio, an asymmetry of cost to consequence.

Still, terrorism is not a subcategory of revolutionary warfare as some might suppose. The terrorist, despite what may appear to be similarities of circumstance, is not a guerrilla. While the "urban guerrilla" may reside in the heart of the modern metropolis, it is certainly not a "guerrilla." The distinction lies in character more than semantics.

Many, for example, subscribe to the notion that terrorism is altogether novel. Since their argument is limited to those cases of contemporary relevance, history has little if any useful lessons to inform their views. Likewise, many falsely conclude that terrorism is either the greatest existential threat to society or one of the most precarious challenges facing the world today. Such notions might be the result of availability bias, the tendency to believe whatever solution first springs to mind when evaluating a problem. Others see terrorism as the consequence of injustice or cruelty. Their argument presupposes that freedom from civil disorder would result in the absence of terrorism. Such conclusions can be as naïve as they are misdirected. Proponents of these arguments might determine, for example, that by resolving grievances and addressing what are perceived to be the underlying problems that caused a terrorist response, the incidents of terrorism would also decrease. Some mistakenly believe that terrorists are fanatics consumed by ideology and compelled by cruel circumstance. Another fallacy in this list of widely held but poorly founded notions about terrorism is the notion that terrorism can occur anywhere at any time. The purpose here is not to systematically reject common misconceptions but to stimulate a fresh view on the subject of terrorism.

Of course, some methodological challenges arise, prime among them the availability of data on terrorism. Some groups such as the Baader-Meinhof movement, or the Symbionese Liberation Army, or even the Narodnaya Volya, have been well documented. Interestingly, because of the fascination among the public these movements kindled (because they were able to attract a great deal of attention through their activities), they sparked the creation of books, articles, and nuanced studies on each. Other terrorist groups have meanwhile gone unnoticed, failing in their pursuits to exploit the public's attention. Some have never achieved notoriety outside of their region, while others still have long since been forgotten. A general theory on terrorism cannot exclude outliers. The focus here is on the main stages of the development of terrorism; its waves, its phases, and the essential characteristics of the doctrines that motivate terrorism; and its principal problems.

The term *terrorism*, as noted earlier, is fairly new. In 1796, the British Edmund Burke published his *Letters on a Regicide Peace* where he mentions the "object of terror," and just one year prior, in 1795, he described "thousands of those hellhounds called terrorists." While the "reign of terror" generally refers to the period between March 1793 and July 1794 during the French Revolution, by 1796, the Jacobins accustomed themselves to the self-referential title with pride. The definition of *terrorism* is first ascribed to a 1798 supplement to the *Dictionnaire de l'Académie Française*, where it was referenced as a *"systeme, regime de la terreur."* Not until after the ninth of Thermidor (i.e., the fall of Robespierre) did *terrorist* take on a derogatory meaning, and then typically with an association to crime.

After its wider circulation, a *terrorist* generally denoted those who advanced their ideology by coercion or intimidation. In most recent times, the term *terrorism* has been applied so widely and to such drastically different actors that its current circulation has nearly devolved into a meaningless label applicable to any arbitrary act of violence whether political or not. Some even argue against the study of terrorism and political violence, citing frequently the greater number of deaths due to violence from above (i.e., drone war, aerial bombing, misplaced artillery fire, and other atrocities committed by governments) than those killed by violence from below (i.e., as the result of actions taken by terrorists). The present study concerns itself with the specific phenomenon of terrorism as one of the many manifestations of political violence in the world. Further, even as narrow as that approach may be, nonetheless, a single unifying definition of terrorism addressing the nuance and variety of its occurrence remains as elusive as it is improbable.

Terrorism is constrained little by established institutions. Cases of terrorism can be found in a wide array of different situations: smaller disputes between the labor and management classes, wars of independence and revolution, civil wars and wars for national survival, resistance movements to counter foreign occupation—all can have terrorist components. Yet, in the majority of these cases, terrorism is a subordinate factor to the aggregate conflict. There are many cases where terrorism is simply one tactic among many others, selected for its momentary feasibility. The concern in the present study is with groups that have employed terrorism as their primary weapon and in a systematic way.

Many regard systematic political violence and terrorism as a novel phenomenon, or at least a recent one, emerging only in the past century. While the "philosophy of the bomb" appears new, it has been implemented since the earliest days of recorded history. The Russian tsars had foes real and imagined. The Roman emperors likewise. The Ottoman sultans eliminated foes only to seemingly clear the way for the next competitors hungry enough to seize a seat of power. Terrorism from "below" manifested itself in a variety of forms and fashions and with a broad range of motivations, from religious protests movements, to social uprisings and labor movements, to outright political revolts.

Perhaps one of the earliest terrorist movements was the Sicarii. The Sicarii was a religiously zealous, well-organized male sect that participated in the early struggle for Palestine from AD 66 to AD 73. Much that is written about the Sicarii is unclear or contradictory, but some of the more consistent accounts, such as those written by first-century scholar Josephus, maintain that the Sicarii employed a mixture of unconventional and outright criminal tactics. They sometimes attacked on holidays or during the daytime. They would conceal a *sica* (i.e., a short sword) underneath their coats. They trashed public archives, ruined palaces, and destroyed bonds from moneylenders in an effort to prevent debt repayments. They would also avoid apprehension by hiding within densely populated urban areas. In David Morrell's historical novel *Murder as a Fine Art*, the expert in De Quincy's club describes this best, stating, "Just considering that the great crowds are in themselves a sort of darkness by means of the dense pressure, and the impossibility of finding out who it was that gave the blow, they mingled with crowds everywhere . . . and when it was asked, who was the murderer and where he was—why, then it was answered '*Non est inventus.*'"* These Sicarii, mentioned by Tacitus as well, were vehemently anti-Roman nationalists whose targets included Palestinian and Egyptian moderates who aligned with the Jewish peace party, which was composed mainly of high priests, Pharisees, and followers of Herod.

The intellectual underpinning of the Sicarii was the Fourth Philosophy. This doctrine regarded God as the one and only Lord. In this movement, the "earthly power" of the clergy eschewed political involvement; priests could no longer be mediators between God and man. Critics viewed the Sicarii antics as a protest of the rich. Josephus portrayed them as bandits disguised by ideological patriotism. However, even he acknowledged the pressure to be always outwardly religious, even to the point of glorifying martyrdom. He was unable to accept their belief that the Romans would be delivered unto glory by God after the fall of Jerusalem.

Similarly, in the eleventh century, an Ismaili splinter called the Assassins formed their doctrine as a mixture of messianic message and political terror. Suppressed only by the Mongols in the thirteenth century, the Assassins spread from Persia to Syria, targeting politicians, government officials, and caliphs. The leader of the Assassins, a man named Hassan Sibai, quickly realized their inability to succeed in open battle and elected to challenge others through a systematic, long-term campaign of terror consisting of the accumulation of small but decisive acts of violence by his disciplined

---

* Literally, "He is not found."

political force. The Assassins always cloaked their behavior in secrecy, and fighters (*fidaiin*) even disguised themselves as Christians. Like the Sicarii, they used a small sacramental dagger, maintained ascetic discipline, and firmly believed in a new millennium in their preoccupation with martyrdom. Their primary aim was to defend their religious autonomy and way of life against Seljuk suppression. Yet while they initially garnered widespread notoriety (legends of the Old Man of the Mountain settled deeply into the popular imagination of generations), theirs was ultimately a fruitless attempt. The Assassins held beliefs akin to the Sicarii, enacting a blend of religious aspiration and political intervention. This branch of the Ismaili was extant for two centuries, overtaken in the thirteenth century by the Mongols.

Similar secret societies existed in India and even farther east for centuries. Secret societies in China typically had their own "enforcers," and while some only engaged in extortion, many were paid assassins who auctioned their services to the highest bidder. China's secret societies organized gambling houses and small smuggling rings. Many had political aspirations and shared a disdain for foreigners and Manchu. These were among those that helped Sun Yat-sen in the 1920s and early days of his Red Spears, who were behind the Boxer Rebellion. Not dissimilar to the counterculture of the 1960s, they combined politics with alternative practices like deep breathing exercises and magic formulas.* They shared perhaps more characteristics with the modern Mafia than with contemporary political terrorist movements. Politics was but one of many of their preferred activities, which included illicit trade.

Secret societies were not exclusive to the Old World. The Ku Klux Klan is an example. The Ku Klux Klan's interest in politics was even deeper than either the Red Spears or the Assassins. Still, the KKK was not a mainstream terrorist movement. Many forget that there was not a single, consolidated Klan that persisted through the decades, but three or more. The first Klan was a secret society that emerged during the post–Civil War Reconstruction period and targeted emancipated black people, often employing rape, murder, and mutilation. The second Klan (1915–1944), preoccupied with ritualistic ceremony and the "great wizard," maintained

---

* This is out of the scope of this book, but for an extended discussion, see Avron A. Boretz, "Martial Gods and Magic Swords: Identity, Myth, and Violence in Chinese Popular Religion," *Journal of Popular Culture* 29, no. 1 (1995): 93–109, doi:10.1111/j.0022-3840.1995.2901_93.x.

the violent behavior and ideology of white supremacy as they permeated Southern politics at the state and local level and became a legal business, incorporating as a society and trading in emulsified asphalt for road construction. It was their business activities that ended the second era. In April 1944, a federal suit for over $685,000 in delinquent income tax resulted in the termination of their charter and their going out of business. The Klan rose from the grave for its third era, fighting civil rights and the liberalism of the 1960s.

The Sicarii, the Assassins, the Red Spears, and the various iterations of the Ku Klux Klan all engaged in illicit activities, yet when compared to modern terrorist groups, these seem like a different type of organizational behavior altogether. Certainly, they share characteristics with the modern breed of terrorists, such as the manipulation of fear to achieve some religious or political goal or asymmetric tactics. Theirs were parochial interests, though, and lacked the revolutionary character of the terrorism most people imagine. Ultimately, they were conservative and orthodox groups interested in maintaining the status quo, whether political or religious. They were not interested in reverting society back to some imagined halcyon past, nor did they have the utopianism that characterizes contemporary terrorism. Rather, they were the ultimate conservatives, lacking faith in violence's ability to social-engineer an ideal. Therefore, for this study, we must return to the Wilhelm Tell syndrome.

In the era of absolutism, political assassinations were relatively less frequent. Regardless of personal differences between monarchs, including competing interests and familial clashes, still, there was a measure of solidarity. Warring factions rarely attempted to kill rivals or order the assassination of other monarchs; the frequency of regicide declined until it was virtually nonexistent. The French Revolution and the rise of nationalism in Europe changed this. Previously, political murders occurred between rival groups or as military coups, as the actions of fanatics, and less frequently during dynastic quarrels and clashes. But in the latter half of the nineteenth century, systematic terrorism emerged with distinct characteristics.

From 1878 to 1881, revolutionaries fought the autocratic Russian government. Then again, in the beginning of the twentieth century, revolutionaries in Russia fought their government. Among the Irish, Macedonian, Serbians, and Armenians emerged radical, nationalist groups that used terrorist methods in their campaigns for autonomy. During the 1890s in Europe, among the anarchists in France, Italy, Spain, and even across the ocean in the United States, arose the "propaganda by the deed" (or in French, *propagande par le fait*). *Propaganda by the deed* meant to commit a political action, such as assassination, that was intended to serve as a catalyst for others to emulate toward the realization of a political goal. The relatively few assassinations in Europe that did occur captivated enormous attention. While assassinations effectively commanded widespread publicity, they were not altogether part of a systematic strategy. Spain and the United States were exceptional cases where terrorism garnered the support of specific populations. For instance, in the United States, working-class terrorism was practiced by the Molly Maguires and the Western Federation of Miners. Similarly, terrorism plagued Spain's agrarian and industrial centers. In hindsight, terrorism appears with a variety of aims and in the context of widely divergent political circumstances. Yet one can argue that modern terrorism, in its various manifestations and despite widely different aims and circumstances, has a shared origin. Indeed, the different manifestations of terrorism share more in common with each other than with other forms of violence.

In brief, modern terrorism has a common origin—all manifestations of terrorism are connected with the rise of democracy and nationalism. Grievances certainly existed before, but with the allure of nationalism and the proliferation of ideas from the Enlightenment, what once was tolerable now became unacceptable. Autocracy had dominated government. Empires had denied smaller nations and colonies their independence. Minorities had suffered, had compromised, and had been suppressed. Still, armed protestors only had a shot at success if given the willingness (or acquiescence) of those in power to accommodate the new institutions along with the rules and enforcement of the law. This, more than not, obstructed violent repression. Thus, terrorist movements only stood a small chance at taking on nonterrorist governments. The same paradox applies, *a fortiori*, to totalitarian systems that emerged in the twentieth century—the first wave of modern terrorism.

The Narodnaya Volya (National Will) of Russia, whose activities lasted only briefly from early 1878 to spring 1881, was one such important terrorist movement. They began their armed struggle when a member of an antecedent organization, Ivan Martynovich Kovalski, resisted arrest in 1878 during a raid by the tsarist police in January of that year. He was later hanged in August, sparking furor among the revolutionaries in Russia. They continued their operations later that same year with Vera Zasulich's attempted assassination of the governor general of Saint Petersburg. Then, in August 1878, they assassinated the head of the tsarist political police (the Third Section), one General Mezentsev. By early 1879, friends of these individuals coalesced into the Nardodnaya Volya, and that April, a member, Alexander Soloviev, tried and failed to assassinate the Russian tsar Alexander II. The following September, the revolutionary tribunal of the Narodnaya Volya ostensibly "sentenced" the tsar to death. More failures followed. On one occasion the Narodnaya Volya failed to blow up the tsar's train. On another, they blew up a mine in the Winter Palace while the tsar was incidentally away. They persisted. By early 1881, police had nearly apprehended most of the movement's members. On March 1, two of Narodnaya Volya's younger members each threw separate bombs at the tsar's caravan. The first landed under the tsar's carriage. It failed to kill him but forced him to evacuate the caravan—which allowed his attackers to throw a second bomb at his feet, resulting in his death.

The second wave of modern terrorism was also concentrated in political assassinations. One of the most important groups of the second wave was the Socialist Revolutionary Party in Russia. In 1901, a young man of the nobility, Mikhail Karpovich, shot and killed the Russian minister of education, Nikolai Bogolepov. The next year, they murdered the minister of the interior, Dmitry Sipyagin. Three additional attacks occurred in the following two years resulting in the 1902 botched assassination attempt against Ivan Mikhailovic Obolensky, the governor of Kharkov, and the death of N. M. Bogdanovich, the governor of Ufa, in 1903. The following year, two more assassinations occurred, including the minister of the interior, Vyacheslav von Plehve, known as a "strong man" in the regime. In 1905, the number rose to fifty-four, including the Grand Duke Serge Aleksandrovich. The Socialist Revolutionary Party then intensified their campaign of assassinations, and in 1906, the group killed eighty-two. The following year, they killed an additional seventy-one. Operations subsequently decreased to one in 1908, three in 1909, and two in 1910. Apart from minor incidents, the group appears to have ceased its operations against individuals after 1911. This was largely a factor of the controversy terrorism elicited within the group. The matter of assassination led to the group splintering, as discussed later.

Prior to World War I, terrorism was frequently assumed to be a tool of the left wing. Paradoxically, the targeting of individuals associated with this period of terrorist acts did not align with the ideological foundations of the early left. None of the groups emerged as socialist or anarchist. A third wave of modern terrorism emerged in Russia with the Bolshevik coup in 1917. Aimed primarily at Communist leaders such as Lenin and Volodarski (the first was wounded and the latter was killed), the third wave also aimed to undermine negotiations between Russia and Germany by targeting German military leaders and diplomats.

During this same period, Irish terrorism emerged. While their accomplishments may be less dramatic than the Bolshevik coup, they lasted much longer. The Society of United Irishmen emerged in part due to agrarian unrest in 1791. Roughly seventy years later, they initiated an ill-fated policy of open force. In the 1870s and 1880s, the Invincibles achieved notoriety with the Phoenix Park murders and then fell into relative obscurity until renewed surges in 1916, 1919, and 1921. Their operations again fell out of public view, perhaps aggregated into World War II, later reemerging in the 1970s.

Armenian terrorism emerged in the 1890s against the backdrop of Turkish oppression and quickly flickered out. Unlike the Irish, the Armenians opposed an impulsive enemy. Still, political assassinations of select Turkish leaders occurred in 1918, targeting individuals involved in massacres during World War I. This practice continued in the region, including assassinations of Turkish ambassadors in Vienna, in Paris, and the assassination of the first secretary of the Turkish embassy in Istanbul.

As the Armenian terrorists spread, another separatist group, the Internal Macedonian Revolutionary Organization (IMRO), also appeared, aimed at the Turkish leaders as well. Led by one Damyan Gruev, the IMRO began as an underground propagandist society among civilians that quickly evolved into a militant group ready to foment mass insurrection and acts of terrorism. Their initial attempts at mass insurrection were catastrophic failures. Adding to their ignominy, Macedonia was divvied up among the Greeks, Bulgarians, and Serbians in 1912 and 1913. Directing its attacks against Yugoslavia from 1924 to 1934, the IMRO suffered more losses than it inflicted. By the mid-1930s, when a new Bulgarian government managed to suppress their activities, the IMRO had changed so much that it no longer resembled what it had been under Gruev.

Polish and Indian nationalist-oriented terrorist groups also emerged before the war. In each case, terrorism persisted after national independence was secured. There is little doubt, for example, that terrorism plagued relations between communities, contributing to the Indian partition in 1947. Similarly, Polish terrorist groups persisted well beyond World War I among the western Ukrainians when their demands for independence were rejected by the Warsaw government.

By the 1890s, the primary tactic of terrorism in western Europe was "propaganda by the deed," propagated by anarchists such as Ravachol, Émile Henry, and Auguste Vaillant between the years 1892 and 1894. The impact was dramatic and captivating. Europe became enamored with the concept of a giant international conspiracy driven by anarchist propaganda and individual bomb throwers. But such a supranational organization never existed. Ravachol was more a criminal than a systematic terrorist. He likely would have murdered and plundered without the anarchist movement in Europe. Henry's behavior might best be explained as the exploits of a high-strung youth. And Vaillant was really just a bohemian.

The increased urbanization due to industrial changes in late-nineteenth-century France explains public uncertainty but does not account for the motives of the terrorist movements. Europe was captivated with the mysterious anarchists, but their views aggregated all nonconformists, including socialists, nihilists, and radicals, so that they all seemed to spring from one group. Official accounts took few pains to correct this misperception.

From the 1880s and through the early 1900s, many assassination attempts were orchestrated against leading European and American officials. U.S. presidents Garfield and McKinley, for example, were both victims of the deed, as was French president Marie François Sadi Carnot. In 1897, the Spanish prime minister Antonio Cánovas del Castillo was assassinated. The Austrian empress Elisabeth was murdered in 1898, and the Italian king Umberto in 1900. During this period, the majority of assassinations were committed by anarchists. Yet none of these were part of a broader, more systematic approach. In each case, anarchists acted alone. At the time, this was a significant departure from years prior. For example, assassination attempts against Napoleon and Napoleon III were plotted by conspirators. These individuals had plans to fill the power vacuum post-regicide themselves. But these were concerted efforts, not plots by individuals as increasingly became the case. In this sense, they are a historical approximation of the modern concept of lone-wolf terrorism. One historian even observed that "it is difficult to assign to them any participation in the various outrages, notably the assassination of rulers." What our observer meant was that the anarchists were of a different mind from that of the regicidal assassins of not many years prior.

In the United States, violence concentrated on addressing economic factors played a more prominent role than in Europe. Even from the early 1870s, the Molly Maguires represented a transplantation of Irish terrorism more violent than in Europe. Feeling disaffected, exploited, and discriminated against, the Molly Maguires fought mine owners and foreign nationals like Welsh and German workers. In 1886, the Haymarket Square bombing pitted militant miners and steelworkers against factory police, resulting in a bloody escalation. Similarly, the Industrial Workers of the World (IWW), acknowledging inspiration from the "Russian struggle," assassinated Frank Steunenberg, the former governor of Idaho, in 1905. In 1910, the McNamara brothers bombed the *LA Times* building. Terrorism in the United States, for all its violence, was narrowly focused. There was never an underlying agenda to spark a revolution, instigate a coup, or even overthrow local government.

Spain was different. The emergence of a working-class movement, inspired to some extent by the Russian revolutionary Mikhail Bakunin, engaged in a great deal of violence and spread terrorism across trade unions. Unlike terrorism in the United States, the systematic terrorism in Spain galvanized around political change. While rural violence in southern Spain constantly simmered, the most militant force, in fact, was the Iberian Anarchist Federation (Federación Anarquista Ibérica, or FAI). "We are not afraid of ruins," declared one of their leaders. Terrorism resurged again and again, from 1904 to 1909, during World War I, and compounded the events of 1936–1939. Terrorism plagued Catalonia even during the Spanish Civil War, and inside the left wing, the impact contributed to constant infighting. Toward the end of the Franco regime, the regional concentration of attacks shifted to the Basque region. Once there, separatism and ethnic ideology were the principle catalysts of terrorism. At times, terrorist acts were even perpetrated under the banner of Marxism.

Following World War I, terrorism was frequently sponsored by nationalistic, right-wing groups. Many groups were simultaneously right-wing and separatist. One such group existed in Croatia's Ustacha, which was supported by fascists in Hungary and Italy. The Croatians sought autonomy, and they were little concerned about the origins of outside support. Emerging fascist movements that traced their origins to the Freikorps of Germany or the Iron Guard of Romania fostered an environment from which systematic terrorism grew in the 1920s. While some governments opposed terrorism, and in fact the League of Nations intervened with resolutions targeting international terrorism, the fact is that many governments still favored any means of securing their interests, thereby undermining both international and local coalitions against terrorism.

Interestingly, outside of Europe, terrorism was much less frequent. In Egypt in 1910, Prime Minister Boutros Ghali Pasha was murdered. Another Egyptian as well—the commander in chief of the Egyptian Army, Sir Lee Stack—was assassinated in 1924. But from the 1930s to the 1950s, individual acts of terror were abandoned for more systematic terrorism. One possible explanation is that the Muslim Brotherhood, Young Egypt, and a host of other right-wing radicals embraced this type of mass terrorism. These developments of course later played a major role in exacerbating the current terrorism problem. Ayman al-Zawahiri, the current leader of al-Qaeda, first joined the Muslim Brotherhood.

Perhaps one pronounced exception was Palestine. In then Mandatory Palestine, the Irgun Zvai Leumi, the Fighters for the Freedom of Israel (Lehi), and others adopted individual terrorism. Lord Moyne was the victim of assassination. While the Irgun discontinued their anti-British operations by 1939, the Lehi movement continued unabated. In India too, anti-British activities spread. Downplaying terrorism, Jawaharlal Nehru contended that terrorism was simply their revolutionary urges in their infancy. In his view, India had nearly outgrown terrorism by the 1920s. Nehru's wishful thinking may come across as naïve today, but he continued to denounce terrorism in a campaign in which he argued that the appeal of terrorism held little value more than a detective story.

Initially, many of the groups we might now categorize as terrorists—the Irish, Macedonian, Armenian, and Bengali "freedom fighters"—were neither socialist nor anarchist. In fact, even the Black Hundred was motivated less by socialism and fought primarily to withstand the Russian Revolution and remove opponents of tsarism (typically liberal democrats). The Black Hundred also supported anti-Jewish pogroms, and while they emerged from the right wing of domestic Russian politics, initially at least they had the support of the police as well. As the tsar's government began redistributing property and labor, members of the once-supportive group began to voice their discontent at what they saw as exploitation. The very organization that emerged to support the monarchy turned against it, concluding that the absence of government altogether would be preferable to the tsar. Some even darkly reminisced about past occurrences in Serbia—a reference to the Serbian regicides.

2

WRITINGS ON TYRANNY AND THE ORIGINS OF THE PHILOSOPHY OF THE BOMB

IN ANCIENT TIMES, SOME RELIGIOUS LEADERS SAW TYRANNY AS A violation of divine law. Terrorism is not new. Even in antiquity, acts of terror were justified by their proponents as a necessary resistance to evil. Plato, in fact, regarded tyranny as a deviation. Aristotle in turn considered it the worst form of government. The ancient Greeks regarded the Tyrannicides as national heroes, and in his monumental work *De Officiis*, Cicero maintained that while Romans often acclaimed tyrants, the tyrants always met a violent end. Seneca often gets credit for the saying that, to the gods, nothing tastes sweeter than the blood of tyrants. The concept of violently resisting tyranny predates the invention of explosives. The philosophy of the bomb emerged long before the modern tools that would be incorporated into its practice.

Early discourse within the Catholic Church was contentious about the "merits" of regicide. Yet on tyranny, a unifying school of thought promoted the divine resistance against tyranny. According to Saint Isidore and others, the call of the ruler was the promotion of justice. Tyranny, Isidore noted, could have no claim on loyalty. Thomas Aquinas likewise distinguished the *tyrannus ex parte exercitii* or the tyrant punishable by the *publica auctoritas* alone, and the defecting usurper *tyrannus ex defectu tituli* a threat to any one individual and society combined.

In the twelfth century, John of Salisbury extolled the merits of tyrannicide. He makes note of the good king—one who observes the law and champions the well-being of those he leads. Salisbury also decries the oppressor. He observes the legends of Jael and Sisera, then of Judith and Holofernes. He concludes that those who rule by force, who maintain power solely through violence and oppression, are themselves worthy of a violent end.

Dante too lent his pen to the collection of writing on tyranny, casting Caesar's murderers to the depths of the Inferno. Later attempts such as the 1418 Council of Constance attempted to outlaw tyrannicide, losing sight of the shibboleth that any opposition to tyrannical rule is a rejection of the institutions held by those in power. The council's efforts were ignored as both Catholic and Protestant thinkers maintained their "inherent" right to resist commands contrary to the divine law of God. In fact, some went so far, such as Juan de Mariana of the late 1500s, to suggest that a ruler's power should be based on a contract with the people. Mariana goes further still and argues that the ruler's violation of the social contract with the people meant the entitlement of any citizen to remove the same ruler from power by any force necessary.

This brief survey on the evolution of Western thought regarding tyrannicide was not just an intellectual exercise for students of terrorism and political violence. These tracts and ideas influenced idealists for centuries. Indeed, the justification of tyrannicide laid the intellectual foundations from which nineteenth-century terrorists would later draw inspiration and, subsequently, all terrorist movements onward. Examples taken from Russian terrorism illustrate this point. In June 1879, the Narodnaya Volya held a convention at Lipetsk, where they explicitly stated in their drafted manifesto, "We will fight with the means employed by Wilhelm Tell." Every one of them knew of Friedrich Schiller and Wilhelm Tell, and often they knew all the stories compiled by Stephen Junius Brutus contained in *Vindiciae Contra Tyrannos* by heart. Nikolai Morozov, for example, justified the executions of tyrants without legal notice based on a reading of Saint-Just and Robespierre. Still, a tyrant's execution did not mean the summary end of tyranny. Tyranny involved a concerted bureaucratic effort to maintain its hold on power. The tyrant was but the figurehead of a system designed to exploit and abuse millions for the privilege of the very few. Many recognized that to truly defeat tyranny, it had to be attacked from multiple

fronts. To this end, many of those drawing inspiration from the tyrannicide literature of the medieval era formed secret societies where they
could multiply their strength with an organizational machine designed for
revolutionary change. This set the stage for the terrorist groups that oper-
ated throughout Europe in the 1800s. To be sure, secret societies existed
before their reemergence in the eighteenth century. Many groups certainly
existed before that with religious preoccupations or magical rites. Yet the
eighteenth-century secret societies that engaged in the political debates of
their day did not violently conspire to topple the existing political order.

The idea of effecting the systematic removal of tyranny really began
with Thermidor. True, the Italian poet Alfieri in his work "Un istante e
con tutta certezza"* reflected on the most effective means to end tyranny
when writing on liberty in 1770. However, such popular slogans declaring
"all means are legitimate against tyrants" by the likes of Babeuf, or even
"no means are criminal which are employed to obtain a sacred end" by
Buonarroti, were all in the vein of Thermidor. In fact, Buonarroti's *History of Babeuf's Conspiracy for Equality* would become the inspiration of
revolutionaries for generations to follow. It both preceded Blanquism
(with its embrace of insurrection rather than individual acts of terror) and
influenced what has now come to be thought of as modern terrorism (due
to its promotion of violence and disregard for life). Justification of the means
by the ends entered into the calculus as well. If a few can mobilize a revolution of the many, some rationalized, then the fate of those few catalysts
mattered less than the future of the many. Interestingly, this rationalization was a departure from its origins, where the foundational belief was
that the many should have some say in their future rather than a few deter-
mining the fate of many.

The French Revolution was a defining moment in the evolution of political violence. Terror gained currency in fits and starts but later matured
into a doctrine. Ultimately, terror as a doctrine lost prominence as proponents fell victim to their own excesses. Yet terror, or *terreur*, was quite different from the long-term terrorism that followed. Among the French
revolutionaries, the Jacobins failed to identify clear long-term aims. Coin-
cidentally, they also lacked public favor and policing. Nonetheless, this ep-
och gave early intellectual underpinnings to the critical belief among

---

* Literally, "In an instant and with all certainty."

terrorists that fear could effectuate revolutionary change. Certainly, there were differences with what people consider terrorism. During the Reign of Terror, terrorism was associated with state violence and, as explained elsewhere, it lacked the pejorative meaning ascribed to it today. For those learning from these experiences, though, they saw how the very fear of death created sufficient panic among opponents of the revolution that it helped protect the republican values animating it.

Students of the French Revolution also forget that Spain, Piedmont, and Sicily managed to overthrow their governments. These campaigns were insurrections, more akin to what people today would call an insurgency than actual terrorist campaigns. Yet terror did occur. In Piedmont and Sicily, the Carbonari were said to have fomented terror, setting fire to their enemies' houses and helping prisoners to escape. When this was too risky, poison was used. The Carbonari were said to be pitiless professional revolutionaries, ready to kill anyone. Once having joined the conspiracy, their members lost all individuality, without family or fatherland, and belonged totally to their masters. When signaled, they had to obey them blindly, knife in hand. It is true that the language used by the Carbonari was bloodthirsty. The following passage conveys something of its flavor:

> The cross should serve to crucify the tyrant who persecutes us and troubles our sacred operations. The crown of thorns should serve to pierce his head. The thread denotes the cord to lead him to the gibbet; the ladder will aid him to mount. The leaves are nails to pierce his hands and feet. The pickaxe will penetrate his breast, and shed the impure blood that flows in his veins. The axe will separate his head from his body, as the wolf who disturbs our pacific labors. The salt will prevent the corruption of his head, that it may last as a monument of the eternal infamy of despots [etc., etc.].*

Little is known to this day about the origins of the Carbonari other than the mere fact that the movement appeared first in Naples in 1807. Whether it drew its inspiration from earlier anti-Austrian secret societies in northern Italy or whether French republicans and freemasons had a hand in founding the movement is still a matter of contention. It is

---

* Giuseppe Bertoldi, *Memoirs of the Secret Societies of the South of Italy* (London: John Murray, 1821), 30.

certain, however, that the terrorist element in Carbonari activities was grossly exaggerated. Occasional terrorist acts were perpetrated, but they did not amount to a systematic campaign.

This was a distant prelude to political violence on the peninsula. In later decades, Felice Orsini tried to kill Napoleon III, and Cavour denounced the "villainous doctrine of political assassination practiced by the execrable sectarians." Giuseppe Mazzini, the great Italian advocate for unification, wrote, "You exhumed the theory of the dagger, a theory unknown in Italy. Do you take us for villains and madmen? For whom and to what end could the death of Victor Emmanuel serve?" If Mazzini's words here appear unclear, his personal letters to friends shed further light on his attitude toward assassination. "Holy was the sword in the hand of Judith," he said, "the dagger of Harmodios and Brutus, the poniard of the Sicilian who had initiated the Vespers and the arrow of Wilhelm Tell— was not the finger of God to be discerned in the individual who rose against the tyrant's despotism?"

These acts of terror in France and Italy did not amount to a doctrine. The first underpinnings of a terror doctrine emerged within secret societies in central Europe, although they would eventually reject it. The League of the Just (later, the Communist League) was an example of this. Wilhelm Weitling, the first German Communist, advocated to his friends in Paris for the "founding of the kingdom of heaven by unleashing the furies of hell." He did not discriminate in terms of who he thought should participate in this particularly violent project. For example, he believed a community of women would serve this purpose just as well. His friends were immediately horrified by his proposal of stirring up the "thieving proletariat" against society. Weitling continued. He ambitiously concluded that he could amass tens of thousands of "smart and courageous" murderers and thieves. Weitling's correspondents balked at his ideas. They believed it was possible that a desirable end could be attained by what they termed "Jesuit tactics." They added that they thought Weitling's idea would do the revolutionary cause irreparable harm were murderers and thieves to style themselves as Communists. If they prevailed, their argument, they would not support the cause of Communism, and they would likely kill Weitling.

This exchange of letters took place in 1843, unknown to Marx and Engels, who had misgivings about Weitling's capacity as a systematic thinker. They argued that it was fraudulent to rouse the people to action without a sound and considered basis for action. But Weitling was not deterred by the arguments of his friends in Paris, and the idea of the noble robber continued to figure in his writings in later years. In a new edition of his main opus, *Garantien der Harmonie und Freiheit*,* published after the failure of the revolution of 1848, he wrote that public opinion ought to be persuaded that a robber who found his death in the fight was a martyr in a holy cause. Anyone who informed on such a man should not rest secure for a single moment from the people's vengeance, and those who sought to take revenge upon him should be given protection and cover. The year of the revolution, 1848, also gave fresh impetus to the concept of terrorism, expressed most succinctly perhaps in an essay entitled "Murder" (*Der Mord*) written by the German radical democrat Karl Heinzen (1809–1880). He argued that while murder was forbidden in principle, this prohibition did not apply to politics. The physical liquidation of hundreds or thousands of people could still be in the higher interests of humanity. Heinzen took tyrannicide as his starting point; he pointed out that such acts of liberation had been undertaken at all times and in all places. But it soon emerged that he was willing to justify terrorist tactics on a much more massive scale: "If you have to blow up half a continent and pour out a sea of blood in order to destroy the party of the barbarians, have no scruples of conscience. He is no true republican who would not gladly pay with his life for the satisfaction of exterminating a million barbarians." There could be no social and political progress unless kings and generals, the foes of liberty, were removed.

Karl Heinzen was the first to provide a full-fledged doctrine of modern terrorism. In fact, most elements of modern terrorist thought can be found in the writings of this long-forgotten German radical democrat. To be sure, it was confused. For instance, he argued against killing, saying that it was always a crime. Yet he claimed that murder might well be a "physical necessity," that the atmosphere or the soil of the earth needed a certain quantity of blood.† He maintained that the forces of progress would prevail over the reactionaries in any case but doubted whether the spirit of freedom and the "good cause" would win without using daggers, poison, and explosives: "We have to become more energetic, more desperate."

* Literally, *Guarantees of Harmony and Freedom*.
† *Die Evolution*, January 26, 1849.

This led him to speculate about the use of arms for mass destruction. For the greater strength, training, and discipline of the forces of repression could be counterbalanced only by weapons that could be employed by a few people and that would cause great havoc against many. These weapons, Heinzen thought, could not be used by armies against a few individual fighters. Hence the great hope attached to the potential of poison gas, to ballistic missiles (known at the time as Congreve rockets), and mines that one day "could destroy whole cities with 100,000 inhabitants."* Heinzen blamed the revolutionaries of 1848 for not having shown sufficient ruthlessness; the party of freedom would be defeated unless it gave the highest priority to the development of the art of murder. Heinzen, like Johann Most after him, came to see the key to revolution in modern technology: new explosives would have to be invented, bombs planted under pavements, new means of poisoning food explored. To expedite progress, he advocated prizes for research in these fields. Heinzen's subsequent career was not, however, in the field of professional terrorism; he did not blow up half a continent but migrated to the United States and became an editor of various short-lived German-language newspapers, first in Louisville, Kentucky, and eventually in Boston, "the most civilized city in America."

The alliance between the revolutionary avant-garde and the criminal underworld recurred throughout the nineteenth-century terrorist movements (as in the case of the Narodnaya Volya) and again among the American and West German New Left militants of the 1960s. Pavel Akselrod, one of the fathers of Russian socialism, relates in his autobiography how in 1874 he and Catherine Breshkovskaya, the future "grandmother of the Russian Revolution," went searching the forests of southern Russia, without evident success, for a famous robber who had the reputation of plundering rich landowners and Jews and distributing his booty among poor peasants. Weitling's theory had been forgotten by that time, but like all revolutionaries of his generation, Akselrod had read Bakunin; Bakunin, in turn, had met Weitling in Zurich and had been deeply influenced by him. This meeting was one of the formative events of Bakunin's life, "completing his transformation from a speculative philosopher into a practical revolutionary."

---

* *Die Evolution*, February 16, 1849.

Mikhail Bakunin, one of the key historical figures in anarchist thought, placed high hopes on the religious sectarians in his never-ending search for the main catalysts of the forthcoming Russian Revolution. He was even more sanguine about the rebel-robbers in the tradition of Stenka Razin and Yemelyan Pugachov and had nothing but contempt for the Marxists and "Liberals," who preferred not to appeal to the so-called evil passions of the people. The robber, Bakunin wrote, was the only sincere revolutionary in Russia—a revolutionary without phraseology, without bookish rhetoric, irreconcilable and indefatigable, a revolutionary of the deed. The robber was traditionally a hero, a savior of the people, the enemy par excellence of the state and its entire social order. Without an understanding of the robber, one could not understand the history of the Russian people; whosoever wanted a real popular revolution had to go to this world. It was a cruel, merciless world, but this was only the outcome of government oppression. An end to this underworld would spell either the death of the people or their final liberation. Hence Bakunin's conclusion that a truly popular revolution would emerge only if a peasants' revolt merged with a rebellion of the robbers. And the season was at hand to accomplish this task. Bakunin, however, placed no emphasis on individual terror or even on guerrilla warfare. In 1848, he envisaged the emergence of a regular revolutionary army, trained with the help of former Polish officers and, perhaps, by some junior Austrian officers. It was only after Bakunin's death that his anarchist followers committed themselves to "propaganda of the deed."

Bakunin had been fervent in his devotion to the revolutionary cause since his emergence in the 1840s. Sergey Nechaev, however, inspired a drastic change in him. Meeting for the first time while Nechaev was a student at Saint Petersburg University in 1868, Bakunin came to call him that "magnificent young fanatic, that believer without God, hero without rhetoric." This relationship in turn inspired Bakunin's theory of destruction. His major book, *Principles of Revolution*, outlined his thoughts: "We recognize no other action save destruction, though we admit that the forms in which such action will show itself will be exceedingly varied—poison, the knife, the rope, etc." This work, dating to 1869, noted that those meant for death had been chosen already. Sorrow was imminent. The revolution meant that no compromise or remorse could be expressed. He echoed future terrorists, by noting the condemnations that would be hurled at them but stating that this should not stop them. Their aims were holy and just, and therefore, they were above criticism. Russia would be purified.

Nechaev himself built on many of Bakunin's ideas. As the great nihilist of Russia during the 1860s and 1870s, he absorbed fully the ideals of revolution. That violence should become a hallowed and divine thing came to the fore in Nechaev's most important work. In *The Revolutionary Catechism*, Nechaev provides an anthropological assessment of what defines a revolutionary, including lacking a name, his or her attitude, and rules for organizing as such. The revolutionary is a person with no attachment to anything but the cause of revolution. The revolutionary is nameless and it is a nameless soldier fighting for a higher purpose—an idea absorbed, learned, and internalized by terrorists in Ireland and Serbia many years later. The revolutionary above all else is one who exists outside the laws of society, shrugs off public opinion, and is committed to withstand torture and death to realize the goals of the revolution. This is a lonely path, devoid of human needs and wants such as love, friendship, gratitude, and honor. Nechaev's manifesto permits revolutionary passion and nothing more. The success of a revolution would be the revolutionary's reward.

This assessment of the revolutionary's anatomy serves as a prelude to the rest of Nechaev's work. He provides tactical advice on how to proceed. He urges revolutionaries to infiltrate all of society's institutions in secret: churches, the world of business, government, the military, and even the royal house. Nechaev catalogues "society" into six separate categories:

1. Above all, those who are especially inimical to the revolutionary organization must be destroyed; their violent and sudden deaths will produce the utmost panic in the government, depriving it of its will to action by removing the cleverest and most energetic supporters.
2. The second group comprises those who will be spared for the time being in order that, by a series of monstrous acts, they may drive the people into inevitable revolt.
3. The third category consists of a great many brutes in high positions, distinguished neither by their cleverness nor their energy, while enjoying riches, influence, power, and high positions by virtue of their rank. These must be exploited in every possible way; they

must be implicated and embroiled in our affairs, their dirty secrets must be ferreted out, and they must be transformed into
slaves.

4. The fourth category comprises ambitious office-holders and liberals of various shades of opinion . . . they must be so compromised
that there is no way out for them, and then they can be used to
create disorder in the State.

5. The fifth category consists of those doctrinaires, conspirators, and
revolutionists who cut a great figure on paper or in their cliques.
They must be constantly driven on to make compromising declarations: as a result, the majority of them will be destroyed, while a
minority will become genuine revolutionaries.

6. The sixth category is especially important: women . . . [whom can
be] divided into three main groups. First, those frivolous, thought-
less, and vapid women, whom we shall use as we use the third and
fourth category of men. Second, women who are ardent, capable,
and devoted, but whom do not belong to us because they have not
yet achieved a passionless and austere revolutionary understanding; these must be used like the men of the fifth category. Finally,
there are the women who are completely on our side—i.e., those
who are wholly dedicated and who have accepted our program in
its entirety. We should regard these women as the most valuable
or our treasures.

For all the furor within his manifesto, no real group existed to make it
a reality. Certainly, Nechaev wanted people to believe this, and he created
the Narodnaya Rasprava, or People's Reprisal. That being said, once
Nechaev's fanaticism and distrust overwhelmed him, his group did manage to kill a student named Ivan Ivanovich Ivanov. Nechaev was beginning
to see conspiracies everywhere. This lack of a real organization held true
for Bakunin as well. His "World Revolutionary Union" was nonexistent,
but even if he did have comrades, Bakunin was not the type of man to
manifest his philosophy.

Of course, what Bakunin and Nechaev advocated was neither new nor
unique. Youths from all over history had articulated curious ideas about
changing the world without the means of making them come to life. Peter
Zaichnevski was one of them. Coming from a well-off family in Orel,

Zaichnevski wrote and published *Young Russia* when he was twenty-one. He surrounded himself with young ideologues like himself who viewed themselves as true revolutionaries. He thought that, as was the case with his cohort, all people ought to be ready for any plot despite the obvious danger, such as storming the tsar's Winter Palace and killing everyone there, whether it be the tsar and his family or the elite that made up the backbone of the Russian nobility. The pamphlet also included the usual diatribes against those who opposed the revolutionaries, enemies who merited destruction. Zaichnevski relished the criticism of Russia's liberal opposition, which reciprocated by pointing out his immaturity and detailing the ways in which his ideas were derivative of Schiller, Babeuf, Louis Auguste Blanqui, and Ludwig Feuerbach. Bakunin joined in the attacks because he was not receptive to Zaichnevski's elitist worldview. The outcry generated was reflective of Russia's political climate in the 1860s, but the pamphlet led to no plots or attacks. It's also worth noting that Zaichnevski and some of his conspirators were arrested after its release.

Another youth of the era was Nikolai Ishutin. He established a group named Hell, some two years after Zaichnevski's arrest, which claimed ties across Europe. Hell was supposedly the Russian branch of a pan-European terrorist organization called the European Revolutionary Committee. Threads from Ishutin's predecessors emerged again. They talked heavily of regicide, killing the elite and major landowners. Ishutin came before Nechaev but anticipated many of his ideas, such as the identity-less character of the revolutionaries. Members of his group now belonged to a different world. After having committed to this, the revolutionary was to take even more extreme measures. To really be faceless revolutionaries, they would literally have to be faceless. They had to disfigure their own faces before assassinating the intended target. Revolutionaries executing a plot would have manifestos explaining their cause and a poison capsule to commit suicide if captured, not entirely dissimilar to the martyrdom videos members of al-Qaeda or Islamic State film before executing plots. Not all that followed Ishutin were this extreme, however. Many preferred the traditional method of propaganda and seeking to educate others in the values of socialism. They even sought means of fettering and restraining the extremist that shared Ishutin's vision. Eventually, they toned down Ishutin, who sought to dissuade his cousin Dmitry Karakozov from executing a plot to kill the tsar. Karakozov proceeded, failed, and was executed by the Russian state. They also arrested Ishutin, temporarily blocking all revolutionary activity in the country. Ishutin died in 1879 in Kara Katorga prison, driven insane by years of solitary confinement, never seeing the fruits of his labor.

RUSSIA'S TERRORISM AS A DOCTRINE

Carlo Pisacane is credited with having designed the notion of "propaganda of the deed," but the Russians created their own version of the doctrine after Vera Zasulich attempted to kill Colonel Fyodor Trepov, the governor of Saint Petersburg, in 1878. Afterward, there was a spate of terrorist violence throughout Russia, which seemed to be a reaction to the revolutionaries' failure to recruit or inspire the peasantry to buy into their utopian values. Terrorism was used to draw attention to their cause, demonstrate the revolutionaries' capabilities and their growing strength, and to also delegitimize the Russian government. Everyone—the authorities and even the likes of Georgi Plekhanov—agreed on this point.

This did not occur overnight. The process of systematizing Russian terrorism was spurred by events occurring around them, but all of this was gradual. Authorities penetrated revolutionary groups with spies, whom the terrorists executed publicly upon discovery. The first to take action was Sergey Stepnyak-Kravchinsky. He had assassinated General Nikolai Mezentsov in 1878 with a dagger. Days later, he justified his actions in a pamphlet called A Death for a Death, a fascinating document riddled with inconsistencies. His main point was that Mezentsov had been the head of the tsarist political police and as such had to be killed in just reprisal for all the revolutionaries killed at the hands of the government. The revolutionary movement would continue to punish anyone who harmed the idealists associated with the movement as it progressed and continued to accrete in strength. Kravchinsky for some reason also decided that the middle class and the capitalists should be the main targets of any violence to come, asking the government to remain on the sideline in the conflict. A few lines later, Kravchinsky identified the state as the main capitalist force in the country, claiming that government lands now belonged to the revolutionaries but private lands should remain untouched. In November 1878, Kravchinsky wrote the editorial for the first issue of Zemlya i Volya (Land and Liberty), where he contradicted his pamphlet. In it, he argues that the masses are the key to the revolution and that terrorism's ul-timate effect would be minimal. Only the people could destroy the sys-tem that oppressed them. If terrorism did collapse the state, it would only mean that the bourgeoisie would become the new rulers of Russia.

This period of moderation reduced the talk of terrorism. Plekhanov, a prominent Russian Marxist who maintained ambivalent ties with Lenin and Trotsky, thought it wise to restrict terrorist activities and focus on other more productive actions. By 1879, there was a threefold split between those that advocated mass terrorism, such as Nikolai Morozov, and others who thought it best to copy the approach used by the Jacobins in France. Ter-rorism should be reserved to preserve the values of the impending Russian Revolution, so only those who were anathema to its purpose would die—meaning the tsar and his supporters. Osip Aptekman and Plekhanov, for their part, thought that terrorism should be a measure of last resort.

Eventually, the first group won, and traditional terrorist groups began to emerge, adopting the "armed struggle" approach. This became evident when the conspirators in Russia decided in March 1879 to murder the new head of the political police, Alexander Drenteln. Plekhanov objected be-fore the Central Committee, but he was overruled. The terrorist campaign came in full swing as terrorists soon realized how much more publicity could be generated by a brazen attack for the revolutionaries' cause. Mo-rozov and Lev Tikhomirov, another revolutionary who would renounce violence and later adopt a more conservative worldview, explained this in their newspaper, *Listok Narodnoi Voli*, in March 1879.

This increasing belief in the efficacy of terrorism led to the splinter-ing of *Zemlya i Volya* and the formation of Narodnaya Volya (People's Will). This group, perhaps the most famous terrorist organization of late-nineteenth-century Russia, included luminaries of Russia's revolutionary movement such as Morozov, Andrei Zhelyabov, Vera Figner, and several others. For those in the Narodnaya Volya, terrorism assumed a pedagogical function. Assassinations served two purposes: revenge and agitation. The terrorist's purpose was to show the masses the way to change the system—by destroying the heart of the system. According to the Narodnaya Volya, a terrorist had to kill key government officials, kill those that opposed the revolutionaries, and kill spies. They understood that these mass killings would trigger an overreaction, which would help the masses to perceive their conditions and find ways to fight back. Unlike modern terrorist groups, though, the Narodnaya Volya failed to provide a strategy. Their approach was purely tactical. They never designed an organizational framework for recruiting and mobilizing people after committing attacks or explained how terrorism itself was supposed to fracture the government and allow the revolutionaries to assume control of Russia. Tikhomirov was the most optimistic, arguing that a few years of violence would suffice. There was also a degree of naïveté among the radicals, as they believed that their protracted terrorist campaign would bring the government to the negotiating table and promulgate reforms, such as freedom of speech and the right to assembly. Of course, this extreme view represented a minority of the Narodnaya Volya; only 10 percent of the organization's roughly five hundred members were terrorists. Certainly, not all terrorists were Narodovoltsy, as supporters of terrorism included people from many levels of society, including intellectuals, university radicals, and even garden-variety liberals. Others that blessed the Narodnaya Volya included Lavrov and Mikhailovski, and even Marx and Engels, who saw it as a means for achieving the revolution. Plekhanov even stopped arguing against it, noting that supporters of terrorism believed in it "as they did in God."

Other Narodovoltsy who provided justification for terrorism included Morozov and Romanenko, both of whom published pamphlets abroad that eventually became doctrine. They are of interest because of the rationalization provided for terrorism, but also for the great lengths taken to avoid calling terrorism what it was. Morozov's pamphlet sought to provide a common language for terrorism and to systematize it into a doctrine that all revolutionaries could share, rather than taking their own interpretative approach to the phenomenon. He thought that after achieving this, terrorism could be implemented in such a way that would destroy the Russian monarchy. He begins by tracking the evolution of the terrorists from a defensive movement to one engaged in a frontal assault against the overwhelming power of the government, which struggled in defeating them. Terrorism was an avant-garde, cost-effective fighting method. It had supplanted the mass struggle of the 1850s. From here, Morozov details its strength, ideas that would be revived by terrorist luminaries throughout history. The terrorists' ability to disperse and hide among the people rendered the government's ability to mass-murder useless. In contrast, terrorists could dedicate all their energies to tyrannicide and changing the system. Terrorists were human and inventive, not saddled by the constraints of bureaucracy or law. In addition, the terrorists had grown in strength, and unlike their predecessors, they were not being reactive but rather proactive. They were not tragic figures imposing death sentences on the government in secret; they now had the ability to attack it directly. This would doom the monarchy. Terrorism was an inexorable movement, and the only way to give it pause was by the government making reforms and granting them the constitution the revolutionaries wanted for Russia. It was an approach that could be replicated elsewhere too, like Germany. Morozov thought the destruction of tyrants and dictators was an obligation for all terrorists, and terrorists were capable of confronting them regardless if their power base was martial or pseudodemocratic (Bismarck). Interestingly, Morozov imputed much of the moral value onto terrorism that the French had during the Reign of Terror, arguing that it was a guarantor of freedom and liberty, as it would dissuade naked power grabs.

Romanenko's pamphlet shared many of the same points, but he seemed to take a more nuanced and scientific approach to justifying the violence. For one, he noted that terrorism only eliminated the guiltiest, something that mass revolutions in the past had struggled to do, as they often ended up killing many innocent people along the way. This protection of human life made it much more humanitarian and cost-effective, and it was the culmination of the dialectical struggle between the monarchy and the intelligentsia, waged since 1825. Systemic terrorism was just because it brought freedom, a utilitarian argument. Romanenko's ideas were echoed by Zhelyabov and in Lev Sternberg's pamphlet *Political Terror in Russia*, the latter arguing that terrorism was necessary in order to prevent a mass revolution that would consume all of Russia. Not everybody agreed with these views. M. P. Dragomanov, a Ukrainian who supported the revolutionary cause, disliked the rationalization of death demonstrated by the Narodnaya Volya. He particularly disliked the systematization of terrorism into a method beyond self-defense and reprisals. By committing violence not meant for defense, the terrorists were on the same moral plane as the government they sought to dislodge.

These men all had different fates. Nikolai Alexandrovich Morozov lived to see the revolution he dreamed of, dying in 1946. He was imprisoned between 1885 and 1905 and became a prolific writer on topics as far flung as Christianity and chemistry. Despite becoming a liberal on the eve of the revolution, he lived the rest of his life in Russia. Tikhomirov distanced himself from terrorism later in life, Sternberg became an ethnographer, and Romanenko became a fascist and joined the Black Hundred, to be discussed in a later chapter.

The Narodnaya Volya were interesting because of what they wanted. They were not followers of Bakunin—there was no talk of destroying everything—but they adopted an extreme approach for the simple request of a constitution and amnesty, something they argued to Alexander III in a letter written ten days after killing Alexander II. Their violent program would end if these demands were met, signaling that they were not intent on waging a forever war. They wanted to litigate their rights in the context of the free market of ideas; they were at worst liberals with bombs, forced to take such drastic measures because of the repressiveness of the Russian monarchy. This latter argument was advanced by Lev Deitch, who noted that the Narodonaya Volya was composed of many peace-loving individuals such as Nikolai Kibalchich, the main bomb producer for the group, who was compelled to violence out of necessity. At any rate, Bakunin's ideas did not define this group. Neither did the ideas of Nechaev, who was more of a Jacobin. Interestingly enough, those that followed the latter's example into the early twentieth century were liberals, not socialists.

The Narodonaya Volya represents a unique moment of terrorism in Europe. They were youthful idealists who were able to coalesce around key values to wage a protracted terrorism campaign with a unique operational tempo and a systematized doctrine. The anarchists in Europe throughout the nineteenth century resembled the lone-wolf terrorism of the twenty-first century more than the Narodovoltsy. This spasm of violence led to the formation of a revolutionary socialist party, cementing its originality in the European space. The terrorists themselves recognized this to an extent, with Vera Zasulich comparing it to the explosive potential produced by pressure built up in sealed objects. After this spasm, violence subsided. Kravchinsky detailed the exhaustion felt by Russia's intelligentsia and argued that terrorism had become a thing of the past by the late 1880s. Nonetheless, there remained a potent fear about terrorism in the Russian state. Alexander III, in response to the death of his father, reversed many of his policies. He also promoted a strong counterterrorism program to neutralize the terrorist problem. It was only in the beginning of the twentieth century that terrorism was revived with any fervor in Russia.

In the decades prior to the October Revolution, individuals of all stripes looked at the Narodonaya Volya for inspiration. Its materials circulated in clandestine circles, and people like Alexander Ulyanov attempted to create a student terrorist group based on its ideals. Ulyanov, Lenin's older brother, was hanged in 1887. Ulyanov borrowed heavily from his predecessors, emphasizing the pedagogical, educative, and illustrative value that mass terror had in terms of drawing attention to a cause and serving as a catalyst for mobilization. After Ulyanov came Vladimir Burtsev, who praised the Narodovoltsy's terrorism as the only method for fomenting regime change in Russia. Burtsev published his views in the *Narodovolets*, a journal he founded in London in 1897. The Russian monarchy, understanding the implications of Burtsev's ideas, asked the British government to arrest him, which they did, though they released him shortly thereafter. This only served to motivate Burtsev to expand on his ideas further in a pamphlet, in which he noted that all opposition groups in Russia, regardless of their ideological bent, were beginning to believe that terrorism was the only way to force change. He was not wrong, as diverse individuals across the Russian Empire began advocating its use, including Krichevsky, Zhitlowski, and half a dozen Polish thinkers.

While at the time, it was easy to conclude that these efforts were largely in vain, they were setting the foundations for the terrorist platform in Russia leading to the Bolshevik Revolution. Conditions had degenerated enough that a group of individuals established the Socialist Revolutionary Party in 1900 and turned this into a platform for terrorism. The group included veteran Narodovoltsy, who provided them with a modicum of wisdom. Unlike the Narodonaya Volya, they believed it was imperative to create a party apparatus that was commensurate with the scope of any terrorist plotting. This would be placed alongside other activist methods, not all of them legal, to buttress the mass struggle. Such concerted efforts to sow chaos would overwhelm the monarchy and help fracture it: "Terrorist activity will cease only with victory over autocracy and the complete attainment of political liberty."

To help maintain a separation of the different efforts, they established the Boevaya Organisatsia (Fighting Organization), a subunit of the party that retained organizational independence from the political activities. Complementing this, the party published a pamphlet explaining the rationale for the use of terrorism. Written as an attack against the Social Democrats, the party said that terrorism was the option of last resort adopted when there were no alternative or legitimate ways to register opposition to the government, or when the revolutionaries had to defend themselves against the oppression of the state. The Social Democrats disliked terrorism. They viewed it as an egotistical approach that failed to unite the revolutionary intelligentsia with the masses they proclaimed to be supporting, and moreover, they believed peaceful dialogue with the government was possible. Of course, the Russian monarchy was loath to give up power and repressed the masses viciously, and the party mocked the Social Democrats' desire to use speeches and pamphlets to change people's minds. The party articulated once again the propaganda value of terrorism and discussed the chaos it was creating. The animosity of the Boevaya Organisatsia toward the Social Democrats probably came from the fact that many of its leading members, like Ivan Kalyayev, Stepan Balmashov, Boris Savinkov, and Mikhail Karpovich, had been part of it before switching over to the Socialist Revolutionary Party. The Boevaya Organisatsia made its presence known in Russia quickly with the assassination of Dmitry Sipyagin, the interior minister, in 1902. The power of the Socialist Revolutionary Party's terrorism was made manifest later by Pyotr Durnovo, another interior minister, when he said, "Stupid it may be, but it is a very poisonous idea, a very terrible one, creating power out of impotence." Durnovo, unlike his six predecessors, died of natural causes and not a victim of terrorism.

Those that followed the Narodnaya Volya understood the political impact of the group. The Social Revolutionaries, emerging some twenty-five years later, saw what effect they had on Russia's political class, despite lacking public support. The Social Revolutionaries thought they could magnify this effect with more public support. Terrorism was not their main tool; it was only used sparingly to help generate attention. They did not believe it to be a moral and self-replicating phenomenon that could serve as a panacea for all their problems. Terrorism only made sense in the Russian atmosphere where it was otherwise impossible to register political dissent. Once the situation normalized, they would return to normal political procedures. They opposed the Social Democrats' newspaper *Iskra*, which came out in support of accidental terrorism but wholly rejected systematic terrorism. Accidental terrorism was defined as collateral fear generated from normal revolutionary activity. Systematic terror, in contrast, was a concerted plan of action, targeting specific individuals who carried some symbolic value or were key members of the ruling governing apparatus. The Social Revolutionaries disliked accidental terror because of their lack of control over it and the innocent victims it would claim. The Social Revolutionaries had a strategy for their murders that necessitated planning, debate, dialogue, and proper timing to effectuate the greatest impact without causing innocent deaths. There was a degree of rationalization not seen in contemporary terrorists. Unfortunately, while the party held these views, the terrorists in Russia differed. They let emotion carry them forward and painted themselves as revolutionary heroes driven by hatred, inspired by honor and the willingness to sacrifice themselves. Violence was divine, and bomb-throwing was holy.

Gradually, these terrorist activities shifted public opinion in Russia. In the early years, only the intelligentsia seemed receptive to their cause. By the end of the nineteenth century, the average Russian came to support terrorism as well. Even the likes of Georgi Plekhanov came to justify the assassination of Vyacheslav von Plehve, the interior minister, while noting the value of cooperating with the terrorists.

Sticking to their word, the Social Revolutionaries unilaterally ceased the use of terrorism in 1905 after the tsar established a legislative assembly. This was short-lived. They renewed violence in January 1906 and July 1906—when the Duma opened and was dissolved respectively. Internal bickering led to a splinter group called the Maximalists, which had a more violent outlook and strategy. In these years, terrorism became a daily occurrence throughout imperial Russia. Both the left and the right were active participants. The Black Hundred carried out pogroms and assassinated political opponents, while the Bolsheviks carried out their own plots. The Maximalists, for their part, broke from the Social Revolutionaries because they disliked how hierarchical the organization was in terms of plotting. They believed centralized control was only effective if the right people directed it—men like Grigory Gershuni—but there was not a man like that in charge. A more decentralized approach would allow spontaneity, creativity, and a broader sense of fear because the attack would be random. Besides, a centralized organization was susceptible to undercover police agents (something that did ultimately happen). The downside, of course, was that decentralization would most likely kill more innocents, and it would not stop infiltration from security services. They wanted to rebuild the organization with a strong leader who could provide a strategic vision and tactical guidance while maintaining autonomy at the local level.

By 1909, both the Maximalists and the Social Revolutionaries had ceased being terrorist organizations—the former in 1907, and the latter in 1909, after Yevno Azev was revealed to be a police spy. In May 1909, one of the leaders, Ilya Rubanovich, criticized terrorism in a party conference, and by the end of the year, the entire leadership echoed Rubanovich and decided to suspend terrorist activity. Viktor Chernov thought that the use of terrorism was greatly compromised after the outing of Azev, but it remained an effective tactic. His opponents just wanted to end the program writ large. The conditions in Russia had changed as well. The tsarist regime had lost much of its power. There was a major class struggle occurring with various groups holding disparate ideologies that were competing among themselves. At this point, the individualized terrorism of the late nineteenth century no longer held as much strategic value.

In the Caucasus, terrorism occurred following the 1905 revolution. Anarchist groups preached "ruthless and total people's vengeance." A group called Bezmotivniki (meaning "the ones lacking motives") declared "death to the bourgeoisie" and employed bomb-throwers against soft targets like cafés and theaters. The Hotel Bristol and Café Libman were bombed in Warsaw and Odessa, respectively, but none of these plots compared to what was occurring in Russia. On the whole, they were ineffective. Perhaps their only real contributions were their belligerent appeals, such as the one from the 1909 futurist manifesto: "Poisonous breath of civilization: Take the picks and hammers! Undermine the foundations of venerable towns! Everything is ours, outside us is only death. . . . All to the street! Forward! Destroy! Kill!"

3

TURKEY, INDIA, AND THE RUSSIAN EXAMPLE

THE RUSSIAN LEGACY IN THE HISTORY OF TERRORISM IS UNDENIABLE. Across the world, from Europe to North America, terrorists studied the Russian methods in depth. Anarchists in the United States honed their craft based on what they read, and the Irish used it to advance their cause of separation from the United Kingdom. Unfortunately for Russia, Polish socialists learned these methods as well and were soon engaged in assassinations and robberies of banks and trains. Neither was the Balkan region immune to the contagion of terrorism. For many decades, terrorism was studied and practiced there, and even came to influence the Russians. Sergey Stepnyak-Kravchinsky had gone to fight in Herzegovina in the 1870s, and Ivan Kalyayev once told a comrade that while there were only a few Russian terrorists as yet, he hoped he would live to see the existence of a really popular terrorist movement as existed in Macedonia. Their ideology, though, was not that of the Russians. Probably a few knew of Mikhail Bakunin and Peter Kropotkin, but they were nationalists. They most likely found inspiration from the likes of Giuseppe Mazzini rather than anything produced by the Narodnaya Volya. Of course, they observed some of the practices. They were ascetic, much like the Narodniki, and valued chastity, much like the Russians. They also believed virtue was necessary for political assassination, and only those who had the necessary nobility of the mind could engage in the practice.

The Russian example also mattered in Asia. The Armenians sought to emulate them in their bid for independence, especially in the form of Avetis Nazarbeck. He seems to have been influenced by the Narodnaya Volya after converting to socialism, largely due to the influence of his Russian fiancée, who had participated in Russian revolutionary movements. The program of the Dashnak Party (1892) stated that the revolutionary bands intended "to terrorize government officials, informers, traitors, usurers and every kind of exploiter." Nazarbeck and his cohorts cultivated relationships with Armenians living in Russia as well, with these acquiring weapons made in the Tula factory or clandestinely purchased in the Russian armory in Tiflis.

The Armenian revolutionary movements had an impossible task. As a minority, they were disliked by the autocratic Ottoman Empire and by the local population as well. They were intellectual and engaged in dialectic practices of fomenting strategy. Some thought it was foolish to engage the Ottomans while they were not engaged in some war involving the Arabs or a major European power, and others thought it best to engage immediately. Eventually, the latter group won, but given their numerical inferiority, they sought to provoke the Ottomans. Their aim was that of all terrorist groups from their era: to force an overreaction. The assumption was that any attack by the Armenians against the Turks would provoke a large enough reprisal to mobilize the Armenian public to rise up against the Ottoman Empire. They also believed that a major massacre committed by the Turks would lead to intervention of some great European power, which would help them achieve freedom. This approach had worked for the Bulgarians, and they believed it could work for them as well. If not that, they hoped to inspire other minority groups in the empire to rise up. Their attempts proved futile. They staged some important attacks, including the seizure of the Ottoman Bank in Constantinople in 1896, but all it did was provoke the massacre of thousands of Armenians. There was no help from the major European powers.

What happened in Armenia was emblematic of many nationalist movements employing terrorism. The larger population distrusted nationalists. This was the case even with the Russians. When Dmitry Karakozov was apprehended after shooting the tsar in 1866, he called his captors fools for remaining loyal to the Russian government. This was the same for the Turks. To them, the Armenian nationalists were fifth columnists committing treason, as such requiring little reason to react so viciously against the general Armenian population. For them, the attack was not only an affront to the Ottoman Empire; it was an attack against Islam and the Turkish people themselves.

TERRORISM BY INDIAN NATIONALISTS AND FORMER PACIFISTS

Nonetheless, Russian ideas continued to spread like the plague. Indian revolutionaries found a method for their goals of achieving independence from Britain. Bal Gangadhar Tilak, writing in 1906, noted that "protests are of no avail and the days of prayer have gone . . . look to the examples of Ireland, Japan, and Russia and follow their methods." Some Russians also saw an opportunity to interact directly. In 1908, Senapati Bapat sent a bomb-making manual to India, which was given to him by a Russian chemical engineer and was translated by another sympathetic Russian for Bapat's Free India Society based in London. Of course, much like the Armenians discussed earlier, not everything the Russians did worked for them as well. They did not share the same love for socialism and much preferred what Mazzini had to say about patriotism to treatises by the Narodnaya Volya. So important was Mazzini to the vanguard of the Indian revolutionary terrorists that one of their most important leaders, Vinayak Damodar Savarkar, wrote a biography of the Italian, which was later banned under the Indian Press Act of 1910.

The efficacy of these ideas was limited in the Indian context. Rarely did they kill the intended person; instead, they killed civilians. The significance of Indian terrorism is not necessarily its tactical innovations but rather the syncretism between Western terrorist doctrine and its own homegrown ideas. First, there was a revivalism and retroactive worship of assassinations from prior eras. In 1897, Tilak noted how a Hindu by the name of Shivaji had killed a Muslim general named Afzal Khan, leading to celebrations and adulations toward Shivaji. The murder notably occurred during a peace parley. Gandhi later condemned Shivaji as misguided. Using Shivaji and others as examples, editorials in *Marathi* offered justifications for murder if they occurred for some noble cause. Most of

Marathi's readership were orthodox Hindus who disparaged reformist politicians for their assimilationist tendencies toward the West, going against their religious views. In their manifestos, they announced, "We shall assuredly shed upon the earth the lifeblood of the enemies who destroy religion." A decade later, *Jugantar*, the most popular daily in its time, reaffirmed this message: theft, criminality, and murder were okay if they served a higher good—that of religion. Killing foreigners was regarded as *jagna*, or a religious ceremony. *Jugantar* and other dailies advised where to manufacture bombs and the most reliable sources for importing weapons in secrecy. Tilak, in an echo of the Thuggee cult, would often praise Kali, the goddess of death, in his speeches: "We are all Hindus and idolaters and I am not ashamed of it." He also imputed magical properties to bombs and guns. Savarkar and his followers learned from this and shed their previous pacifism as a result. He remarked that this former stance stymied the "faculty of resisting sin" and enervated the cause of independence. Following his predecessors, he wrote a book on the Indian War of Independence of 1857, and in it, he praised Brutus's sword and Wilhelm Tell's arrows as divine. He juxtaposed these alongside key events from Indian history, citing acts of vengeance against evildoers as examples of excellence. These tracts blatantly advocating assassination and rebellion were subsequently banned in the United Kingdom, and the publisher of these dailies moved to India.

London suffered terrorist acts at the hands of these Indian nationals. In 1909, a student of Krishna Varma—a sociologist who advocated assassination—killed Sir William Curzon Wyllie, Lord Morley's political secretary. Other lesser plots occurred, but the next upswing came in the 1920s. Savarkar's preaching had amplified from targeting Britons to attacking Muslims and perceived other Indians to be enemies as well. Savarkar would eventually become the leader of the Hindu Mahasabha and assert control over its military wing, the Rashtriya Swayamsevak Sangh (RSS). The Mahasabha took a hard-line stance that India could not be divided and that anyone opposed to this was a traitor. RSS's membership came mainly from Savarkar's hometown of Poona. One of the Brahmins of RSS, Savarkar's assistant, would later kill Gandhi in 1948. The Indian judiciary never managed to link Savarkar to the death, and he remained free. He died at eighty-two in 1966.

The next important Indian terrorist group emerged, ironically, from Gandhi's following. These individuals had adhered to Gandhi's philosophy of nonviolence, but reneged after they came to believe that his goals were unobtainable. In 1928, they formed the Hindustan Socialist Republican Association (HSRA). These individuals took inspiration from socialists and communists. Bhagat Singh, for example, had studied Marx and supported the USSR. They explained their ideology in the "Philosophy of the Bomb," noting that they neither wanted mercy nor planned to offer it: "Ours is a war to the end—to Victory or Death." Curiously, they did not want to be labeled a violent nationalist revolution that used bombs and pistols. They saw themselves as the revolutionary vanguard for the proletariat. They qualified their stance, however, by noting that most of the peasants and the poor remained too uneducated to understand why their cause mattered. The more widely held view was that the only viable vanguard was the nationalist terrorists the HSRA had criticized earlier. This culminated in a bloody idea: that India's youth needed to be mobilized if anything was going to change. These young men and women would give purchase not only to propaganda of the deed but also to the propaganda of death. This confusing mess of ideas had precedence and, to some extent, logical coherence given the underdevelopment of most of India at the time. Much like Mao's revolutionaries, who thought they could skip the advance of capitalism and move directly on to socialism, the members of the HSRA were impatient. Unlike Mao, who came from a peasant family and understood the peasant's political culture, these individuals were from the upper classes. They did not bother to emulate the Russians or the Chinese, who were both politically organized. As a result, the majority of their actions were attached to nationalist goals rather than a more universal revolutionary conscience.

The allusion to the "Philosophy of the Bomb" manifesto deserves a brief exploration. In 1929, the HSRA tried blowing up the vice-regal special train. Gandhi was horrified by this event and gave a speech at a meeting of the Indian Congress, where he rejected terrorism. Gandhi declaimed the terrorists as cowards, adding that he would abandon the path of nonviolence were he not certain that bomb-throwing was futile, nothing more than "froth coming to the surface in an agitated liquid." In the same speech, Gandhi seemed to foretell his own death. He noted that the logical consequence of killing foreigners was attacking perceived interlopers in India, people the terrorists believed impeded their revolutionary aims. This is exactly what happened to Gandhi in 1948.

Indian terrorists were not fond of these arguments. They countered that terrorism was not a foreign import. It was a homegrown strategy necessary for political change: "Terrorism instills fear in the hearts of the oppressors, it brings hope of revenge and redemption to the oppressed masses. It gives courage and self-confidence to the wavering, it shatters the spell of the subject race in the eyes of the world, because it is the most convincing proof of a nation's hunger for freedom." Echoing their manifesto, these individuals argued that the Indian peasantry lacked the education to understand the religious significance of Gandhi's message of peace and that talk about love for one's fellow human beings would do nothing to convince the British to end their violence against India. They then uttered the age-old argument used by terrorists. They noted that given all the atrocities the British monarchy had meted out to India, their violence was justified morally: "As a race and as a people we stand dishonored and outraged. Do people still expect us to forget and to forgive? We shall have our revenge, a people's righteous revenge on the tyrant." They noted as well, citing Russia and Turkey, that violence could be a means for achieving social progress in spite of Gandhi's rebukes.

It goes without saying that in the historic battle of ideologies, Gandhi's message resonated better. Gandhi's superior organizational abilities and his appeals to the masses were hard to beat. Regardless, the HSRA disseminated their manifesto, and it did inspire a few attacks, including the murder of a police officer in Lahore in 1928 and the bomb attack on the Central Legislative Assembly by Bhagat Singh and Batukeshwar Dutt. When arrested, they claimed they wanted to give voice to the voiceless and gave a mishmash of historical examples ranging from George Washington and Giuseppe Garibaldi to Kemal Pasha and Guru Gobind Singh. Following this, the HSRA conducted the 1930 Chittagong raid. The Calcutta Jugantar Party, inspired by their ideology, wrote a similar manifesto. But by the mid-1930s, the British had blunted their efforts and rendered Gandhi's movement less effective as well. Terrorism had one last outburst during World War II, but after independence and partition, terrorism metastasized into various forms of repression and civil war.

4

PROPAGANDA BY THE DEED

THE CONCEPT OF PROPAGANDA BY THE DEED, OR THE NOTION THAT
the actions of terrorists can serve a pedagogical purpose, originates with
Carlo Pisacane. Pisacane is a legendary figure in Italy. A patriot, he participated in the revolution of 1848 and would later try to overthrow the
Kingdom of Naples, an effort that resulted in his death after he embarked
on an expedition to Calabria in 1857. Outside of Italy, though, he is best
known for popularizing the idea that violence had an important propagandistic purpose that should be exploited. He wrote that ideas did not
suffice in inspiring change; people lacked either the wisdom to understand
or the very awareness that there was a problem until they could see it for
themselves. The only way to get people to understand what needed to be
done was through action. Pisacane was not unique in having these
thoughts. That Pisacane's ideas were put into practice made them unique.
Errico Malatesta and Carlo Cafiero, two Italian anarchists, were the first
to make this happen, proclaiming "the insurrectional fact destined to af-
firm socialist principles by deeds is the most effective means of propaganda
and the only one which, without tricking and corrupting the masses, can
penetrate the deepest social layers and draw the living forces of humanity
into the struggle sustained by the International." While the idea has its

origin in Pisacane's writing, the phrase *propaganda by the deed* was coined by Paul Brousse, a French physician whose writing appeared in the same journal in which Malatesta and Cafiero first published their doctrine. Brousse thought that traditional propaganda could only be consumed by the middle classes, who had the luxury to read and understand the likes of Pierre-Joseph Proudhon, and not the laborers, whom the socialists wished to mobilize. Given this reality, forceful action was the key to mobilizing the public.

Interestingly enough, Brousse did not advocate assassination, doubting its efficacy. For that, the anarchists have Peter Kropotkin to thank, as he exposed Brousse to the idea of permanent incitement through words, knives, rifles, dynamite, and anything that was not legal. Although the media back then was not what it is today, with social media and other forms of communication transmitting global events in an instant, Kropotkin was aware that violent actions attracted attention in a more widespread fashion than mere words, even in the primitive days of global media. For Kropotkin, the action built on itself: governments overreacted, which served to spread the propaganda further and incited others to react and mobilize against it. This, of course, is the hallmark terrorist goal, and it is still copied today. Al-Qaeda staged 9/11 with the hope of forcing the United States to overreact, invade Afghanistan, and thus inspire the Muslim community to rise up against all apostate governments.

Kropotkin is a notable figure in the history of terrorism. He came from an established military family, but, after coming of age, quickly evolved into a conspirator actively participating in the various anarchist movements engulfing Russia. Despite being arrested in 1874, he escaped a few years later and continued propagating his ideas. Yet in contrast to the likes of contemporary terrorists belonging to al-Qaeda or IS, Kropotkin eventually came to shirk "mindless terror." This made him different from Nechaev and those who seemed primarily to lust for blood. Before taking this approach, though, he was the key advocate of the individual terror characterized as regicide or tyrannicide. He thought such assassinations would help inspire the revolutionary fervor most anarchists and socialists found wanting among the masses. Kropotkin later provided moral justification to the assassination of Alexander II and other political figures killed at the end of the nineteenth century, blaming society for making the assassins desperate enough to take such actions to remedy their unbearable social conditions. Society had filled these people with contempt for life. This idea still finds purchase in contemporary terrorism.

Consumers of anarchist and socialist literature found much inspiration in the ideas postulated by Pisacane, Brousse, and Kropotkin. Propaganda by the deed was a major point of discussion in the July 1881 International Anarchist Congress held in London, leading many in attendance to advocate the study of chemistry to disseminate bomb-making techniques. Kropotkin participated in that meeting. He supported these ideas to an extent, but he qualified his support from a sociological perspective. In his mind, what was more important was knowing the impetus to radicalize and mobilize people rather than making bombs. Bombs and other forms of pyrotechnics were of no use if they served no tactical or strategic function. Moreover, these were rigorous sciences that necessitated an elite cadre that could quickly learn and manufacture these items; it was a waste of time to have everyone try to study chemistry. Again, Kropotkin provided the blueprint for the likes of Osama bin Laden, generating a cohort that specialized in making bombs rather than tasking everyone to do so. Regardless, the congress passed a resolution that those in attendance should study chemistry and other related disciplines, for it already had provided a revolutionary service and its need would only increase as the fervor for change increased. The resolution stated "that a general conflagration was not far distant; 'propaganda by deed' had to reinforce oral and written propaganda and arouse the spirit of the masses insofar as illusions still existed about the effectiveness of legal methods." This resolution had little effect. It was another ten years before anarchists throughout Western Europe would attempt propaganda by the deed.

Despite the inaction, general panic spread along with calls for greater scrutiny of their activities by security forces. Strangely enough, in seeking to penetrate these groups, police actually enabled their activity. Evidence suggests they may have provided money for some of their propaganda pieces and even funded some plots. It is at least certain that the police sponsored the publication of an anarchist piece written in a French-language periodical based in London that advocated violence against all sectors of society, noting that if arson and theft were legitimate, explosions were as well. Again, predating the likes of *Inspire* and *Dabiq*, in the 1880s, *La Révolution Sociale*, a French newspaper, gave bomb-making instructions. Unlike its more contemporary examples, the editor was Serreaux, a police spy working in cooperation with the Paris police prefect. Similar instructions appeared in legitimate anarchist papers across Europe. Alongside instructions for manufacturing incendiary devices, they also gave guidance on where to place these weapons, usually around places that were highly flammable, but ultimately what mattered was: *"L'action ne se conseille, ni ne se parle, ni ne s'ecrit—elle se fait."** Propaganda by the deed even made it into revolutionary songs, with Marie Constant ending one of her songs by saying: *Maintenant la danse tragique vent une plus forte musique: Dynamitons, dynamitons.*[†]

These anarchists were opportunists. They were happy to use any weapon. After the conviction and execution of Ravachol for a series of bombing in the 1890s, *ravacholiser* became a verb and "La Ravachole" became a popular tune based off "La Carmagnole": *"Vive le son d'l'explosion."*[‡] Propaganda of the deed became fashionable, as Ravachol evolved into a cult. The latter in turn advocated all sorts of devious plots. Servants should poison their masters. Anarchists should douse rats with gasoline and light them on fire to raze the houses of the enemy. The goal of the anarchist in the 1890s was to co-opt science for revolutionary aims in order to destroy society. The strategy of revolutionaries across the world no longer revolved around confrontation, but rather *"une guerre des partisans menés de façon occulte."*[§]

Even with this literature in the public sphere, there was not much to show for it. As noted before, the French were the first to put propaganda by the deed into action in the 1890s, but this wave seemed to end around 1894. In Italy, by the time propaganda by the deed became central to all anarchist enterprises, the revolutionary fervor had receded in the peninsula. Some attempted to reignite the passions of their coconspirators. Between 1882 and 1884, anarchists killed a shoemaker, a police inspector, a police agent, and a moneylender, but with little to show for it. Dampening the spirit of these attacks was a tragedy: the anarchists had killed a small child in order to hide evidence, which proved repugnant for Italian society. North of Italy, others killed a pharmacist and a banker, in Strasburg and

---

* Literally, "An action is not recommended, nor spoken or written of—it is done."
† Literally, "Now the tragic dance plays stronger music: Dynamite, dynamite."
‡ "Long live the sound of the explosion."
§ "A war of partisans fought in a [hidden] way."

Mannheim respectively, but both seemed to be botched robberies onto which the police imputed political motives after the fact. In 1894, Italians assassinated several political figures, but these were likely acts by individuals and not planned by an organization. The only instance of a strategic assassination conducted by a group was that of King Umberto in 1900. There is evidence to suggest that Gaetano Bresci, the man who killed him, received support from an Italian anarchist group based in New Jersey.

This is to say that despite these limited outbursts of violence, there was no grand anarchist conspiracy. More than anything, the "revolution" was a product of the political imagination of various police chiefs across Europe, and while the movement provided valuable referential material to the great writers of that time (James, Conrad, Zola, and others), it did not change the established order of things. What did happen resembled the contemporary lone-wolf problem—individuals who were influenced by the literature but lacked any material or organizational support from a larger entity. In this respect, Émile Henry's words at his trial for bombing Café Terminus seem quaintly hollow: "We ask no pity in this pitiless war which we have declared on the bourgeoisie." It was around this time that the last true anarchist publications renounced propaganda by the deed as ineffective. It was too idealistic to hope that such activity could inspire mass uprising without any concomitant organizing by anarchists across the world. Kropotkin himself agreed to this sentiment. The Russian example again proved wanting. Explosions could destroy buildings but not institutions. Yet despite these appeals by the leading anarchist intellectuals of the 1890s, individuals still bought into the rhetoric of the 1880s and acted on it. Regardless of the nonexistence of some constituted global conspiracy to destroy the state, explosions were speech for individuals who wanted the world to hear and know their minds.

ARMS AND THE CLASS STRUGGLE:
SPAIN AND THE UNITED STATES

In Europe, the nation that felt the outburst of anarchist violence for the longest period of time was undoubtedly Spain. In the 1880s, there were reports of a peasant uprising organized by an anarchist group called La Mano Negra, or the Black Hand. Whether this group was real or invented by the police to justify a crackdown in Andalusia is debatable. Nonetheless, there were anarchist revolts throughout Catalonia, afflicting Barcelona particularly badly from 1904 to 1909 and again from 1917 to 1922. These plots had a noticeable labor flavor to them. Violence seemed to follow labor disputes, either with the owners of factories or intra-syndicalist rivalries. They also included common thieves who would participate in the violence in an opportunistic fashion. These efforts were remarkably better organized than those in other parts of Europe. In 1905, there was a plot to kill King Alfonso in order to inspire a true revolutionary movement on the Iberian Peninsula. Whatever noble quality this anarchist violence had managed to create, degenerated completely during the First World War. Ángel Pestaña characterized the prewar violence as "mystical and apocalyptic idealism," but after the war, anarchism became an excuse for score settling, avenging disputes, or fee collection among rival syndicalist groups. Anarchism seemed more of an organizing principle than the main motivator of violence in the country. Spain of course had a unique history of political violence, being the country of origin for the term *guerrilla*. In the early twentieth century, Spain was home to unique social conditions that made it amenable to this type of violence. This is to say that ideology mattered little for many of these disputes.

Conditions were similar in the United States. As it industrialized, there were major labor disputes. The Homestead Massacre is only one of multiple examples of the bloody fights that occurred. Organized fights began with the Molly Maguires and continued with various labor unions such as the Western Federation of Miners and the IWW. With German and Eastern European immigrants commingling with these already radicalized laborers, ideology helped inspire others to become anarchists who promoted propaganda by the deed. There were some differences, however. In 1883, the International Working People's Association was established in Pittsburgh, and it did not advocate terrorism. The IWPA thought mass strikes and sabotage were more productive. Nonetheless, propaganda by the deed did find purchase among the laborers in Chicago.

In that midwestern city, emblematic of America's industrialization, industrial conflicts arose continuously. Blue-collar workers railed against the owners of factories, asking for more equitable pay and for the eight-hour workday, but as the factory owners became more and more reluctant to concede, newspapers like *The Alarm* and the *Chicagoer Arbeiter-Zeitung* were published, both of which advocated the use of terrorism. They borrowed the words of their counterparts in Europe, noting that in the same way the guillotine a century earlier had equalized capital punishment for both rich and poor, dynamite could advance their cause. They wrote pamphlets with instructions on how to use these new industrialized tools of revolution: "The Weapons of the Social Revolutionist Placed within the Reach of All." One reader wrote to them arguing that "[dynamite] of all good stuff, this is the stuff. . . . It is something not very ornamental but exceedingly useful. It can be used against persons and things, it is better to use it against the former than against bricks and masonry."

There were important ideological agitators in these circles. C. S. Griffin argued that a government required a head to function, and "by assassinating the head just as fast as a government head appeared, the government could be destroyed, and, generally speaking all governments be kept out of existence. Those least offensive to the people should be destroyed last." These advocates of terrorism also believed it to have an important democratizing effect. Albert Parsons, the editor of *The Alarm* who was accused of participating in the Haymarket affair, defended the use of dynamite. "It was democratic," he said. "It made everybody equal. It was a peacemaker, man's best friend. As force was the law of the universe, dynamite made all men equal and therefore free." Parsons claimed innocence in that particular incident. Apparently, the ones who did participate had been followers of Johann Most, the high priest of terrorism in America.

European immigrants continued plotting throughout the 1890s. Alexander Berkman arrived from Lithuania in 1887, when he was sixteen years old, and came to idolize Yevgeny Bazarov, G. W. F. Hegel, the idea of "liberty," and Nikolay Chernyshevsky in that order. Inspired by these individuals and ideas, he came to view the proletariat as the only ones that mattered in society, and inverting the logic of another Eastern European émigré (Ayn Rand), he thought the owners of capital were the true parasites. Because of the latter's control of the means of production, he believed all actions were morally justified and advisable if the goal was to change the system. Berkman compared the system to an infirm individual that required immediate surgery. As such, any capitalist who acted like a tyrant had to be removed. For Berkman, assassination attempts against these targets had to be weighed differently from blatant murder. To kill a capitalist was a noble activity. He put his words into action in July 1892 when he tried shooting Henry C. Frick of the Carnegie Steel Company, making him responsible for the denouement of the Homestead Strike. The United States was not ready for this type of conceptual tyrannicide, with most of society rejecting it outright. He was denounced in *Freiheit* but defended by Emma Goldman. Surprising many of their contemporaries, Johann Most actually attacked Berkman for the plot.

TERRORISM AND NATIONALISM

There is a contemporary belief that for much of the nineteenth and twentieth centuries, terrorism was associated with the left wing and only recently has it become associated with the right. The truth is different. While certainly the left has discussed terrorism more extensively and the theoretical implications of it, the right has always used it. Terrorism in India, prior to the HSRA and others, inculcated it with religiosity through the worship of the gods Kali and Durga. It manifested clearly with the Thuggee cult, but also in the anti-cow-killing campaigns, both activities that usually included high-caste Brahmins. The Irish, while definitely having a religious element, also had a nationalist flair when it came to their terrorism campaigns in the late nineteenth and early twentieth centuries. For much of this period, Irish radicals used the United States as a foreign base of operations against the British Crown and established Clan na Gael. This group did not wish to target individuals but rather symbolic objects, like buildings and other public places of power. In contrast, Jeremiah O'Donovan Rossa, another leading Irish nationalist from the era, had no remorse about killing civilians. Likewise, the Invincibles carried out violent plots like the Phoenix Park murders in the 1880s. The Irish tried every sort of weapon, shirking doctrine or the idolatry of dynamite, like the Russians. They built submarines, Rossa plotted to gas the House of Commons, and groups tried to acquire lucifer matches and poisoned stiletto-blade knives.

The Irish adopted similar arguments to those used by Indians to justify their plots: the British had done far worse. This was the era of pronounced British colonialism throughout Africa and Asia. In 1893, during the Battle of the Shangani, the British regulars killed sixteen hundred men while only suffering four casualties through the industrial use of the

Maxim gun. Given these atrocities, among others, the Irish felt they were justified in their campaign. In the 1880s, the Irish inaugurated the dynamite campaign throughout the United Kingdom. They attacked the London Underground, symbolic barracks around the country, the Liverpool town hall, and other targets. Their goal was to disrupt the daily lives of Britons, their tourist industry, and to generate panic. The Invincibles, learning from the Russians, had similar expectations that such bloody campaigns would lead to an overreaction by the Crown, which would lead to the radicalization and mobilization of the Irish. The Irish terrorists, although they lacked an ideology like the anarchists or the socialists, were quite educated and provided some very telling quotes about terrorism: "Despotism violates the moral frontier as invasion violates the geographical frontier," one of them wrote. "To drive out the tyrant or to drive out the English is in either case to retake your territory. There comes an hour when protest no longer suffices. After philosophy there must be action. The strong hand finishes what the idea has planned. Prometheus Bound begins, Aristogeiton completes; the Encyclopaedics enlighten souls, the 6th of May electrifies them." Or on mass psychology, they quoted Victor Hugo: "The multitude has a tendency to accept a master. Their mass deposits apathy. A mob easily 'totalizes' itself into obedience. Men must be aroused, pushed, shocked by the very benefits of their deliverance, their eyes wounded with the truth, light thrown in terrible handfuls."*

With this type of wisdom, intense dialogue and discussion were inevitable among the Irish nationalist leaders. It was generally agreed among them that their cause was just. The only matter that needed to be settled were tactics. John Devoy criticized Rossa and his dynamite campaign as a foolish enterprise that depicted the Irish as ignorant individuals incapable of comprehending the consequences of their actions. Yet, despite these criticisms, he maintained an eye-for-an-eye mentality toward violence committed against the Irish by the British Crown. In 1881, he made a direct threat against the British government, saying he would kill a minister for each Irish person killed by the Crown. This sentiment was shared widely by others, including Rossa. In 1886, Devoy personally threatened British ministers, telling them one would die for every skirmisher executed, and later started fires in the cities where each execution

---

* P. J. P. Tynan, *The Irish Invincibles* (New York: Irish National Invincible Publishing, 1894), 488–490.

occurred. It is likely that Devoy's attempt to avoid reprisals was motivated by his concern about the weakness of the Irish cause in the face of concerted British oppression. He most likely thought it impossible to win given their current situation. This was the position taken by Charles Stewart Parnell, who publicly rebuked terrorism, but in private, he held a different opinion. Constitutional reforms were most likely the best way to achieve Irish independence, and this could certainly be buttressed by clandestine murders.

5

THE PHILOSOPHY OF THE BOMB
AND THE FAR RIGHT

THE PREVIOUS CHAPTER TOUCHED PARTIALLY ON RIGHT-WING TERRORISM, but a broader survey is warranted, especially when it comes to the extreme right. A good example of this violence is the Black Hundred from Russia. These individuals carried out numerous assassinations before the beginning of World War I. Assassinations by the far right continued after the war across Europe. Hitler was a big advocate for them: "Heads would roll," he said, "ours, or the others." Later, when he was taken to court after a spate of assassinations committed by the Nazis, he tried to mitigate his words by saying they were hyperbole intended to force an ideological confrontation. The Nazis, according to Hitler, prioritized constitutionality and the rule of law. The idea that Hitler might approve of someone who dared break the law, causing reckless death and mayhem, was anathema to the values of the Nazis. Hitler had to maintain this façade because of his leadership role. Joseph Goebbels, for his part, argued that "whoever defended his own Weltanschauung with terror and brutality would one day gain power," and that political decisions depended on the common person out in the streets, not those in government offices. Goebbels, much like Hitler, was a populist, and he thought it important to win over the masses. That was the only way they would take power. With people, they could disrupt state functions and opposition party meetings, and conquer the street. And, of course, part of this involved using terrorism, taking inspiration from Mussolini: "Terror? Never. It simply is social hygiene, taking those individuals out of circulation like a doctor would take out a bacillus."

Mussolini, the erstwhile socialist, in his younger days remarked, *"Il proletario deve essere psicologicamente preparato all'uso della violenza liberatice."** This concept of psychologically liberating violence was a hallmark of his Fascism, and he contrasted it as a progressive. What his enemies did was nothing more than stupid reactive violence: "the Socialists ask what is our program? Our program is to smash the heads of the Socialists." Violence for both Mussolini and the Nazis had a political element, but it was no longer revolutionary in scope and aim. There were no assassinations, no sabotage. This was violence of the masses—or hyper-democratic, if you will—designed to express the people's will by intimidating opponents. They claimed self-defense, noting they only engaged in terrorism after others had done them ill. But even the right wing saw the value in the doctrine of the left-wing anarchist of the previous century. The Nazis exploited their violence to enrapture the media. Whenever they committed attacks, newspapers had to print what they had done, and of course this catapulted the Nazis to new heights in Germany's political imagination. This small group, lacking any elite support, soon became the leading party in Germany. Goebbels, the master propagandist, of course was the mastermind behind this strategy. In his "conquest of Berlin," he gave the example for others to copy his style.

Why were the Nazis and the Fascists so committed to this violence? These were the heady years after the first great war, and many of their members were veterans of these conflicts. They saw how might made right, or so they believed. The struggle for power made violence permissible. Much like the populists in the final years of the Roman Republic, these individuals saw legalism as a make-believe obstacle that could be overcome by sheer force. There was no room for polite debate or persuasion. The enemy was liberal democracy, and this system had to be destroyed. Again, the socialist undertones reemerged in how they sought to destroy this system, something promulgated both by Mussolini and the Nazis during the Kampfzeit. Count Helldorf, during a trial against Nazi storm troopers, remarked "that it was quite absurd to accuse them of having attacked Jews,

* Literally, "The proletarian worker must be psychologically prepared for the use of liberating violence."

for they were fighting against the capitalist system, which was represented, after all, not only by Jews."

The Nazis and the Fascists were large organizations, however, so the targeted small-scale terrorism that characterized the left-wing groups from the previous century was not present. The ones who did practice it, though, identified with the smaller extreme right wing. This is a catchall term for these individuals and does little to convey their strategy. The Organisation Consul, a German Freikorps movement, practiced systemic terror as a manifestation of radicalism, not conservatism, as they cared little to defend the ongoing German capitalist system. Others, like Ernst von Salomon, were conservatives who thought little about human life: "We killed whoever fell into our hands, we burned whatever could be burned. . . . The march into an uncertain future was for us sufficiently meaningful and suited the demands of our blood." Nihilism prevailed in many of the extreme right-wing circles. Walther Rathenau was not killed because of what he represented or because of his role as foreign minister. On the contrary, they had respect for him. Rathenau was killed because he was too important a symbol and his death would reverberate more so than others. This "duel between giants" was prominent among Central European terrorists. The Freikorps plotted the death of General Hans von Seeckt, who led the Reichswehr, the main military body in Germany until 1935, while Hungarian fascists sought to kill the interior minister, a man of the right. The Iron Guard in Romania killed two conservative prime ministers in the 1930s as well. These were not left-wing individuals. These were firmly in the establishment and seemed to share their values. What mattered was the symbolism of their deaths.

THE RIGHT WING ELSEWHERE

While the Central European example spread throughout the continent, there was still enough variety to identify noticeable differences among the various right-wing terrorist groups of this era. In Hungary, the Arrow Cross included many criminals, and the Internal Macedonian Revolutionary Organization degenerated into a Mafia-style group after shedding its patriotic motives. Over time, the IMRO would perform assassinations for the highest bidder and later participate in the drug trade. By contrast, Romanian nationalists remained committed to their values. The Iron Guard always kept its youthful image, identifying their members as "legionnaires," seeking to bring back the old values of Romanian society: religion, patriotism, and all those ideals that were swept away with modernity. Their problem was that they identified as Christians, for whom the act of forgiveness mattered, but the nation could not be saved by acting like proper Christians. Sometimes murder was necessary, but it had to be followed immediately by expiation. They also adopted the anarchists' ideology of propaganda by the deed, taking it to heart and making it part of their strategy. They thought violence, when used properly, had a moral component that made it legitimate. They also seemed to revere death, writing songs saying, "Legionnaires are born to die," or "Death is a gladsome wedding for us." This bloodlust and worship of death made them similar to the anarchists with their suicidal impulse.

What is interesting about the previously discussed groups is that they all were protesting the ills of modern Europe. This was true of both the left and the right. They railed against the political parties of their era and the control of wealth by a select few, calling them a plutocracy. The right needed a way to distinguish itself from the left, and the way it accomplished this was through the use of patriotic and religious symbolism. Terrorists from all over the world looked to the past for guidance and inspiration. In Japan, the cult of the samurai, which had existed well into the nineteenth century, inspired terrorists in that country. These individuals had an interesting trajectory. Many of them started as anarchists or identified as "lovers of the native soil," before coming to support the annihilation of the Western style of life. They formed groups like the League of Blood and separated themselves from all their known contacts, much like Nikolai Ishutin and Sergey Nechaev, to restore the traditions of Japan. Of course, these terrorists were political pawns like so many throughout history. The military saw value in these men terrorizing Japanese society, and it made the notion of a more aggressive military policy palatable to the political classes. Furthermore, the example of these terrorists wishing to preserve the honor of Japan served as a moralizing force, which further pressured politicians into supporting Japan's "historical mission" of greatness throughout East Asia and the world.

Terrorism was a variegated phenomenon in Europe during the years before World War II. In France, the targets were mainly universities. The far right enjoyed employing journalism to menace professors they deemed offensive and playwrights who wrote scripts they saw as profane. Some smaller groups practiced a more intense and violent form of terrorism, such as the CSAR, which eventually expanded the repertory of terrorism in France to include murder. This type of terrorism belies the typical view that extremist groups dislike the press. There was no such easy relationship with the press in the case of the Austrian Nazis or the Japanese terrorist groups. They viewed journalists and the press alike as hostile enemies that needed to be destroyed. An early advocate of Austrian terrorism wrote, "One kills these dogs by shooting or poisoning them, every means is right," an idea his coconspirators agreed with and which manifested itself in their plots to poison journalists. In Finland, the Lapua did not kill, but they engaged in kidnapping and torture. After roughing up their victims badly, they made sure the message was received in Russia.

The Fascists rarely engaged in terrorist plots against individual targets. In Italy, they were notorious for making their victims drink castor oil, but this was not a frequent thing they did. In Germany, Walther Rathenau and Matthias Erzberger were indeed killed, but this was not to advance a coherent political program like the anarchists. There were exceptions to this. In 1924, Fascists killed opposition leader Giacomo Matteotti, and, ten years later, in 1934, Austrian Nazis killed Chancellor Engelbert Dollfuss during an attempted coup d'état. While an effective and deadly tool, the far right in both Italy and Germany seemed to shirk assassination as a tool because they did not find it effective. Carl Schmitt explained why when he wrote on the "political soldier": "The ethics of the Sermon on the Mount applied to the private enemy, the inimicus, not to the hostis, the public foe." Contrary to the liberal-democratic thinkers of the time, the fascists did not believe discussion and debate would resolve the differences plaguing the different political parties. They viewed politics as a struggle, but somehow recognized, almost out of instinct, that "love your enemies" was not applicable to politics. Yet, in this warped worldview, terrorism played a minor role.

Some terrorist groups did develop their own doctrines to explain their worldview somewhat, but the value of these statements and manifestos were of limited use if the goal was an understanding of all terrorist activities. There were many things that radicalized and mobilized people to cause harm during that era. The aforementioned IMRO and the Croatian Ustasha were established by patriots, but later became political pawns for foreign powers that wished to sow havoc in their countries. The IMRO understood its numerical inferiority relative to the task at hand and recognized the importance of having foreign backers to help them achieve their independence goals. The Croatians similarly ceded Dalmatia to their Italian overlords with the hope that this would facilitate their cause. This lack of doctrinal rigidity meant that the IMRO eventually degenerated into a band of glorified hit men, with the Bulgarians exploiting them to fight their rivals, and the Croatians engaging in indiscriminate terrorism throughout Yugoslavia. The reality aside, these individuals thought such foreign interference was still useful in helping them achieve their goals of independence. Yet given how depraved their actions became later on, there is debate as to whether any of this emerged from legitimate political convictions or if it was merely depraved social behavior.

Indeed, at times, terrorists of the far right engaged in something called *instinctive terrorism*, a form of violence that arose from generational hatred between various national groups. These individuals lacked ideological doctrine but understood the propaganda value of violence. This was the case with the Ukrainians in eastern Poland and the peasants in Schleswig-Holstein. They had that innate insight that during times of extreme crisis, like the Great Depression, the most effective way to register political protest was not by airing one's grievances but through the use of violence. They still had enough political sense to separate the two approaches to avoid being scrutinized by authorities and to maintain plausible deniability. They would often create two distinct groups—a moderate political one that sought traditional means of protests and the more violent direct-action groups. Since the beginning of time, people have been making love and cooking without the help of textbooks, and the same principle applies to terrorism. Certainly, there were times that these terrorists of the extreme right combined their violence with a well-considered strategy, but this was normally figured out on a post hoc basis, after the conflict had been initiated. When these discussions did occur, there was usually bitter debate, which engendered more squabbling. But terrorism also took place without precise doctrine and systematic strategy, with only hazy notions about the direction of the struggle and its aim. Like Faust, the terrorists could truly claim, *"Im Anfang war die Tat"*—in the beginning there was the deed.

The similarities between terrorists on the left and the right were many. They understood the value of propaganda of the deed; they disliked democracy, liberalism, and their attendant institutions; they sought reform or revolution by any means possible, regardless of the outcome; they saw themselves as heaven-sent. Even Carl Schmitt, quoted earlier, understood these connections. The same individual, considered the most preeminent jurist for the Nazis, came to praise Mao and other leaders of the left in his work on partisans. Schmitt, like many contemporary terrorists, believed that it was a tool that could undermine and destroy from within the governance and the broader systems of a nation. The SS regarded their mission as quasi-divine and viewed themselves as "chosen" to purge the world of any and all evil and sin that existed. The Narodovoltsy were pained to kill people and suffered intense remorse from their actions. The fascists lacked that moral compunction, because they truly did see themselves as purifying the world. The anarchists, also believers in propaganda by the deed, thought similarly. Émile Henry, the man who bombed Café Terminus, boldly proclaimed, "There are no innocent bourgeois." Others who shared his worldview came to despise all humans, saying none could be innocent. Yet there is something to be said about the Narodnaya Volya and its view on life, compared to later fascists. These former individuals understood their government to be intractable and incapable of reform without the impetus provided by terrorism, as the regime had outlawed most forms of political activity. When there were venues for debate and means of reforming the system without violence, they condemned this violence. After the assassination of President Garfield, they denounced his murder specifically because they believed in a free and nonviolent society. They were optimistic about life—the right-wing terrorists were not.

THE HISTORY OF TERRORISM

The foregoing is largely a highly compressed survey of two chapters of *The History of Terrorism*, originally published some forty years ago. What happened during the four decades that have passed since then remains well remembered. Some of the events and developments will be described in detail in the following pages. Others have been fully and competently described and need no repeating. Forty years ago, terrorism was mainly found in Europe and Latin America. There were a few instances elsewhere such as the Palestinian conflict and later on also in the Caucasus. But over the years, terrorism in Western Europe died out, and it also faded away in Latin America, with the last of the terrorist groups there fading from the scene in Colombia in 2016. On the other hand, there was a great upsurge of terrorist operations in the Middle East and other Muslim countries. Following the Russian and American invasion of Afghanistan, al-Qaeda came into being, and the invasion of Iraq led to circumstances that facilitated an expansion of terrorist operations. Syria became the major battlefield, and terrorism also appeared in African countries such as Nigeria, where it had been, on the whole, unknown.

The new terrorist groups that appeared expanded their activities worldwide. Noteworthy also was the fact that they engaged in a great deal of propaganda, often successfully, which led to the radicalization of local Muslim communities in Europe and America. Major attacks in American and European cities are well remembered, ranging from 9/11 to the attacks in Madrid, Paris, London, Copenhagen, and other European cities. These events prominently figured in the media, often overshadowing all other news. However, the political attacks were quite limited. No government was overthrown as the result of these attacks, and few if any new converts joined the Muslim communities. Some thousands of radicalized young men and women proceeded to the battlefields in the Middle East and other Asian countries, but more than a few returned, disappointed, to their native countries after a couple of months or years. The issue of terrorism had become a major political force, but at the same time, its limits clearly appeared. How far would it advance or retreat from its position? How great was its staying power? These issues will be discussed in the sections that follow.

6

FINAL REMARKS ON THE HISTORY OF TERRORISM

THIS BOOK IS NOT EXHAUSTIVE IN DISCUSSING THE HISTORY OF TERrorism. Left out of this history are the majority of twentieth-century terrorist events, including the rise of the anti-colonialism movement before and after World War II across Africa and Asia, the subsequent ethno-nationalist terrorism of the Basques in Spain and the IRA in Northern Ireland, the youthful utopianism of left-wing terrorists in Europe and Latin America, the rise of state-sponsored terrorism led by Qaddafi in Libya and Hezbollah with the patronage of Iran, and finally, the rise of religious terrorism in the form of Sunni extremists in Afghanistan and elsewhere. Such full accounting of terrorist movements is useful, for it showcases the remarkable continuity in strategies and tactics pursued by the terrorists of the nineteenth and twentieth century. While it would be beneficial to give an accounting of all these movements, there is insufficient space in this book to permit a proper accounting of them. They emerged in the context of their times, with large overarching political ideologies governing their worldviews and technologies dictating how they executed their particular acts of terrorism. Nonetheless, their operational tempos, their strategic frameworks, and their goals were based on the idea that a small number of individuals with no access to high-tech weaponry could change the world.

Yet this early history of terrorism dating back to antiquity and stretching all the way into the early twentieth century conditioned and informed all subsequent terrorist movements. Not all the methods associated with terrorism today appeared in those days, such as vehicle-borne improvised explosive devices (IEDs), suicide attackers on jetliners, or drones, but they provided the blueprints for the successful use of violence for the purposes of forcing change. If one focused exclusively on the recent history of terrorism, starting in the year that Osama bin Laden died, the myopic perspective would delimit activities by al-Qaeda and IS as exceptionally unique and unprecedented, which they are, but not for the reasons furnished typically by commentators. Notions about propaganda by the deed, the importance of complementing terrorism with correlative political organizations, the pedagogical purpose of terrorism, and the use of provocations to force a government to overreact were all part of the political programs discussed by the terrorists of this era. In other words, this introductory history gives a paradigm for evaluating the successes and failures of the movements that followed throughout time.

Indeed, there is something to be said about this worldview given what it accomplished. In the nineteenth century, terrorists of all stripes committed regicide or tyrannicide in one form or another, whether it was killing a tsar, a king, or a president. These violent movements never threatened the survival of a regime directly. This was both a function of the restraint displayed by these brave young men and women in seeking to use violence in a surgical fashion, along with the rudimentary tools at their disposal—antique pistols, poisons, knives, and dynamite—not to mention their limited numbers. Yet many were active participants in history, adding political pressure to recalcitrant regimes that were hesitant or unwilling to moderate, liberalize, and ultimately usher in the modern political liberal-democratic order in Europe and North America. It is remarkable how influential they were, given how little support terrorists had for much of the nineteenth century. They were the inspiration for many idealists who changed the world during the twentieth century as we knew it: Gavrilo Princip and the death of Archduke Franz Ferdinand, the Bolsheviks as acolytes of the Narodonaya Volya establishing the Soviet Union, Menachem Begin and the bombing of the King David Hotel, and Michael Collins in the struggle for Irish independence.

Of course, there is a dark side to all of this. Many terrorists killed innocent people unnecessarily. Others had starkly racist and cruel worldviews, committing untold and unrecorded atrocities against ethnic and religious minorities. Blacks in the United States, Jews across Europe, and other powerless individuals became victims of violence designed to enforce an antediluvian social order, one that sought to impede or reverse the changes wrought by industrialization and the rise of political liberalism in the West. For all the exuberance and romanticism of terrorism, which even Marx and Engels lauded, there was a side of unmitigated evil that deprived the world of valuable and innocent souls. This loss of opportunity needs to be weighed alongside the fruit of evil actions. Needless to say, the Reign of Terror and the various political pogroms enacted by the Nazis once they achieved power and set about conquering the world do not fall into this category.

While not explicitly articulated in this history, what is evident is that terrorism itself never caused historical events directly. There had to be a mass uprising like the Jacobins in France or the Russian revolutionaries who took part in the October Revolution. Violence was used to enact the will of a political subset—the terrorists—and governments found themselves overreacting and, with that, adding to the incipient social catastrophe of the day, leading to tragedies and ultimately their defeat, as in the case of World War I or the British and French withdrawals from numerous colonies between 1930 and 1970. This book has maintained that terrorism is not an existential threat to the existing order for the same reason that the terrorists of the nineteenth century were not an existentialist threat to Russia or to Britain. That said, it does provide a subtler and more pernicious problem—namely, it directly challenges the relationship between the individual and the state. By the criterion that Thomas Hobbes offered some four hundred years ago to evaluate the state, a government is legitimate if it can offer security to its people. Hobbes was writing during the bloody seventeenth century, focusing primarily on physical security, but his ideas also encompassed material and financial security. Terrorists challenge this relationship by making the state seem weak, impotent, and unable to respond to the seemingly randomness of terrorist-driven chaos. The breakdown of this relationship is what creates mass discontent, political uprisings, revolutions, and, at its worst, civil wars.

The normal tendency among states is to overreact or overcorrect for this deficiency, and their primary tool is generally the use of force, as terrorists threaten the body politic's physical security. For liberal-democratic societies whose constitutions and firmaments are based off humanistic princi-ples and the works of Enlightenment-age writers, such physical overreaction is repugnant and repulsive if it is not calibrated and proportional, espe-cially since oftentimes it can erode into the very values that legitimize secular-democratic governments in the first place. This has happened many times throughout history. The extensive use of torture, the suspension of the constitution, limits on civil liberties, and targeted discrimination based on preconceived notions of race, religion, and ethnicity are all different results of the same mistake. While one could use the Russian monarchy's response to terrorism or the British government's use of torture against sus-pected members of the IRA during the troubles, there are much more re-cent examples. The very fact that terrorists can produce such an overreaction that states themselves are willing to self-immolate and destroy their values for the purpose of protecting those very values should give the public pause when considering whether or not terrorism is really deadly to the state it seeks to destroy. Aside from the victims, this overreaction causes the quality of life for much of society to suffer and can lead to complete turmoil.

This has been the approach perfected by both al-Qaeda and IS over the past three decades. These entities, either consciously or unconsciously, have internalized the lessons of the propaganda by the deed and have seen how relatively minor plots can cause governments to react so repugnantly that they end up directly undermining their goals. The United States was baited into an extreme counterterrorism program that saw it engage in sys-tematic torture after denouncing the practice as being opposed to its very values for decades. The United Kingdom has increased its domestic sur-veillance, eroding the notion of the right to privacy. Both of these govern-ments are by no means evil; they were simply trying to act in an expedient and efficient manner to physically protect their populations, without think-ing of the moral and ethical costs of their activities. Elsewhere, Assad found himself confronting a mass uprising that he sought to quell by mas-sive repression, which only generated more grievances and turned his country into the worst humanitarian disaster of the early twentieth century. At the time of this writing, Iraq finds itself engulfed in a brutal counterin-surgency campaign to uproot IS fighters who use car bombs against their position and have instituted a policy of systemic rape, torture, and execution against individuals they believe to be sinners.

The overreaction has given rise to bigger problems; terrorist groups no longer seek simplistic reforms and have instead moved to seize sovereignty over territory and to formulate their own taxation policy. What is important to remember, though, is that terrorism is born out of the existence of grievances and because people find a situation unjust and intolerable. This was evident in the groups covered in this section and will be evident in the following section that focuses on the events of the past three decades. Before a terrorist movement can form, there has to be some perceived inequity that can mobilize intelligent youth to take up arms to fix these problems. Terrorism is the result of bad governance and bad policy. In Russia, the government proved to be too repressive and unwilling to accommodate the liberals wanting freedom of expression and assembly. In the American South, the Ku Klux Klan emerged because the governments of the southern United States were complicit and thus unable to enforce the rule of law, which allowed these hooded men and women to terrorize minorities for generations. In Europe, the breakdown of government facilitated the rise of the Italian Fascists, who felt they could act with impunity. In other words, terrorism is not only the product of bad governance but also a manifestation of youthful idealism.

These two structural features of the world go a long way in explaining the terrorism that followed in the twentieth and twenty-first centuries. In discussing these events, the book will reference and expand upon these ideas, giving concrete examples and demonstrating the intellectual continuity between the violent intellectuals of the past with those who have adopted the mantle of terrorism today.

PART 2

Contemporary Terrorism

7

THE NEW FACE OF TERRORISM

THE RAPID ADVANCE OF THE ISLAMIC STATE OF IRAQ AND SYRIA (ISIS) across northern Iraq in the first half of 2014 shocked the world. Appearing to arise out of nowhere, the group overwhelmed the Iraqi military, which the United States had trained and armed at a price tag of billions of dollars, and seemed poised to destroy the fragile political order that took a decade to reestablish. As it conquered city after city, including Fallujah and Mosul, ISIS circulated via social media stunning images and videos of massacres, crucifixions, decapitations, and other atrocities, cementing its ruthless and bloody image across the world. Culminating in its declaration of a caliphate in June 2014 and the adoption of a new name, Islamic State (IS), IS wanted the world to know that this was the inauguration of a new political order in the Middle East set on erasing century-old political truths. In its stead, it would resurrect a theocratic system imported from the seventh century and impose it by sheer force. It further communicated that it was not stopping there. As a self-declared state, IS wanted the entire world to believe it was ready to continue its offensive to reconquer territory it believed had fallen under the control of apostates and of territory it believed was usurped by nonbelievers. The new map it envisioned had large swaths of Europe and Asia under its control, and would further its objective of bringing about the end of times. Thanks to these battlefield successes, highly stylized propaganda videos, and impressive recruiting efforts saw its ranks swell even more, as people flocked from Europe, North America, and East Asia to the so-called caliphate. If people took its rhetoric at face value, it seemed unstoppable.

In many ways, this was truly the beginning of a new form of terrorism. The IS phenomenon was not concentrated solely in Iraq and Syria, as the group found devotees across North and West Africa, parts of the Arabian Peninsula, Afghanistan, and in places in East Asia. It immersed itself in preexisting conflicts in Libya and South Asia, it feuded with al-Qaeda— the leader of the global jihadist movement—and seemed like the next evolution of the polymorphous threat that al-Qaeda had represented over the previous fifteen years. Indeed, its successes, combined with the declaration of the caliphate, allowed it to co-opt groups formally aligned with al-Qaeda and other groups immersed in the broader jihadist movement. Many of these allegiances were opportunistic, capitalizing on the rising prominence of IS relative to al-Qaeda, the parent organization from which it split in 2014, while others represented concerted efforts by IS to expand the reach of its caliphate to other parts of the world. IS also exploited its network of foreign fighters, training thousands in urban guerrilla tactics and bomb-making skills before sending them back to their home countries to set up support networks and cells that could later execute future plots. In instances where they could not rely on a trained operative, the group took advantage of its vast global network of online supporters to plan further attacks and to increase the perception of its expansiveness and the danger it posed for the entire world. Not surprisingly, the number of so-called lone-wolf terrorists increased.

However, in the years since that fateful summer, things have not turned out how IS's propaganda suggested it would. Within a year, it had lost a sizable portion of the territory it controlled and had suffered significant attrition among its leadership. This was a product of then president Obama's decision to deploy American troops as advisors to Iraq and to use air strikes against IS to slowly dismantle, degrade, and ultimately destroy the organization. Combined with political reforms the United States forced onto the Iraqi government to win back the support of the Sunni population so critical to Islamic State's success, IS began to collapse within Iraq and parts of Syria. Most tellingly, by the end of 2016, the Iraqi military IS had humiliated had been rebuilt and by July 2017 had retaken

Mosul after having won back Fallujah earlier in 2016. This is not to say that IS is no longer a threat to the world or that the organization has been defeated. Rather, that much like other terrorist organizations that transformed into an insurgency, they came upon the stumbling block of needing to govern and holding territory to maintain their support base and to maintain their legitimacy.

WHY WAS IS SUCCESSFUL?

As the group fades, questions remain as to why it succeeded in the first place. The reality is that the group's tactics and strategy are neither new nor unique in terms of scale and devastation. As this book will explain in further chapters, in its push forward, IS relied on the same approaches used by other protracted insurgencies and meted out violence similar to numerous contemporary and historical terror organizations. Even their most brazen action, the creation of a pseudostate, has a strong historical precedent. The formation and expansion of a shadow government in areas where it maintained a degree of support before exporting it and expanding it was a practice pioneered by violent nonstate actors in East Asia, Latin America, and Africa, adapting Mao's guide for insurgent warfare to their local circumstances. Similarly, the use of ceremonial violence to generate attention for the group and to both intimidate locals and fracture the ties between the individual and the state was used by the FLN in Algeria and the Vietcong at various times. Attacking public infrastructure to enervate the state's ability to assert its ability to govern was part of the strategy used by the likes of Sendero Luminoso (Shining Path) in Peru and the Taliban against the American-backed government in Kabul after 2005 in order to erode the legitimacy of the national government. Meanwhile, the scale and ferocity of its violence is easily matched, if not surpassed in many ways, by Boko Haram in Nigeria.

Its ideology too is something it adapted from other extremist organizations, most notably al-Qaeda and the multitude of groups that form the global jihadist umbrella. If anything, the main difference is their willingness to assert the apocalyptical essence of Islam to justify the formation and expansion of the caliphate. As will be explained in subsequent chapters, its relationship with al-Qaeda is critical for understanding both its approach and its ideology. Representing the newest iteration of al-Qaeda in Iraq (AQI), IS relies on the same assemblage of ideologues and theologians to legitimize its violence, its vision of Islam, and its right to govern as a caliphate that was first deployed by AQ.

This is to say that in purely practical terms, IS is a hodgepodge of the best approaches from the history of terrorism. To an extent, on the face of things, this seems to belie the idea that it marks a new inflection in terrorist violence the same way the regicides of the nineteenth century paved the way for the liberal and communist revolutions of the following century. This would be selling the group short if the analysis ended here. Despite its repackaging of terrorism's greatest hits, IS has galvanized an entire generation of would-be jihadists across the world and has changed the rhetoric about the threat posed by terrorist organizations. If before the fear surrounding groups like IS or AQ operating in ungoverned spaces was that they could use these environments to safely plot attacks against the West, it has now metastasized into the implications of a terrorist group actually governing and having the industrial capacity of a nation-state to support its revolutionary aims. Moreover, by Americanizing its violence through the exploitation of modern telecommunication platforms to broadcast its message across the world, all neatly packaged in dramatic videos shared on YouTube and sleek online magazines, it has provided a new model for terrorist groups to imitate. In fact, at the same time that IS has lost territory the size of the United Kingdom and tens of thousands of fighters, it has retained an aura of invincibility due to its widely disseminated propaganda, which keeps implying the continued expansion of its caliphate, giving the group more credibility than is deserved.

If then what made Islamic State successful was the use of insurgency strategies with only the added benefit of being able to disseminate its propaganda far and wide, the question remains why it succeeded where others did not. Therefore, it is worth exploring not only its origins but also the implications for terror movements moving forward into the coming decades. This will become increasingly important as well when other groups operating in environments similar to IS begin dissecting the lessons of its rise and fall. Apart from providing a path forward for others to emulate, it will provide the blueprints for creating and consolidating a state. Certainly, when these actors do arise, they will need to be studied within the context of their times and politics, but at the very least, as this section of this book will try to demonstrate, there are certain generalizable trends about IS that will be present in the future. In the case of IS, while its declaration of the caliphate made it appear like a truly potent revolutionary power, the moment it sought to establish the framework of a state, it weakened its overall position, as it had to govern in a manner acceptable to the people it intended to rule while attempting to consolidate the territory captured to maintain its legitimacy. These problems, evident from the outset, were masked by the ineffective and corrupt central government in Iraq, as well as the continued civil war buffeting Syria. This is the problem that affects all terror groups eventually unless they reform their approach.

The possibility of another movement like Islamic State expanding rapidly and violently is not a reach. In the same temporal frame that IS devastated Iraq, terrorism has continued and evolved in key parts of the greater Islamic world. At the time of this writing, Boko Haram and the Taliban have yet to slow down the tempo of their insurgencies in Nigeria and Afghanistan, respectively, while Libya and Yemen continue experiencing bloody civil wars, joining Syria as contested states. In each of these cases, similar political realities animate the bloodshed that inspired IS initially. Additionally, the group that initiated the current wave of terrorism, al-Qaeda, is still dangerous, as it has taken advantage of the mistakes committed by Islamic State to rebuild its organization and adapt its strategy to capitalize on the emerging political realities once IS is no longer a threat.

8

A TRUNCATED HISTORY OF IS

WHERE DID ISLAMIC STATE EMERGE? LONG BEFORE ISLAMIC STATE declared its caliphate, it was the radical and genocidal brainchild of Abu Musab al-Zarqawi. Born in Jordan, al-Zarqawi was a troubled youth for most of his life. Involved in crime, he was arrested several times. Things changed when he went abroad. Around 1989, he arrived in Afghanistan just as the Soviets were leaving. He did not participate in the fighting, but he cut his teeth participating in the subsequent civil war erupting. Reportedly not very religious before arriving in Afghanistan, he began his radicalization process here. He first acted as a journalist, reporting on the incipient conflict among rival warlords before becoming immersed in the war. It was in Afghanistan where he befriended his mentor, the Jordanian Abu Muhammad al-Maqdisi, a notorious Salafist, who set him on his ultimate trajectory.

Both men returned to Jordan in 1993 and were arrested following a failed bomb plot. Prison was a bountiful time for al-Zarqawi, as he distinguished himself as an experienced jihadist with a radical, if not so erudite, interpretation of the Qur'an, bringing to himself untold attention from his prison-mates and recruiting members for his organization, including Iraqis and Syrians. These individuals would become important fighters for al-Zarqawi and, later, IS during the following two decades. Reports suggest that al-Zarqawi had a falling out with al-Maqdisi in prison because of the former's more aggressive and muscular interpretation of jihad, which made him more popular among the inmates and which saw al-Maqdisi sidelined. Eventually, in 1999, the Jordanian government released al-Zarqawi and others arrested for terrorist activities during an amnesty program.

After his release in 1999, al-Zarqawi traveled to Afghanistan, where he met with Osama bin Laden. Reports from the era suggest their meeting was frosty. Bin Laden was not impressed by the brash and impetuous jihadist who seemed set on achieving his own agenda at the expense of others. Al-Zarqawi, for his part, disliked bin Laden's relatively tempered approach to jihadism, finding him too cautious and disliking his approach of targeting Western targets over governments in the Middle East he deemed as apostates. Crucially too the first divergence in strategic preference emerged here. Even though al-Qaeda had killed hundreds of Muslims at this point, bin Laden sought to limit the deaths of his fellow coreligionists, as his priority was to unite all Muslims against the West. Al-Zarqawi, coming from an even more extreme perspective, felt that the priority of jihad should be to kill apostate Muslims, mainly Shiites, but also other confessional sects that deviated from his rigid interpretation of Islam. Bin Laden found these ideas to be anathema and abhorrent. He had a Shiite mother, and al-Zarqawi seemed unlikely to listen to him. There was also the not-so-minor issue of both men coming from disparate socio-economic backgrounds. Osama bin Laden came off as the more educated of the two relative to the mostly self-taught al-Zarqawi. In some ways, this meeting set the stage for the eventual separation of IS from al-Qaeda due to differing outlooks about the world. Regardless, this meeting proved propitious for IS. After the intervention of others, bin Laden gave al-Zarqawi seed money to start a training camp for other Jordanian radicals released in 1999, out in Herat.

Herat, in western Afghanistan, would serve as al-Zarqawi's base of operations for two years. Relations with al-Qaeda proper remained precarious, as al-Zarqawi supposedly refused to swear a *bayat,* or oath of allegiance, to Osama bin Laden. After 9/11 and the subsequent American invasion, al-Zarqawi participated in the counteroffensive but was regarded as an unreliable follower of Osama bin Laden. Soon after, he fled to Iran and remained there for over a year, where he husbanded his troops and prepared his organization for the inevitable war in Iraq being planned by the United States. Working with an extremist Kurdish organization in northern Iraq, al-Zarqawi infiltrated the country in February 2003 and by March was organizing one of the more prominent elements of the Iraqi insurgency, although not the only one. Also worth remembering is that while al-Zarqawi was associated with Osama bin Laden and the global jihadist movement, al-Zarqawi still maintained a large degree of independence and was not necessarily a formal part of al-Qaeda, as the Bush administration maintained at the time.

THE IRAQ WAR AND THE EMERGENCE OF AL-QAEDA IN IRAQ

To understand the history of Islamic State, one must be cognizant that it is only partially explained by the American invasion of Iraq in 2003 and the policies adopted by the Bush administration in the immediate aftermath. The irony of this invasion is that one of the pretexts for it was the claim by the Bush administration that Saddam Hussein and al-Qaeda were working together. Very little evidence backs this up. In spite of this, the invasion catalyzed the group that would manifest into Islamic State by destroying the safeguards against sectarianism and creating the conditions for any insurgent group to organize and mobilize. Like many things in war, the invasion improved the probability that a group like it would emerge but was not entirely deterministic. IS, in its current manifestation, is primarily an Iraqi group that uses foreigners. The organization that al-Zarqawi was building initially relied on largely foreign Arab cadres that lacked social buy-in from locals and in many ways represented an alien power taking advantages of a fractured government. Up until 2003, Iraq was more or less a secular state ruled by the Arab Socialist Ba'ath Party (referred to here as the Baath Party), with Saddam Hussein as its figurehead. Although sectarian divisions existed within the country prior to the war, largely because of the paramount role played by Sunnis in the Baath Party, these cleavages were regulated through heavy repression designed to produce an Iraqi national identity capable of mobilizing for war, whether against the United States or Iran. This identity was shattered by the invasion.

There are two key reasons for this. First, by removing Saddam Hussein from power, the United States and its coalition partners changed the political calculus for the various elite entities operating at the regional and provincial level and mobilized elements capable of competing with the

Baath Party for influence. Hussein, brutal as he was, served as a referential point in terms of an individual to fear and to respect, creating a singular target for these groups to focus on. In this regard, Hussein's repression of the worst political excesses in the country simultaneously limited the formation of secondary or tertiary identities capable of rivaling the national Iraqi character and also created a political cleavage that played the paramount role over parochial interests of these sub-elites. Phrased differently, the personality cult around Hussein helped instill an imagined political community that united people in the country from across immense geographic expanses, giving the impression of a united Iraqi nation. Second and related to the previous point, although the Baath Party largely favored Sunnis in a country where they were not a majority, it still created cross-cultural exchanges among Iraqis of various political backgrounds hoping to persevere, survive, and perhaps excel under the dictatorship. This type of contact helped ordinary Iraqis maintain a collective identity that deprioritized perceived cultural differences from a religious background. The destruction of the Baath Party demolished the one civil body that prioritized interethnic and interfaith exchanges among ordinary Iraqi citizens.

The importance of Saddam Hussein and the Baath Party in terms of unifying Iraq was made evident shortly after the invasion. After the United States and its coalition partners defeated the Iraqi military in a matter of weeks and took control of Baghdad by April 2003, the real fighting began in earnest in May 2003. Lacking a viable plan for reconstruction that integrated the various ethnic and sectarian groups into a monolithic whole, the Bush administration prioritized de-Baathification to stamp out any lingering influence from Saddam Hussein. The process of excising out remaining former-regime elements from a new government is an old practice designed to help exorcize an emerging government from the evils of its predecessors. The goal is not necessarily to collapse a government wholesale, but only the elements that animated it to commit evil. The United States engaged in a similar process in both Germany and Japan at the conclusion of World War II to delegitimize the old regime and impose a new government free of "original sin." These efforts recognized the importance of basic government services and maintained a degree of continuity in terms of bureaucracy.

De-Baathification was more extreme. Paul Bremer, the American proconsul in Iraq tasked with rebuilding the country, extended the order to include the full dismantling of the entire Iraqi government and civil service, smashing any semblance of order in the country. Regardless of their background or degree of fidelity to the Baath Party, many midranking government employees lost their jobs. This created chaos as public service jobs, such as trash collection or mail delivery, had to be refilled, but it also created a groundswell of resentment among the newly unemployed, many of whom were Sunnis. More worryingly, de-Baathification included wholesale dismembering of the Iraqi military, displacing tens of thousands of trained soldiers who suddenly lacked a way to earn a living. Sunnis in the country felt threatened, as the transition government imposed by the United States was mainly Shiite in character.

Into this chaos, al-Zarqawi inserted his organization, exploiting the mounting grievances experienced by many in the country. T. X. Hammes has characterized the Iraqi insurgency as a leaderless networked mosaic insurgency involving various rival groups coordinating their activities against the coalition and against themselves. There was no particular Islamist strain to it initially, but it became prominent with the passing of time. While the coalition forces, mostly formed from democratic countries susceptible to public opinion, were attacked to dissuade them from remaining in Iraq, much of the heavy violence took on a particular genocidal character as Sunnis and Shiites began targeting each other. This was a by-product itself of the paucity of strategic knowledge the United States had of the country, as it never made an effort to reconcile the secular national identity that characterized Iraq under Hussein. Al-Zarqawi sought to exacerbate these tensions by targeting Shiites as much as possible starting in the summer of 2003 and disseminating extremist propaganda to unite the Sunnis under one banner. Aside from employing religious rhetoric to demonize Shiites as apostates, al-Zarqawi also played on Sunni fears of invasion from Iran through the fifth column composed of Shiites. Not surprisingly, various religious groups emerged and began proffering protections to their neighborhoods and religious sects.

Al-Zarqawi complemented his attacks on Shiites by launching grand attacks against foreign targets, including the Jordanian embassy and the Canal Hotel, which killed the main UN representative in the country, Sérgio Vieira de Mello. He later began circulating gruesome beheading videos, most notably the Nicholas Berg video, further bolstering his organization as the forefront of the insurgency. These widely shared videos attracted thousands of recruits from across the Middle East and soon made al-Zarqawi's group the most visible element of the global jihadist movement. These developments angered Osama bin Laden, as it seemed that his group was being eclipsed by an upstart group differing in tactics and strategy. This was at a time too when the United States was arguing publicly that core al-Qaeda was no longer a threat after being destroyed in Afghanistan, burnishing al-Zarqawi's credentials even more. For a year and a half, al-Zarqawi maintained communications with al-Qaeda's senior leadership. Osama bin Laden and his deputy, Ayman al-Zawahiri, criticized al-Zarqawi for singling out Shiites and for the excessive use of violence against Muslims in general. Nonetheless, al-Qaeda offered resources necessary for the insurgency to continue, leading to al-Zarqawi officially pledging an oath of loyalty to Osama bin Laden by the end of 2004. Al-Zarqawi also renamed his organization al-Qaeda in Mesopotamia, or al-Qaeda in Iraq (AQI).

The transition toward an official al-Qaeda franchise did little in tempering AQI's violence. Throughout 2005, high rates of killings continued, but increasingly, much of it was directed toward Sunnis living in areas controlled by the group, which increased as leaders in Iraq's Sunni triangle were either assassinated or began fleeing the country. Presaging IS, AQI governed like a strict theocracy, punishing locals for the slightest perceived infraction, which only served to generate even more grievances against al-Zarqawi. Al-Qaeda's leadership recognized this and chastised al-Zarqawi, admonishing him to focus on organization building and reducing the violence. This culminated with an infamous letter intercepted by American intelligence and later shared publicly in late 2005. AQI ignored this advice and bombed al-Askari mosque in Samarra in February 2006, one of the holiest Shiite shrines. The blast caused no deaths, but it triggered a violent wave of reprisals and counterreprisals, leading to the deaths of thousands. This incident transformed the war in Iraq from an insurgency to an all-out civil war between the various religious groups. Concomitantly, al-Zarqawi began reorganizing AQI to cement its position as the paramount rebel organization in the country, creating the Mujahideen Shura Council, which brought other Salafist jihadist movements under one banner. This eventually metastasized into IS.

Al-Zarqawi did not live to see the fruits of his labor. In May 2006, an American air strike killed him. Combined with the United States adopting a population-centric counterinsurgency strategy that sought to win over the disenchanted Sunni tribes, AQI's influence waned, and the level of violence decreased significantly over the coming years. The seeds of IS were planted, though.

HOW IRAQI POLITICS CREATED ISLAMIC STATE

In 2006, Iraq was a country without a government amenable to the needs of the various ethnic groups trying to form a new state. Tactically and operationally, the United States sought to fix the situation by co-opting the disenchanted Sunni tribes and giving them a buy-in into the new Iraqi government. It accomplished this by paying off Sunni fighters, increasing the number of ground troops to help secure the population, and taking a more anthropological approach to fighting AQI. This helped generate large amounts of human intelligence, which slowly led to the United States and the new Iraqi army uprooting AQI from large portions of the country. Most of the success centered on Anbar Province where the United States and its coalition partners cooperated with the so-called Sons of Iraq. The latter was a movement of disenchanted Sunni tribe members opposed to AQI's violence and its attempt to supersede tribal customs and laws. These individuals knew their environment better than the United States, its allies, and the newly reconstituted Iraqi army, which consisted of mostly Shiites, and were able to identify AQI sympathizers, supporters, and members, pushing the group further into the periphery.

Starting in 2007, the levels of violence from sectarianism decreased. There was optimism that Iraq had been pulled from the brink and it could slowly bring itself back together. From this perspective, the United States succeeded. Politically, it also gave the American public the illusion of success as it sought to withdraw from the country by the end of 2011. These victories aside, it failed to address the main strategic problem plaguing Iraq: the lack of a viable government seen as legitimate by the majority of the country.

Ever since the American-led transitional government took shape in 2004, and through the country's formulation and adoption of its constitution and its first election for a full-term government in 2005, Sunnis had rejected these efforts because of their overt Shiite influence. Much of the propaganda distributed by AQI, other Sunni insurgents, former Baathists, and other elements of the Iraqi resistance portrayed these efforts as a means for Iran to take over the country. This was worsened by the election of Nouri al-Maliki as prime minister, the leader of the Islamic Dawa Party. Dawa is an organization that formed in the 1950s and has maintained ties to Iran since the 1980s. Indeed, it was part of the constellation of proxies used by Iran to try to destabilize Iraq during the Iraq-Iran War in the 1980s. Al-Maliki himself was a hard-line anti-Baathist—which, given the preponderance of Sunnis in the party under Saddam Hussein, easily took on harsh sectarian emphasis. After 2003, he was part of the committee tasked with executing de-Baathification, giving credence to al-Zarqawi's propaganda.

Over the next nine years, with al-Maliki leading the country, efforts were made to soothe the tensions between the various regions and confessional sects. The United States committed itself to continue funding and training the Iraqi army and providing strong economic support to Iraq, which would further facilitate the reconstruction efforts. These moves were designed to help separate the country from the overt and covert influence played by Iran, either through its ties to Shiite groups in the country or through its direct connections to Iraq's governing elites. Apart from being a geopolitical rival for the United States and its allies, many hoped that severing Iran's influence would help foster, again, the notion of a national and secular Iraqi identity while easing some of the concerns and worries held by Sunnis in the country. Building on these efforts, the United States took advantage of the federalism built into the 2005 constitution. Using the promise of economic aid plus the new national strategy proposed during the 2007 Iraq War troop surge, the Bush administration pressured Iraq's new government to cede more authority to Sunnis and Kurds. Most of these efforts translated into yielding authority to provincial governments in Sunni-dominated areas, but they stopped short of giving the degree of autonomy the Kurds experienced.

These efforts were half-hearted for a variety of reasons. Just by their sheer numbers, Shiites dominate the country, with anywhere from 60 to 70 percent of the population identifying as such. Sunnis, in contrast, only make up around 20 percent of the population. Regardless of the interests of the party or prime minister in power, Shiite interests would likely dominate over the wants of other groups, especially after the decades of repression and brutality experienced under Saddam Hussein. This came to pass in the form of Prime Minister al-Maliki. As noted previously, from the out-set, al-Maliki took a stringent anti-Sunni tone, but this was downplayed when the United States backed his candidacy in 2005. At the time, he appeared weak and reliant on other power brokers. However, decades of operating covertly as a member of Dawa also made him wary of political rivals, habits he demonstrated later into his tenure. For the most part, beginning with his ascendency in December 2005 to the end of 2008, right before President Bush left office, al-Maliki cultivated the impression that he was hardworking, pliable, and moderate. This was partially a product of the circumstances, as Iraq was at the height of sectarianism. Even then, though, he showed his teeth by initially rebuffing American efforts to pay the Sunnis who had taken up arms against al-Qaeda.

After 2008, with President Obama in office and a stabilized country in hand, al-Maliki asserted himself. He first acted against his immediate Shiite rivals by seeking to take control of the militia headed by Muqtada al-Sadr, which was one of the most dangerous Shiite groups during the insurgency. Then al-Maliki went about intimidating political rivals, preventing Sunni politicians from participating in local elections, and moving close friends and associates of his into seats of power. He consolidated these moves by sacking many of Iraq's senior military leaders in favor of those most loyal to him, changing the composition and the quality of command of this institution. Al-Maliki also backed away from promises of continuing to pay the Sunni fighters who had participated in the fight against AQI and from integrating them into Iraq's security forces. So obvious were these largely anti-Sunni maneuvers that by 2014, when IS stormed across northern Iraq, around 80 percent of the military was Shiite. This overt sectarianism, in conjunction with al-Maliki's evident ties to Iran, including the notorious General Qasem Soleimani—the head of Iran's Quds Force—gave many Sunnis the impression that Iraq had become an extension of Iran.

The last real chance at preventing the future catastrophe came with the March 2010 national elections. The results showed al-Maliki losing to al-Iraqiya, a coalition formed by Sunni Arabs, Kurds, Turkmens, and Christians. Al-Maliki questioned the results, accusing many of the same Western governments that were supporting him of rigging the vote, which led to a political crisis. Because of a decision by Iraq's Federal Supreme Court, al-Maliki was given the first chance to form a government. Negotiations stalled for nearly six months. Nonetheless, after pressure from Iran, all Shiite organizations agreed to support al-Maliki, enabling him to form a government. This came at the cost of making concessions to ideological and religious rivals, which he would later renege upon and would help feed the tensions that engulfed the country four years later.

These moves by Iraq's government created a political vacuum among Sunnis, who were never entirely convinced of the new model of governance in Iraq. Sunnis were distrustful of the Iraqi security forces and aware of how al-Maliki was centralizing power at the expense of the Sunnis, including jailing the Iraqi vice president. A major reservoir of discontent was building. This was compounded by the fact that the United States never fully eliminated al-Qaeda in Iraq, leaving enough of the organization intact, despite a constant game of whack-a-mole with its leaders. AQI recognized the increased sectarianism pervading the country and began reconfiguring in the shadows.

The first thing AQI admitted was that its model of governance had proven to be its key weakness. After al-Zarqawi's death in late 2006, it still governed overtly in Anbar Province. There it imposed a Taliban-style rule, enforcing a strict interpretation of sharia law, which countervailed traditional tribal and local politics in the region. Reassembling itself and attempting to co-opt Sunnis, AQI started reforming itself with a less severe and capricious governing model. Helping it in this goal was the immense wealth the organization had garnered during the insurgency. Although IS is now recognized to be one of the wealthiest terrorist-cum-insurgent groups in history, it started accumulating a significant portion of its money during the Iraq War. Participating in banditry, kidnapping, and oil smuggling, AQI was bringing in hundreds of millions of dollars a year. With such copious amounts of money, it could finance its shadow army.

The second thing that it did was a process of Iraqization of its organization. When al-Zarqawi entered the country in 2003, the core of his group was a mixture of Arabs from Syria, Jordan, and other parts of the Levant. In this sense, they were truly outsiders seeking to insert themselves in local politics. With the constant elimination of its leadership, either through arrest or assassinations, AQI adopted a more native posture, which helped it appeal to the disenchanted Iraqi Sunnis. Combined with its absorption of other Sunni insurgent groups and the gradual rebuilding of its fighting forces through prison breakouts, the terrorist group underwent a transformation until it became Islamic State of Iraq (ISI). Important as well, Abu Bakr al-Baghdadi assumed the role of emir in 2010.

Much criticism for the emergence of Islamic State is laid upon President Obama's decision to withdraw troops from Iraq at the end of 2011. In many ways, this accusation is unfair. First, after 2005, Iraq was a sovereign country once more, meaning al-Maliki had the right to govern as he pleased. Regardless of the desires of the United States, any decision to remain in the country had to be approved by Iraq's leadership. Second, President Bush, in the closing days of his administration, had signed the status of forces agreement (SOFA), which stipulated the withdrawal of American troops by 2011. National security hawks pushed for a continued American presence after this point to maintain the peace and keep leverage over al-Maliki, who was increasingly imitating other authoritarian governments in the region. President Obama did push to have this agreement extended, but al-Maliki played politics and refused to change domestic laws that would have subjugated American service members to Iraqi laws. He did put the matter to a vote shortly before the mandated departure date, but it did not garner sufficient support from parliament to extend and amend the 2008 SOFA. And besides, this vote was only permitted after Iran acquiesced, as it had been the true victor of the Iraq War. If anything, President Obama deserves blame for not using greater diplomacy after the 2010 Iraqi elections to force out al-Maliki and for ignoring signs that al-Maliki was transforming into a veritable autocrat in his own right. Perhaps with a more inclusive Iraqi leader, the organization that would transform into IS would have lacked the popular legitimacy necessary to govern.

THE ARAB SPRING, AL-QAEDA, AND ISLAMIC STATE OF IRAQ AND SYRIA

The next big inflection point was the onset of the civil war in Syria during the Arab Spring in 2011. As was true of many countries in the broader Middle East, the Syrian public became inflamed and sought reforms. Bashar al-Assad, Syria's president, witnessed what happened to the presidents of Tunisia and Egypt, and later how the international community turned on Muammar Qaddafi in Libya. Initially, he sought to buy off the protestors with token political reforms and a policy of general amnesty. The latter released an untold number of jihadists, many of whom had participated in the Iraq War and had ties to al-Qaeda. These peaceful over-tures quickly turned violent, as Assad sought to crush dissent and quell the uprising before it consumed his regime. Having learned from his father's brutal crackdown of the Syrian Muslim Brotherhood in the 1980s, he soon unleashed the Syrian war machine upon the restive public.

During the Iraq War, Syria had been the main conduit for foreign fight-ers wishing to join AQI, making it a fertile ground for jihad. Al-Baghdadi and al-Qaeda's central leadership realized this. Al-Baghdadi, with his group having been re-formed and expanding in the Sunni-dominated areas of Iraq, dispatched Abu Mohammad al-Julani, a Syrian deputy of his, to start developing an expansion group in the late summer of 2011. Taking advantage of the cadre of Islamist fighting, al-Julani began form-ing what would become Jabhat al-Nusra (JN), later renamed Jabhat Fateh al-Sham in 2016. The group committed its first attack in December 2011 and released a video announcing its formation in January 2012. Initially, it did not associate with al-Qaeda or ISI, but reports noted that many of its fighters had fought with AQI. JN proved itself a capable fighting force and increased its support among local Syrians as Assad's brutality in-creased. It claimed responsibility for the dual car bombings in Damascus in March 2012 that killed twenty-seven people, as well as for executing thirteen men, whose bodies were later discovered in a mass grave, near Deir ez-Zor in May 2012. In October of that year, it set off three suicide car bombs in Aleppo that killed forty-eight people. By December 2012, the group was formidable enough that it had developed an anti-aircraft doc-trine, declaring a no-fly zone over Aleppo. These and other attacks cre-ated a large public profile, which enabled it to become the public face of the Syrian fight and, at that point, the most visible element of the global jihadist movement.

Al-Baghdadi, authoritarian in nature—as his rule would later show—revealed JN's links to ISI in April 2013 and sought to subsume the orga-nization, using the name of Islamic State of Iraq and Syria (ISIS). Al-Julani was adamant about maintaining his independence and largely fended off al-Baghdadi's efforts. He reaffirmed his loyalty to AQ, and that summer, Ayman al-Zawahiri, the leader of AQ, rejected al-Baghdadi's moves. Both men exchanged insults with each other for the remainder of the year, each issuing edicts undercutting the other. Al-Zawahiri finally incorporated JN into al-Qaeda's global franchise system in December 2013, but this failed to end the dispute. At the same time, JN and the so-called ISIS began fighting each other, openly contesting territory and assassinating each other's leaders. In January 2014, ISIS took over Raqqa, a city that JN had captured in March 2013. The fighting between both groups escalated in February 2014, when Ayman al-Zawahiri formally cut ties with ISIS because of its intransigence.

But many Syrian members of JN remained loyal during the split. ISIS still managed to poach a significant number of foreign fighters from JN and used this as the basis of its expansion into western Syria. Bitter infighting between both organizations ensued. JN had the upper hand among the other insurgent groups in Syria because it sought a more conciliatory and compromising approach to asserting its rule compared to ISIS's more brutal and rigid approach to governance, which jealously maintained power. In addition, ISIS inherited its ideology from al-Zarqawi. It regarded all non-Sunnis to be apostates and pursued its same genocidal fervor into Syria. Wanting to provoke further sectarianism in the region, it brutally attacked other groups fighting against Assad. As such, JN maintained its paramount role in the Syrian insurgency. ISIS, though, apart from taking control of the Syrian city of Raqqa, which would become its capital after declaring the caliphate, also captured large swaths of the western Syrian desert near Deir ez-Zor. Combined with its efforts at breaking out imprisoned members of ISIS in Iraq, by the end of 2013, ISIS was primed and ready for its assault against Iraq. In January 2014, it captured Fallujah and Ramadi and in June 2014 captured Mosul. That month it declared the caliphate and renamed itself Islamic State, making al-Baghdadi's organization the new go-to group for the global jihadist movement. The name change also implied that its focus extended beyond Iraq and the Levant. By calling itself Islamic State, it wanted the world to know that it claimed sovereignty over all Muslims and that its ultimate goal was world domination.

THE JABHAT AL-NUSRA THREAT, THE KHORASAN GROUP, AND THE CO-OPTATION OF ISLAMIC STATE'S CREDIBILITY

While Islamic State was ravaging Iraq and Syria, al-Qaeda continued expanding its presence in Syria, making it the most important piece of the Syrian resistance in the beginning of 2015. When Jabhat al-Nusra emerged in 2012, it lacked the infrastructure and organizational capacity to wage an intense war against Assad. Furthermore, it had poor situational awareness of the politics affecting the Syrian theater. Because it did not appreciate the secular and demonstrative character of the Syrian opposition, its initial forays into the conflict saw it emphasizing terrorism against civilians rather than military targets. It also attempted to force a strict interpretation of sharia law, which was not appealing to the nationalist Syrians. The unpopularity of its initial moves forced it to recalibrate its approach. Fortunately for it, its Islamic image made it the initial beneficiary of the various foreign fighters arriving. Charles Lister, a senior fellow at the Washington-based Middle East Institute and an expert on the Syrian conflict, cites the importance of Syria in jihadist eschatology as the place where Jesus Christ will return, making it an attractive destination for radicals across the world. The influx of human capital helped it readjust its strategy and convert its focus into a purely Syrian issue rather than a pan-Islamic cause like Islamic State. Adopting this approach made it more amenable to other Syrian groups, facilitating alliance formation. Moreover, its leader, al-Julani, was a veteran of AQI and was witness to the effect an extremist approach to governance had on negating a group its popular appeal.

The intensity of the fighting created the need for alliances among the constellation of groups fighting Assad. From the secular to the Islamic, all agreed that Assad had to be removed from power. JN's ability to fight made it a visible figure in the rebellion, making it one of the more popular elements among the opposition. It further grew in stature when it began doling out social services in places like Aleppo and Deir ez-Zor. In this moderated manner, JN managed to change popular attitudes toward it by imposing a type of fair, if strict, governance model that lacked the brutality or the capriciousness of Assad.

JN formally split from ISIS in April 2013 after al-Julani affirmed his allegiance to al-Qaeda. As mentioned above, the organization lost a significant portion of its fighting cadre. It also lost a significant source of funding. It, nonetheless, maintained important ties to AQ, which represented another source of funding, guidance, and experience. By summer 2013, AQ had deployed veteran jihadists to Syria and formed an interlinked group nicknamed, by Western governments, the Khorasan Group (KG). KG's purpose was to use the safe haven afforded by the Syrian fight to recruit, plot, and execute major attacks against Western targets, allowing it to continue Osama bin Laden's strategic priorities. KG also helped Jabhat al-Nusra rebuild and was important in the rebranding of the centrality of Syria in the global jihadist movement, giving it international legitimacy.

In August 2013, the world became aware of Assad's use of chemical weapons against the Syrian opposition. Viewing the opportunity to brandish its Syrian outlook, JN ferociously attacked regime targets, helping maintain its support among the forces fighting Assad, especially as the Free Syrian Army, the main secular fighting force backed by the West, began losing steam. This demonstration of power created the intra-jihadist war between JN and ISIS in 2013, causing JN to lose large amounts of territory. Even with this loss of territory, it maintained the upper hand in Syria. Most important, Charles Lister notes that the group avoided the temptation of mimicking Islamic State's hard-line theological approach or plotting attacks against the West to avoid becoming targets of American air strikes. Maintaining its moderate outlook kept it as the paramount leader of the jihadist movement in Syria once IS began retracting and losing ground.

Over the next two years, the Syrian rebels continued gaining ground and nearly defeated the Assad regime. In November 2015, Russia intervened to prevent this from happening, changing the tide of the conflict in favor of Assad. The evolving facts on the ground led to a series of failed diplomatic talks to end the conflict, which marginalized JN because of its ties to AQ. Recognizing that the al-Qaeda label made other Syrian Islamic groups uncomfortable being associated with it, most notably Ahrar al-Sham—a Syrian focused group with ties to the Syrian brotherhood—Jabhat al-Nusra nominally split away from AQ and renamed itself Jabhat Fateh al-Sham (JFS). This split was actually approved by Ayman al-Zawahiri, suggesting this was an effort to rebrand itself more so than a complete abdication of its role in AQ's universe. By the end of 2016, it retained a strong force of nearly ten thousand fighters across Syria. Its contribution to lift the siege of Aleppo was not enough to prevent Assad from crushing the rebellion there, though.

The fall of Aleppo is significant for the future of IS and JFS. Assad crushed the heart of the non-Islamic opposition, making the only viable forces Salafi jihadist groups. JFS is already in position to exploit the changing political situation. IS will too, because plausible alternatives will be few and far between. Furthermore, Assad retook Aleppo with a thorough disregard for civilian casualties and with ample support from Hezbollah in Lebanon, Iran, and Russia, giving his victory a stringent sectarian character that will likely energize other radical Salafi jihadists. As the International Crisis Group argued in January 2017, Aleppo's fall will not end the Syrian civil war and will most likely embolden Islamic groups, meaning both JFS and IS still have room to build.

STYMIED IRAQI REFORMS, ISLAMIC STATE'S DECLINE SINCE 2014, AND THE FUTURE OF TERRORISM

In August 2014, the United States launched Operation Inherent Resolve to push back Islamic State. Under President Obama, the strategy focused on reforming the Iraqi government to win back the disenchanted Sunnis, training the Iraqi military, ending the war in Syria, and cutting off the flow of foreign fighters. The first step was forcing Prime Minister al-Maliki to step aside in favor of Haider al-Abadi, a figure perceived as more moderate and inclusive. He immediately set out on building a more inclusive government and fighting corruption in the Iraqi military. His efforts at accomplishing significant reform stalled for a variety of reasons. First, Iraqi politics remained plagued by factionalism and sectarianism, limiting al-Abadi's ability to pass legislation. Second, even though he was willing to integrate Sunnis, al-Abadi still depended on Shiite militias politically, further stymieing his reform programs. As such, by the beginning of 2018, Iraq had improved somewhat politically but remains fractured along sectarian lines.

The military effort was more successful. The use of air strikes and American-trained soldiers led to the slow erosion of IS positions over the next two and a half years, beginning by retaking Kobani in Syria and the Mosul Dam. The high rate of air strikes vitiated and weakened IS dramatically. The training effort took some time to commence, with an inability to field a capable fighting force by summer 2015. Things began to change in early 2016 with the seizure of Ramadi by the Iraqi military, which was done without using Shiite militias. The use of purely Iraqi military forces rather than Iranian-trained Shiite militias helped legitimize the war effort among Sunnis, who were concerned because of Iran's overt role in the retaking of Tikrit in 2015. In 2016, the Pentagon claimed that IS had lost 43 percent of its territory and around 45,000 fighters by August of that year. The loss of Mosul and Tel Afar in 2017 deprived it of its last major cities in Iraq, making its power base exclusively Syrian despite it being largely an Iraqi organization. With JFS remaining the primary Islamic group there, IS will have a hard time operating in Syria. IS's situation has worsened significantly since the group lost Raqqa, its territorial capital, in 2017. Seemingly aware of the challenge posed by continuing to hold territory, IS, shortly before losing Raqqa, made an organized effort to move its governing apparatus to Mayadin, a Syrian border town. The anti-IS coalition expected the group to continue its overt governance model in Mayadin, as it permitted easy access to both Syria and Iraq. But this was not to be the case, because Assad's forces retook the town in October without much of a fight and with no sign of IS's senior leadership, as IS had fled into the desert.

According to Hassan Hassan, a prominent security analyst at the Washington-based Tahrir Institute for Middle East Policy, what is likely happening is that IS is shifting its Middle East strategy away from conquest to one based on insurgent warfare. Hassan notes that in various IS propaganda tracts in 2017, the group has sought to portray its activities between 2013 and 2014 as its most successful period, because of how rapidly it organized and took control of territory, suggesting the group is trying to prime its followers to accept this strategic setback as progress. In these circumstances, IS will most likely resume clandestine operations in Iraq's Sunni regions, using both the carrot and the stick to rebuild its base. The group retains sufficient manpower to engage in protracted terrorism campaigns to assassinate prominent Sunni leaders and generate fear, and it fields a large cadre of experienced fighters capable of harassing the Iraqi military. Even if it no longer seeks to display its strength by holding territory, IS regains the advantage of being hidden, allowing it to project power through guerrilla actions. Furthermore, this process occurs within the context of a civil war, meaning it has the opportunity to recruit fighters locally and to engage in clandestine institution building. Likewise, its brand still has relevance abroad, even if it's rather diminished, and it will still attract true believers. It has a model in al-Qaeda, as that organization has been engaged in a process of institution building and managing its brand since the death of Osama bin Laden. In the decade since bin Laden's death, AQ has assumed the upper hand in Syria, solidified its position in Yemen, and expanded into India and Nigeria. If IS modifies this model to its own situation, it can easily return stronger and deadlier than before.

So what comes next? This extensive overview of Islamic State from formation to the present brings about a few key points. First, the group's rapid gains in Iraq and Syria destroyed the global community's illusion that terrorism was on the downswing following Osama bin Laden's death and the Arab Spring, both of which happened in 2011. Whereas bin Laden's death seemed to herald the death of terrorism's ultimate mastermind, the Arab Spring initially promised a new form of politics for the Middle East distinct from the violence and autocracy that had characterized the region. Instead, the opposite happened. Autocracy returned with a vengeance, and many of the countries on the road to democracy stumbled and degenerated into civil wars. The two exceptions seemed to be Egypt and Tunisia, but the old problems continue, with terrorism on the rise in both places.

Second, Islamic State forced the broader public to reassess the ontological nature of terrorism. Although it was understood that terrorist groups could morph into insurgencies and hold territory, many dismissed the idea that a radical Islamic terrorist group could forge an ideology and a governing strategy capable of seizing a territory roughly the size of the United Kingdom. Many thought it was unlikely that such brutal tactics could ever find enough of an appeal to win the support of society, while ignoring the fact that the Taliban had accomplished something similar in the 1990s. Fortunately, IS overreached and invited reprisals that have left it a shell of its former self.

Third, Islamic State remains a potent threat not only in Iraq and Syria but also in many parts of the world. The same forces that animated the insurgency still persist. Despite Russian intervention into the Syrian conflict and the defeat of the rebels in Aleppo, Syria will remain a fractured country for years to come. It is unlikely that Assad will moderate his approach after nearly being defeated. He will most likely continue his scorched-earth approach on other rebel-held areas, hoping that he can replicate his success in Aleppo. In fact, he created even more hatred toward his government in April 2017 after reports emerged that he used chemical weapons again against civilians. Unfortunately for him, he will have to contend with the fact that his army is a fraction of the strength of what it was prior to the beginning of the war, that he is politically weakened and continues to survive because of the support provided by Iran and Russia, and that large swaths of Syria remain outside of his control. In addition, as an Alawite who used chemical weapons and is closely associated with

Iran, Assad will remain the centerpiece of propaganda used by groups like JFS and IS to recruit radicals from across the world. Therefore, the Islamic resistance will have both a motive and the space to reorganize and continue fighting another day. JFS is already primed to do this, as the number of troops available to it continues to increase because of defections from IS. Salafi jihadists will be even more motivated if Russia continues supporting Assad, as many might associate the present struggle there with the birth of the modern jihadist threat during the Soviet-Afghan War of the 1980s.

Iraq is in a similar position. Although it has retaken lost land including Mosul, the long-term animosity between Kurds, Sunnis, and Shiites continues. It is even likely that it is worse than during the peak of the civil war in Iraq in 2006/2007, as the Sunnis will have more grievances to make them suspicious of the government in Baghdad. For many Sunnis, given the lethargic pace of political reform and Iran's overt role in helping Iraq counter IS, the impression that Iran has taken over the country will be hard to dismiss. This perspective will likely animate Sunnis to support IS, even if they hate it just as much as they hate Iran. In the case of the Kurds, over the last fifteen years, they have built their society and economy and are seeking any excuse to declare independence. This would greatly reduce the national oil supply, which would also reduce the available finances necessary for rebuilding the country. Kurds, in fact, held a referendum on independence in October 2017, which resulted in the Iraqi military entering the Kurdish town of Kirkuk and the president of Iraqi Kurdistan, Masoud Barzani, stepping down, which stalled the independence process for the time being. However, this may change in the coming years depending on what reforms occur in Iraq. In other words, the challenge for the government in Baghdad is that when it can no longer rally its population against IS, it will actually have to govern a diverse multiethnic state that has still to recover from a civil war. If reconciliation efforts are not made by the central government, then IS will still have a buy-in among key elements of Iraq's civil society and could easily reconstitute itself in the future.

With this context in mind, despite the impending fall of Islamic State, the model it deployed in 2014 is still something worth emulating. If before 9/11 security analysts dismissed terrorism as a strategic nuisance that could not effect global change unless a group used a weapon of mass destruction (WMD), then IS showed that a localized insurgency combining state-building functions and terrorism tactically and operationally could achieve strategic impacts that threatened to undermine the state system itself. In doing so, it sought revolutionary change that would erase historical boundaries and create a supranational theocratic government that claimed sovereignty over all the Middle East and the world's Muslim population. The fact that this nearly occurred is worth studying and exploring, as Iraq and Syria are not the only places suffering from this type of violence.

9

BEYOND ISLAMIC STATE

ALTHOUGH ISLAMIC STATE MONOPOLIZES MEDIA COVERAGE, TERRORISM is a widespread phenomenon that affects all regions of the globe. Unfortunately, covering every act of modern terrorism or every group engaged in the practice is out of the scope of this book. It is worthwhile, nonetheless, to briefly examine global trends and the ideological components of its current manifestation before delving into the bigger battlefields—namely, Yemen, Libya, and Afghanistan.

Before beginning, it is important to note that modern terrorism is largely an Islamic phenomenon. For reasons explained before in this book, secessionist and leftist terror groups have lost much of their appeal, as their animating ideologies no longer carry legitimacy. In Latin America, the only extant terror group of any note is the FARC in Colombia, but even they have come to sign a peace deal with the government. Some wish to make the case for Mexican cartels and Central American drug gangs to be considered terrorist organizations, but they lack any coherent political objective to suggest their violence has any end beyond personal enrichment. Definitions of terrorism abound, but the key facet is the use of violence and the fear generated from it to force some sort of political change within a society. In this sense, the activities by cartels and gangs remain a purely criminal problem that does not threaten the complete upheaval of the system and only precludes economic development. Likewise, in Peru, there is the perennial worry that Sendero Luminoso will take up arms again, but at this point in its history, the group is at best a glorified cartel. Lacking a charismatic leader to resuscitate the organization, not to mention any mass popular appeal as Peru continues modernizing, the group will most likely continue banking off its legacy from the 1980s until it becomes wholly irrelevant. The economic conditions that gave rise to the group in the 1970s no longer exist, and even if they did, their Maoist ideology was rendered quite repugnant by their wholesale violence at the peak of their insurgency.

These trends hold up for much of the rest of the world as well. Most groups are too weak, maintain parochial interests that curtail their potential for violence, adhere to an ideology that few people will buy into, or have eschewed violence in favor of the opportunity to participate in democratic governance. There are certainly violent non-Islamic groups in Africa and Asia with some semblance of political goals, but oftentimes, this rhetoric masks the real end goal of accumulating wealth. Take the Lord's Resistance Army (LRA), for example. It captured the world's attention in 2012 after a social media awareness campaign went viral, yet in practice, the LRA is a fraction of its size in the 1990s. Some estimates suggest their numbers dropped from several thousand to perhaps as few as two hundred fighters. At this point, most of its activity is consigned to banditry and is only one of the many problems affecting Uganda. Similarly, in Asia, the Tamil Tigers (or Liberation Tigers of Tamil Eelam [LTTE]) have largely collapsed following the brutal scorched-earth campaign waged by the Sri Lankan government in 2009. After being one of the most lethal terrorist groups and taking credit for killing two heads of state, the LTTE is largely decimated. This does not mean that another group like it cannot arise or that it cannot rebuild, as the political conditions in Sri Lanka still make it fertile for a similar group to emerge, but it will be a different entity from the one constructed by its main leader, Velupillai Prabhakaran.

In Europe, with the exception of Anders Breivik, most acts of terrorism have been inspired by Islamic entities. Both the IRA and the ETA have opted to forgo violence in favor of the democratic electoral system, which their political constituencies regard as a more legitimate manner for achieving systemic change than threatening violence. The Basque case is telling. After four decades of violence, Basque society has largely turned on the ETA. This is in part because of the great level of prosperity the Basque country has experienced since Spain democratized, but also because they have seen the example of Catalonia, which is close to seceding largely through the power of the ballot. Elsewhere in Europe, prior to the rise of Islamic terrorism, Germany suffered a string of assassinations linked to the National Socialist Underground, a rightist terror group that was dismantled in 2011. However, despite these examples of sporadic right-wing violence, which appear from time to time in the news, there is a lack of coordinated terror campaigns waged by non-Islamic groups on the continent.

The one anomalous country is perhaps the United States, but even then, this is a product of the country's peculiar legal system. Since 9/11, numerous Islamic-inspired attacks have affected the country, including the Boston Marathon bombings in April 2013 and the San Bernardino attacks in December 2015. At the same time, though, it has seen an increase in various right-wing militia groups that threaten violence against the government for perceived violations of the Constitution. More worrisome has been the proliferation of white supremacist groups, especially following Donald Trump's announcement of his candidacy for president of the United States in June 2015. At this point, these groups have yet to act violently in a coordinated fashion against minority groups or government targets, but there have been some worrying events. In June 2015, white supremacist Dylann Roof murdered nine people in a church in Charleston, South Carolina. In April 2014, Cliven Bundy triggered a standoff with federal law enforcement over unpaid fees for grazing land in Nevada. The incident ended without any deaths in May but nonetheless inspired the subsequent Malheur standoff that occurred between January and February 2016 that led to the death of one of the occupiers. In both cases, the people involved belonged to a coterie of right-wing militia groups and the sovereign citizen movement, which worries about government overreach and wishes to fight back. Yet this does not compare to the spate of violence committed by militia members in the 1990s that culminated with the Oklahoma City bombing in 1995. Furthermore, at the same time these events have transpired, the country has seen a significant decrease in levels of violent crime and homicides. The one problem that seems to affect the country is the spate of mass shootings that occur in a nearly clockwork fashion every couple of days. These, though, with a few exceptions, tend to be apolitical and a product of the country's stance on guns. Bloody headlines aside, the country is safer than it has been in a long time when look-ing at raw statistics.

Certainly, all this can change under President Trump. Before and after his election, there was a surge in membership for organizations identify-ing as alt-right. These groups, who on the whole support President Trump, maintain a decidedly racist and nationalist outlook, resurrecting many of the white supremacist tropes previously considered as too extreme and rac-ist for mainstream consumption. The alt-right has the potential to mobi-lize and organize people into violence, as was demonstrated during the August 2017 Charlottesville protests, and President Trump has gone a long way toward legitimizing these groups both in his language and with the people he surrounds himself. This subject will be explored further later in this book.

RELIGION AND A GLOBALIZED DECENTRALIZED IDEOLOGY

All of this can change. Known and unknown chaos always produces new winners and losers in political systems that might encourage new violent movements. However, the main truth about the current state of terrorism is that it is largely concentrated in the Middle East and places with strong Islamic influence. The epicenter is currently in Iraq and Syria, but violence plagues Yemen, many parts of North Africa, Nigeria, South Asia, and Southeast Asia and affects various regions with large Muslim populations, including Europe, Russia, North America, Australia, China, and other parts of Asia. Despite its indelible Islamic character, terrorism in each of these places is motivated by contextual reasons independent of religion or ethnicity. As has been the case historically with terrorist groups, the animat-ing ideology is often a pretext to justify the underlying causes for violence. On a micro level, motivators for terrorism can range from psychological disturbances, personal greed, or the desire to follow the path taken by family members. On a macro scale, terrorism can be caused by power dis-putes between rival groups, secessionist desires, or revolutionary aims.

These caveats aside, the religious aspect of contemporary terrorism makes it more potent than any secessionist or revolutionary ideology of the nineteenth or twentieth century. Even if it is a pretext, it is a powerful one that attracts recruits from across the globe, giving a shared sense of kin-ship that transcends language and culture. This holds true for Islamic

State and others like it. As noted by experts like David C. Rapoport and Bruce Hoffman, unlike its secular counterparts, religiously motivated terrorism advances a coherent framework for understanding the individual and the state, which puts it at odds with the notion of the dominant nation-state and most other secular political orders. According to most religious doctrines, the notion of a temporal secular order is anathema, as the only law that matters is that of a god. In this sense, where revolutionary forces such as the Sendero Luminoso wished to reorder the laws of society in the twentieth century according to a human scale, religious groups deny these laws any legitimacy. This reading too means that the obvious limits on violence are lacking. In the past, insurgent and terrorist groups had to proscribe excessive violence to avoid alienating their base and source of recruits. As was the case with various groups in the past, too much violence could make a group seem repugnant and make it difficult for an organization to acquire funding, find recruits, or maintain the necessary passive support of their communities to avoid capture or arrest by authorities. Brian Jenkins said it best in the 1970s when he noted that the terrorists of that age "wanted many people watching, not many people dead."

In contrast, going back to the Zealots in the first century and extending to the Thuggee cult in India, religiously inspired violence has always maintained an indelible apocalyptic flair to it. Regardless of the spiritual faith behind it, this type of terrorism regards the present as a prologue to the rewards found in heaven, or at the very least, it hastens the eventual end of the world. With religion sanctioning their violence, these groups have no limits in the scope and expanse of their terror, as long as the intention behind it accords to a notion of advancing the interests of their spiritual order. Not surprisingly, since the 1990s, scholars such as Bruce Hoffman and others have feared that religious terrorists are the ones most likely to use weapons of mass destruction if given the opportunity. Aum Shinrikyo demonstrated this vividly when it committed the sarin gas attacks in Tokyo's subway system in 1995, and the world has been fortunate that this has been the only vivid instance until now. Various reports from the late 1990s and early 2000s note that al-Qaeda sought to purchase materials to create its own weapons of mass destruction. As the Harvard professor Graham Allison noted, the world has been quite fortunate that organizational and technical mishaps have prevented tragedies much worse than 9/11.

So in the context of Islamic State, al-Qaeda, and other groups linked to them, what do they believe exactly? Generally, they begin from the Salafist tradition, which emerged in the eighteenth century and called for a return to the practices of the earliest Muslims. In practice, this translates into an ultraconservative worldview that promotes a strict interpretation of sharia law and rejects religious innovation, but it does not necessarily imply violence. IS and AQ take it further by combining Salafism with the ideas of Sayyid Qutb and Ibn Taymiyyah. The former, in his book *Milestones*, argued for an extreme rejection of secular law in favor of sharia and the importance of offensive jihad to bring about the restoration of Islam. The latter, a medieval theologian, is most notable for writing about jihad against fellow Muslims, serving as an inspiration for *takfirism*, the idea of declaring Muslims as apostates to justify their execution. These paramount ideas elevate groups like IS and AQ from mere Salafist organizations to what scholars call *Salafi jihadists* or simply *jihadists*. Other themes central to jihadist ideology are the importance of regime change to create purer Islamic polities, the retaking of lands seen as occupied Muslim territories, and the necessity of defending Muslims from non-Muslims.

Unfettered in this way by religion, modern Islamic terrorists maintain the hallmark of their confessional predecessors from history but have built on it with ambitious state-building projects. Islamic State's success in Syria and Iraq is the best-known example, but it is certainly not the only case. Similar programs have been attempted by its affiliates in Libya and Afghanistan, by al-Qaeda in Yemen and Syria, and by other groups linked to the global jihadist movements. That being said, this indelible religious character does not mean that the current wave of terrorism is monolithic or carries a unified agenda applicable to every jihadist organization out there, in the same manner that Communist insurgents were not fighting under the same banner or cause. For example, takfirism is a core tenet of IS, especially against Shiite Muslims, but it is something that al-Qaeda has only adopted reluctantly in specific situations and in fact was one of the causes of the eventual schism between both organizations in 2014. This problem plagues Boko Haram in Nigeria too, with various groups splintering off, most notably Ansaru, because of its penchant for violence against fellow Muslims.

Similarly, even within affiliated groups, there are differences in objectives, strategies, and tactics. AQ has always prioritized attacking what it regards as the far enemy, meaning the United States and its Western allies, because it believes that as long as they support the local apostate regimes in the Middle East, it will not be able to establish the caliphate. Yet when it comes to al-Qaeda's franchises in Yemen, in the Islamic Maghreb, and elsewhere, although they might attack Western targets in their area of operations, normally they seek to undermine the local government instead. In this regard, their strategic focus resembles that of an insurgency deploying a coordinated political-military campaign replete with information operations, its own sustained rhythm and tempo, control of territory, and uniforms worn when the group engages military targets in pitched battles. This spectrum of strategies makes it hard to argue that there is a centralized or definable characteristic that permeates throughout all modern terrorism. Even then, just because an organization is affiliated with a terrorist group like AQ or IS does not mean that the group is engaged in terrorism.

This is reflected in how AQ and IS target North America and Europe too. In these areas, they tend to rely on their networks of returning foreign fighters, vocal supporters and recruiters, financiers, and so-called lone-wolf terrorists to execute attacks. Generally speaking, most plots involve some degree of command and control or instruction from leaders and usually seek to advance the parochial interests of the group that ordered or planned a plot. Rarely are there ever truly lone-wolf individuals that were not in contact or had training from some individual linked to an organization like al-Qaeda or Islamic State. Interestingly enough, in this arena is where opportunistic behavior among jihadist entities emerges, as seen in the *Charlie Hebdo* attacks in January 2015, when individuals linked to IS and AQ's affiliate in Yemen worked together. In the final analysis, the end result is normally the same, meaning casualties and deaths, but again reflects the decentralized character of jihadist terrorism and belies the notion of a unified jihadist movement fighting for the same cause. And more important, it demonstrates how the classical distinctions for violent nonstate actors have collapsed onto themselves, with organizations mixing their modi operandi depending on circumstance and opportunity, begging greater analytical rigor when it comes to assessing modern terrorism.

Where this issue becomes extremely important is when it comes to defining who is a terrorist. Given the contemporary wave of Islamophobia affecting the polities in the West, it is worth exploring what terrorists look like and what defines a terrorist. A common analytical mistake is to prejudge all Muslims as potential terrorists, arguing that the religion inherently justifies and advocates terrorism because of language within the Qur'an, as if other religious texts have never been used before to justify violence against other religions. Another common mistake is claiming that terrorism from the Middle East is a direct by-product of poverty and the legacy of imperialism without taking note that there are many poor formerly colonized countries that do not experience terrorism. It also denies countries the ability, and the responsibility, to dictate their own affairs, making them perpetual victims of events that happened a long time ago. Both of these views are found wanting empirically for a variety of reasons that are explained later in this book, and failing to address them adequately creates policy imbroglios that are easily avoidable.

Although this book has covered this issue in previous sections, it is worth noting that depending on the circumstance, the people fighting for AQ, IS, or other organizations might vary in individual motivations and demographics. For example, the leadership of AQ on 9/11 belied the traditional image of terrorists being poor and oppressed. Around 75 percent of the organization came from a middle- or upper-class family, 90 percent came from intact families in contrast to broken homes, and around 63 percent had gone to college. Many of these individuals had gone to university at some point in their lives, had actually completed their university degrees, or even had some sort of advanced degree beyond a bachelor's degree. Osama bin Laden was a civil engineer, Mohamed Atta—one of the ringleaders of 9/11—was an architect, and the current leader of the organization, Ayman al-Zawahiri, is a physician. Notably, most were married, and only a few had received training in conservative religious institutions like madrassas. As we look holistically at the phenomenon, the only factor that seems to have influenced whether an individual became a terrorist was whether he or she had friends or family that were already part of a terrorist organization. Curiously enough, this phenomenon extends back to other terrorist groups, such as the Italian Red Brigades. In some regards, these individuals reflected the best and brightest of their societies given their educational backgrounds and trade, but for some reason they found themselves isolated and alienated from their home countries. This is not surprising when one considers that traditional terrorist acts involve a high degree of planning and strategizing and require strong organizational skills to accomplish. Building bombs or planning ways to successfully attack highly protected targets, such as airplanes, requires cognitive processes that are normally associated with people that are highly educated or at least had some sort of training. In contrast, there are numerous reports of lone-wolf terrorists attempting to make homemade bombs using recipes found online or through publicly available resources and failing in their attempts. This pattern is not unique to the current generation of terrorists either, as the Russian anarchists of the nineteenth century and many left-wing terrorists of the twentieth century had similar backgrounds.

This, however, describes the leadership of terrorist organizations and does not necessarily capture foot soldiers who do not engage in traditional terrorist activities. In places where AQ, IS, and others operate more like an insurgency, the armed individuals tend to come from displaced populations seeking alternatives. The stereotype of the poor, the hungry, and the ones lacking opportunity is a better descriptor of those engaged in this type of conflict rather than the typical image of contemporary jihadist terrorists planning attacks in secret. This is neatly reflected in Afghanistan, where many Pashtuns joined the Taliban in the mid-1990s after it managed to establish order and pushed out some vicious warlords that had been terrorizing the population. By promoting an agenda of governance based around their interpretation of Islam, the Taliban was able to recruit individuals by feeding and paying them. This also explains why it so successfully co-opted poppy growers, as it sought to present itself as an organization capable of bestowing economic opportunities with the condition that people cooperated with it. In other words, this pattern of radicalization is quite different from the path of radicalization for individuals like al-Zawahiri or Osama bin Laden. In practice, then, recruiting from this pool makes sense for insurgent organizations, as training an individual to shoot a gun and to follow instructions is a much simpler task than more complex acts of terror, which might require greater planning and operational security. These attributes, though, are normally associated with guerrillas fighting for defense of their homeland and do not necessarily mean that an individual is radicalized or trained enough to turn into a terrorist. This explains why al-Qaeda's training camps in Afghanistan before 9/11 were so dangerous. With a large pool of fighters, many from across the world, AQ needed only to train them to turn them into lethal terrorists, a step beyond simple guerrillas. Again, though, this type of recruitment and radicalization is not exclusive to Muslim countries. The respective histories of Latin American and Southeast Asian insurgent movements demonstrate that given a sufficient wellspring of grievances and a compelling political narrative, any person can become a guerrilla or an insurgent.

Looking outside of the Middle East, radicalization processes are even more diverse and complex than those described above. In spite of the wave of Islamophobia affecting both Europe and North America, religiosity is a poor indicator for why individuals turn toward violence. Multiple security agencies from both continents have noted that religiosity is oftentimes a spurious indicator of when someone is evolving into a terrorist. An MI5 report from 2008 noted that most jihadist terrorists in Britain had only a superficial understanding of religion and rarely practiced the tenets of their religion. A 2011 Brennan Center report expanded on these findings by noting that there is no deterministic explanation for radicalization in Western societies and that it is generally an individual journey. The report goes further and explains that the fluidity in radicalization pathways makes it impossible to place the blame on religion alone, making it a nonbinary variable. A person can adopt some of the beliefs and reject others, or he or she might commit to a radical program but vary in degree of commitment to those ideas, making radicalization a spectrum rather than a binary condition. In fact, it is important to keep in mind that the constellation of beliefs necessary for an individual to become a radical does not necessarily mean a person will act upon those ideas. Lorenzo Vidino and others have written extensively on the difference between cognitive radicalization, which is the process of adopting the beliefs that go against the mainstream, and violent radicalization, which is the belief that one must commit violence to advance the cause of those views.

This is critical when considering how terrorism occurs in both Europe and the United States. Who becomes a terrorist differs from country to country, and there is no monolithic trait or variable that explains who joins. None of the countries with the highest absolute or relative Muslim populations rank among the top exporters of foreign fighters. If we look at individuals who traveled to Syria from Europe to join Islamic State or al-Qaeda since 2013, the countries most affected are those with large second-generation populations. Whether a country follows a strict assimilationist policy or a multicultural approach does not seem to explain the flow of fighters, nor do socioeconomic variables. In essence, then, what is affecting Europe is not so much a political failure of assimilation driven by refugees and immigrants or the reaction to an interventionist foreign policy but rather a continental identity crisis affecting the youths of specific religious communities. In contrast, in places where Muslim populations are well established, such as Bulgaria, very few individuals have joined AQ or IS. This suggests that individuals in these countries have been able to reconcile their secular, political, and religious identities. In fact, this is the general pattern for foreign fighters from the continent writ large, as it is the second generation, which is still trying to come to terms with its connection to its parents' homeland, with its identity in a secular society.

Taken together, what this reflects about contemporary jihadist terrorism is that, to paraphrase Bruce Hoffman and Fernando Reinares, it is a polymorphous threat that changes depending on context, circumstance, and opportunity. This is important to keep in mind given the heated rhetoric surrounding the role Islam plays in current debates about terrorism. While radical interpretations of Islam do serve an important recruiting tool for individuals in a variety of social milieus, it is incorrect to claim that the religion is inherently more prone to terrorism than others. If this were the case, it would not explain why the largely secular LTTE was one of the most lethal terrorist organizations in history, not only in terms of capacity but also in its use of suicide bombings. Given the historical information presented in previous chapters and some of the structural features concerning terrorism today, it becomes imperative to be judicious in assessing the causes for terrorism.

AL-QAEDA AND ISLAMIC STATE:
BATTLE OF EGOS IN THE PROCESS OF FINAL VICTORY

The schism between al-Qaeda and Islamic State is the other major characteristic of the current international terrorist threat, and it is misunderstood by the general public. Regardless of the infighting between both organizations, ideologically, both groups are grounded in the same doctrine. They share the same goal of wanting to establish a caliphate and believe all Muslims have an obligation to wage jihad in advance of this objective. In fact, they both are following the same seven-step strategy first articulated by AQ back in 2005 with minor tweaks to the original timeline. If anything, what separates these organizations is how their leaders have interpreted this common blueprint. According to the original plan, al-Qaeda intended to declare the establishment of the caliphate between 2013 and 2016 after provoking the United States and its allies into a protracted war in the Middle East, which would both destroy the American economy and serve as an inspiration for other jihadists to join AQ's cause. After a series of setbacks, AQ became strategically patient, building its resources in key theaters. However, IS stole its thunder in 2014, thereby fulfilling the narrative AQ first articulated ten years prior.

This strategic difference is a product of the respective personalities of Ayman al-Zawahiri, AQ's leader, and Abu Bakr al-Baghdadi, the leader of IS. Al-Zawahiri is viewed as soft-spoken and scholarly, unable to make inspiring speeches but well versed theologically. In contrast, al-Baghdadi claims direct lineage to the Prophet Muhammad and is known to be brash and egotistical. In this sense, the schism between AQ and IS emerged more from al-Baghdadi's insubordination than his violent proclivities. As Bruce Hoffman maintains, their shared traits outnumber their differences, making it extremely likely that they will eventually reconcile. This is already happening at the tactical level. In Libya, there have been reports of IS and AQ cooperation against the nationalist government in Tobruk, and if this collaboration is maintained, it will pave the way for a strategic reunification down the road. Depending on how the situation in Syria progresses, there might be room for collaboration there as well, given the value of pooling resources together.

All this is often lost in the popular narrative. Islamic State's stunning string of victories in 2014 made many people believe that al-Qaeda had been defanged, making it a bit player in the global jihadist movement. The ironic thing is that such proclamations have been made before by the United States at various moments since 9/11, and each time it has been proven wrong. After Osama bin Laden's death in May 2011, the Obama administration claimed that al-Qaeda was on its deathbed and no longer posed a strategic threat. Although AQ ceded the limelight to IS in 2014, it has remained active in terms of expanding its presence and plotting attacks against the West. As IS continues to decline, AQ will capitalize on that group's losses, consolidate its territorial gains across the Muslim world, and assert itself as the most dangerous jihadist group in the world.

AQ can do all this because it is a truly resilient organization with a potent ideology that will attract like-minded followers for generations to come. Unlike other groups whose coherence revolves around the presence of a charismatic leader articulating an ideology and directing plots, AQ is but the hub of a movement that has seen the most brilliant and violent theologians espouse a unified worldview and provide various strategies and tactical guidance that can be modified and deployed in various operational contexts. AQ is also a learning organization that has researched and studied the most successful insurgencies and terrorist groups of the past. When the United States pushed it out of Afghanistan in 2001, American soldiers discovered a copy of *The Revolt* by Menachem Begin, the great Jewish statesman who bombed the King David Hotel and helped establish the modern state of Israel. AQ has undoubtedly learned from the mistakes IS committed in Iraq and has pushed its regional affiliates to lessen the violence against Shiite Muslims in order to forge broad cultural bonds and to help maintain its image as the vanguard of a global Islamic insurgency.

This type of flexibility allows AQ to continually adapt to changing circumstances, expand its presence to new territories, fund plots and activities of faraway groups, and maintain a globalized bureaucracy that enables it to replenish and be reborn. Soon after IS declared its caliphate, al-Zawahiri announced the establishment of al-Qaeda in the Indian Subcontinent (AQIS), demonstrating its ambitions. This is not only true of AQ's leadership in Afghanistan and Pakistan. Jabhat al-Nusra showed this strategic flexibility when it transformed into Jabhat Fateh al-Sham and sought to moderate its ideology to win over Syrians to its cause. Al-Qaeda in the Arabian Peninsula followed a similar approach, lessening its violence, assuming a governance role, and attempting to position itself as a defender of Yemen against Iranian aggression.

Its most important accomplishment in the past half decade is convincing the world that it is a moderate alternative to IS, which has given its brand of Salafist jihadism a degree of legitimacy among rebels in Syria, Libya, and Yemen. All of this in spite of being the parent organization that birthed IS in the first place and also killed thousands of innocent civilians, many of them Muslims, in various terrorist attacks since the 1990s. Make no mistake, AQ is just as violent and dangerous as IS, but it has learned how to use violence more selectively to enable alliance formation and the establishment of governance. Although it opposes the Westphalian state system and the world it created, it has learned the secrets of the rule of law and how service provision goes a long way towards earning a community's trust. Already this approach is paying rich dividends in Yemen, and it has helped it poach away IS supporters in Afghanistan and Nigeria.

With Islamic State receding, al-Zawahiri's gradualist approach has been validated, as his organization continues growing and consolidating ground. The continued weakness of the state system in Afghanistan, Iraq, Syria, Yemen, and elsewhere means that AQ has room to grow in multiple theaters. This is especially true in the context of the Arab Spring's failure to bring stability and legitimate governments through democracy following the coup in Egypt and the ongoing crises in North Africa and the Levant. Moreover, it has seemingly found the successor to Osama bin Laden through his son Hamza. Throughout 2017, Hamza bin Laden has taken center stage in AQ propaganda, with the group trying to position him as the true successor of his father in order to delegitimize al-Baghdadi's position. Hamza has both the panache and rhetoric to appeal to would-be jihadists, and he is young enough that he can lead the organization for years to come.

THE (NOT) FOREVER WAR: WHAT IS BEYOND ISLAMIC STATE?

The following chapters will provide an overview of the main battlefields outside of Iraq and Syria. Although terrorism differs depending on the context, there are some structural features that define all the places that will be analyzed briefly. Largely what will emerge is the importance of governance and a society's ability to deal with the social alienation that animates jihadists. While the following subject may strike a note of pessimism, what is important to keep in mind is that this violence is mostly a product of weak states. In other words, rather than facing a clash of civilizations with all the implications of a forever war, what the world faces is the technocratic dilemma of establishing strong, legitimate, and capable states with the ability to enforce the rule of law. This is not to say that this is easy, but the global community has experience doing this. More important, it completely undermines the fallacious notion that this is a war against Islam or that most of this terrorism cannot be contained or defeated.

10

THE BATTLEFIELDS OF THE FUTURE

THE BATTLEFIELDS OF THE FUTURE WILL LIKELY CONTINUE BEING THE same as the battlefields of today. Structurally, this makes sense. The countries experiencing the worst spates of terrorism tend to be poor and have a long history of political inequality and repression, which makes them ripe for conflict. Combined with a surplus of tools for war, such as small arms and technically capacitated fighters, and radical entrepreneurs with the necessary organizational skills to mobilize populations, there is political space for this type of violence to continue.

So what are the main battlefields of today? Aside from Iraq and Syria, they are Libya, Yemen, and Afghanistan. As discussed elsewhere in this book, terrorism affects all parts of the globe, but these countries are unique in that they are both weak and geographically positioned to enable truly transnational revolutionary movements to arise and reshape borders. Moreover, given their proximity to key trading ports, influential countries, and natural resources, their continued instability might have profound global effects both politically and economically. However, much like the decentralized character of the global jihadist movement, violence in each of these places has a regional profile even in spite of the transnational rhetoric deployed by the various organizations involved in the fighting. All that being said, much like Iraq and Syria, the key feature that unites them is the fact that they all have weak governments that are easily targeted by nonstate actors promoting a utopian ideology that provides simple solutions for complex problems. This facilitates efforts to recruit and to receive funding from sources abroad.

In addition, there is no single strategic approach that defines these conflicts. Terrorism is used opportunistically by the various groups to delegitimize the local government and to serve as propaganda and as an effective tactic for defeating the opposition. The group plays to either the regional audience, changing up the levels of violence, prioritizing either the winning of hearts and minds or attacking civilian and military targets, and emphasizing different political programs that allow radical groups to hold territory and claim sovereignty. Combined with the slow-motion collapse of Islamic State since 2015, different jihadist organizations are adapting their propaganda to poach fighters and to draw donations from across the world.

Finally, what is interesting about these countries is that all have multiple nonstate actors, not all of them Islamic in character, competing against one another and against the local government. This means that terrorism is only one dimension of these conflicts and that other structural features are at play. Yet surprisingly, not one of these has managed the revolutionary changes accomplished by Islamic State.

YEMEN: A REGIONAL COLD WAR FOUGHT THROUGH PROXIES

Yemen has been at the forefront of the modern terrorist threat since the early 1990s. Being the ancestral home of Osama bin Laden's family, it has been the source of terrorists' plots against the West for the past thirty years. Terrorism, though, is but one of the challenges facing the country, as it is currently engulfed in a civil war that involves Saudi Arabia and Iran. Within this mix are intricate tribal rivalries and politics and a secessionist movement in the southern half of the country. The current conflict owes to the instability plaguing the country in the aftermath of the Arab Spring. In 2011, protestors forced President Ali Abdullah Saleh from power. One of the wiliest politicians in the world, he had been at the forefront of Yemeni politics for over three decades. Although he stepped down peacefully, he began working with the Houthis, a Shiite-inspired movement, which had earlier been his main threat for most of the 2000s, to try to return to power.

It is difficult to grasp the terrorist threat emanating from Yemen without delving into the Houthis and understanding why Saudi Arabia intervened. Since 2015, Yemen has become a veritable humanitarian disaster. Already one of the poorest and most armed societies in the world, Yemen had been the focus of intense fighting for decades. By 2010, shortly before the Arab Spring, the country's oil supplies were dwindling, and in mid-2015, within months of fighting, much of its already decrepit infrastructure had been destroyed, worsening the conditions in the country.

The Houthis emerged in 1992. They were initially sponsored by President Saleh to counteract Saudi Arabian influence in northern Yemen, but by the early 2000s, the group became his main antagonist. The Houthis, a Shiite-inspired minority movement, found themselves in all-out war against President Saleh by 2004, following disputes between him and their founder, Badreddin al-Houthi. By 2010, they were nearly defeated, but they took advantage of the chaos of the Arab Spring to invade Yemen's capital of Sana'a and capture most of northern Yemen. They eventually decamped out of the capital, only using the threat of violence to coerce the government to pass laws favorable to them. Not satisfied with these developments, they arrested Yemen's new president, Abdrabbuh Mansur Hadi, who soon fled to Aden, the ancient capital of southern Yemen.

The mastermind behind these movements has been former president Saleh. Despite fighting the Houthis for over a decade, he directed his tribal allegiances and members of the military still loyal to him to support their advance on Sana'a. This rapid change worried Saudi Arabia, leading to its intervention. Its primary motivation was the fear that the Houthis would become an organization much like Hezbollah in Lebanon. More important, in the context of the broader Saudi-Iranian rivalry for dominance of the Persian Gulf, fought elsewhere in Iraq and Syria, an Iranian proxy on its southern border was unacceptable. By November 2016, Saudi Arabia had liberated Aden and continues to recognize President Hadi as the rightful and legitimate leader of Yemen as of the middle of 2017.

The costs of this intervention have been high for all parties involved. Eighteen months into the conflict, nearly ten thousand had died and around 80 percent of Yemen's population was in dire need of humanitarian support. UNICEF released a report in October 2016, stating that fourteen million Yemenis suffered from malnutrition. Furthermore, in December 2017, Saleh was killed in Sana'a, after renouncing his alliance with the Houthis and siding with Saudi Arabia. The full scope of Saudi Arabia's intervention into Yemen is outside of the scope of this book, but it provides context for al-Qaeda's activities in Yemen. For the past six years, the country has seen its meager quality of life worsen, with no end in sight for the multipronged conflict. This constant warfare has decimated most traditional power structures in the country and wrecked the country's infrastructure. With only a token government in the south and a Shiite-led government in the north, Yemen begins 2018 with a political vacuum ripe for exploitation by a group like IS or AQ.

Al-Qaeda in the Arabian Peninsula

Al-Qaeda in the Arabian Peninsula (AQAP) is considered the most important al-Qaeda (AQ) franchise outside the core organization based in Pakistan. In 2013, the leader of AQ, Ayman al-Zawahiri, named the group's emir, Nasir al-Wuhayshi, his deputy, and since then, the group has been linked with the most serious plots targeting the West, including the foiled 2013 embassy plots. Despite AQ's central relative decline, AQAP has grown in strength, increasing the overall size of its membership.

The origin of the group harkens back to the returning fighters from the Afghan jihad. Osama bin Laden, of Yemeni origin through his father, sought to push out the Soviet-backed government in southern Yemen and funded the formation of jihadist groups based around returning foreign fighters to attack it. Then President Saleh took advantage of these individuals and used them to help reunify the country. Of importance too, in 1992, an AQ-backed group bombed hotels in Aden where U.S. Marines were staying en route to Somalia. No American service members died, but it did mark the first known attempt by AQ to attack the United States. The veterans of these operations later transformed into al-Qaeda in Yemen (AQY). AQY gained international infamy after executing the bombing of the USS *Cole* in 2000. After 9/11, the United States established ties with President Saleh, who likely stoked the jihadist threat in an effort to keep American aid flowing in the country. In November 2002, AQY was the recipient of the first known drone strike by the CIA. With American support, AQY seemed likely to collapse. This was compounded by the fact that many radicals in the country traveled to Iraq to fight against the United States there, giving the impression of a group nearing defeat.

Unfortunately, as alluded to in the introduction to this section, AQ and its affiliates comprise only one actor in Yemen. After 2002, with the increasing threat of the Houthis, President Saleh slowed down his prosecution of the organization and turned his attention elsewhere. AQ has always been a popular entity in conservative Yemen, and Saleh's closeness to the United States saw him lose support among critical components of the country's Sunni community. Indeed, it is worth noting that Yemen is home to Abdul Majeed al-Zindani, a radical cleric who claims to have discovered a cure for AIDS and whom the U.S. Treasury has deemed a foreign terrorist. Al-Zidani also founded Imam University in Sana'a, a place known for peddling extremist ideas, and where Umar Farouk Adbdulmutallab, better known as the "Underwear Bomber," supposedly attended lectures by Anwar al-Awlaki, the American AQAP ideologue who was killed in a drone strike in 2011. As Gregory Johnsen noted, although the West stopped paying attention to Yemen, it remained an important arena for AQ's global ambitions.

In 2006, a major prison breakout occurred. Among the twenty-three that escaped were Jamal Ahmad Mohammad al-Badawi and Jaber Elbanah, two high-profile AQY members, which caused the United States to start paying attention to the country again. Although these two were the focus of American counterterrorism efforts, the most consequential individual to emerge was the aforementioned al-Wuhayshi, who set out to rebuild the organization and to begin plotting attacks domestically and internationally. In 2007, AQY killed a group of Spanish tourists with a suicide bomber. In 2008, in another suicide bombing, the group attacked the American embassy in Yemen. In 2009, it merged with the remnants of AQ's franchise in Saudi Arabia and established AQAP. Later in the year, the group nearly succeeded in assassinating the current deputy crown prince of Saudi Arabia. AQAP further increased its notoriety when it started publishing *Inspire*, the first English-language al-Qaeda magazine, designed to draw recruits to the organization and to provide practical advice on making bombs and committing acts of terrorism. In addition, Anwar al-Awlaki, at this point a senior leader in the organization, began releasing a series of online lectures in English designed to entice Americans to target the United States. Aside from the Underwear Bomber, al-Awlaki maintained contact with Nidal Hasan, the Fort Hood shooter, and reportedly, through his lectures, inspired Faisal Shahzad, the man behind the failed 2010 Times Square bombing.

This increase in operational tempo, and the number of plots emanating from the group, including the 2010 airline plot and the May 2012 cargo plane attack, led to the United States's deploying special operations forces (SOF) and drones, while increasing its aid program to Yemen to counteract the threat posed by the group. From an American perspective, after the death of Osama bin Laden in 2011, AQAP was the most dangerous terrorist group in the world. The government in Sana'a did not view it that way, though. The country was largely overwhelmed by the Arab Spring, causing President Saleh to step down. Operating as Ansar al-Sharia, a token effort to rebrand itself away from AQ, AQAP took advantage of the chaos and managed to assert control of Abyan and Zinjibar provinces until 2012, when they were displaced. The period it ruled saw it restoring social services and governing, in a manner similar to IS. However, it overreached and angered the locals with its strict interpretation of sharia that alienated it from the local tribes, as happened to al-Qaeda in Iraq prior to the Anbar Awakening. Given the other disputes going on in the country, this was not fatal. The group sought to build ties with local tribes, establishing alliances and paying off members. In April 2015, a few months after President Hadi was deposed, the group took over the city of Al-Mukalla and supported a governance program that was more moderate in order to not alienate the locals. It was retaken by a Saudi-backed coalition in April 2016, but it is likely that AQAP still covertly controls key parts of what is Yemen's fifth-largest city.

Nonetheless, the threat posed by the Houthis has allowed AQAP to insert itself into the conflict, concentrating its energies in pushing the Houthis back to curry favor with the country's tribes. With most of the international attention focused either on IS or on the proxy war fought by Saudi Arabia and Iran in Yemen through their local proxies, this has enabled AQAP to remain hidden and to continue building its capabilities. Moreover, even though its leader, al-Wuhayshi, was killed in 2015, organizationally the group remains intact and still retains its chief bomb maker, Ibrahim al-Asiri. It is likely that AQAP will become the most dangerous terrorist group again after IS collapses, especially if it learns how to govern and assert control over key parts of southern Yemen. Its history of online propaganda set the stage for similar efforts by IS, and its influence will resonate for many years. The 2013 Boston bombers reportedly had copies of *Inspire* on their laptops and likely learned how to make the pressure-cooker bombs from instructions found in one of its issues. In January 2015, one of the *Charlie Hebdo* shooters was linked to AQAP. In essence, then, the silence coming from Yemen likely hides the fact that the group continues plotting against Western targets and should not be ignored.

What About the Islamic State?

In late 2014, IS claimed it had expanded into Yemen, and in March 2015, it carried out a suicide-bombing attack against a Zaydi mosque, killing 130 people. Gregory Johnsen has noted that the Yemeni IS branch seems to follow in its parent organization's footsteps in trying to spark sectarianism in a country not familiar with it. He adds that the strategy adopted by IS seems to be the declaration of state while fomenting civil strife to draw recruits, instead of AQAP's more moderated approach of trying to enmesh itself into local tribal society to win support.

This is unlikely to be a winning strategy in the long run. While the violence in Yemen seems to have a Shiite and Sunni divide, these differences are largely artificial. Zaydi Islam is theologically close to Sunnism, and intermarriage has been a common feature between the various faiths in Yemen. Trying to spark a sectarian war in the country will prove fruitless. This is already the case. In December 2015, the Office of the Director of National Intelligence in the United States translated and released a statement by Yemeni IS members explaining that they were defecting to AQAP because of the abuses committed by the organization against fellow Muslims. As Katherine Zimmerman has explained, IS in Yemen is misleading, as the real threat remains AQAP.

Yemen in the Future

At the time of this writing, Yemen is unlikely to reach a political settlement any time soon. Internationally brokered peace agreements have been rejected by President Hadi's government, while the Houthis demand that Hadi abdicate. There is a gulf of opinion between both parties, worsening the humanitarian situation there. The only organization that benefits from this stalemate is AQAP. The humanitarian crisis in Yemen is giving AQAP and its allies ample opportunity to enmesh themselves within local populations and to begin providing shadow government services. In the future, if a peace deal is negotiated, Yemen will have a difficult time trying to uproot the group.

In this context, then, the question becomes, what does AQAP do afterward? As an al-Qaeda affiliate, it will likely continue prioritizing defeating the government in Sana'a and targeting the West. Although its rhetoric may not be as revolutionary or threatening as IS's, it still will remain dangerous. The key dynamic here, though, is how Saudi Arabia responds. Given the Salafi jihadist hatred held toward the government in Riyadh, and the kingdom's own fears about internal instability, it might find itself in a bigger conflict than it initially imagined.

LIBYA: A MOSAIC CIVIL WAR

NATO's intervention into Libya in 2011 led to the downfall of Muammar Qaddafi, ending a brutal dictatorship that had ruled the country for nearly thirty years. Few shed tears at his death, given his history of state-sponsored terrorism like the Lockerbie bombing in 1988, his meddling in the foreign affairs of various countries, including providing support to the IRA against the United Kingdom and the ill-fated invasion of Chad, and his overall erratic behavior. Before his death, the international community was quite optimistic that it could salvage his government and usher in a democratic government, but the resulting history has proven otherwise.

Given Libya's proximity to Europe and Egypt, instability here has secondary and tertiary effects elsewhere. Libya has already been the target of various counterterrorism operations following the 2012 Benghazi attacks, and the situation in the country has become more worrisome following the emergence of IS in 2014. There is no single neat narrative explaining the terrorist threat from Libya, and given the internal conditions, it has yet to morph into a problem state like Yemen or Afghanistan. What is at play instead is a tangled mixture of alliances and conflicts between nationalists, Islamists, tribes, IS, al-Qaeda, and the international community, with plots centering on the question of legitimacy.

How Did Libya Get Here?: Reconstruction and Deconstruction

The United States and NATO made a conscious effort to avoid a prolonged ground war to remove Qaddafi, relying exclusively on air strikes in support of the ground rebellion. This was desired both by NATO and by the rebels themselves, as it gave ownership of the conflict to ground forces and would limit the presence of outside powers in Libya that could undermine the legitimacy of the forming government in waiting, the National Transition Council (NTC). While this was rational in the sense of wishing to avoid another protracted occupation à la Afghanistan, it also limited the actions the international community could take in the aftermath, lacking ground forces to secure the population and suppress rebel entities attempting to undermine the eventual state-building process. It was this latter factor that ultimately created the current civil war in Libya.

During the fight with Qaddafi, various factions of different ideological and tribal affiliations emerged. There was no unified military body coordinating their activities, making their moves more akin to networked swarms than military campaigns with operational tempos dictated by a leading commanding officer. A report by the RAND Corporation notes that estimates about the actual number of fighting groups vary, with some placing these at several hundred and others at several thousand. The pattern varied by region and city. Revolutionary brigades were key in fighting Qaddafi, while military councils provided security and defectors from the Libyan military eagerly participated in the fight. There were also local gangs that wished to take advantage of the chaos and Islamists in the eastern part of the country that had a postwar governance framework anathema to the revolutionary and democratic aims of many of the other fighters. Exacerbating the situation was the surplus of weaponry received through arms transfers from abroad or from Qaddafi's own weapons depot.

Following the end of hostilities, the key challenge for the emerging state was the disarmament and integration of these various groups into a national military structure. This was difficult to accomplish when the NTC had no army to speak of and had to find incentives to convince the various groups operating to lay down their arms. This was only one of a multitude of concurrent challenges the NTC had to resolve without having much of a bureaucracy or civil service to help implement policies. Initially, though, there was cause for optimism. The NTC created the Warrior Affairs Commission to help with disarmament and received a large number of registrants—too many for the NTC to handle. Furthermore, nothing was done to assure their loyalty to the state. Moreover, the extent to which the NTC controlled other bodies, such as the Ministry of Interior

(MOI) and Ministry of Defense (MOD), was questionable, as they also enacted disarmament bodies.

The MOI created the Supreme Security Committee (SSC), which united numerous rebel factions under one banner but lacked enforcement capabilities, granting them high degree of autonomy. The MOD, in contrast, created the Libya Shield Forces, which was supposed to be the main military force for the country. These three bodies, with varying degrees of success in terms of disarming and controlling the militias, failed at pacifying the country. Instead, given the lack of the rule of law, the various fighting groups began renting themselves out to the highest bidders, immersing themselves in local conflicts between tribes and cities and creating general chaos. Yet another addition to this mix was that the SSC recruited Islamist rebel groups from the city of Derna. These groups had no interest in a democratic Libya and sought to push an agenda more akin to that of al-Qaeda or Islamic State. Within a year of Qaddafi's death, terrorism was again prominent throughout the country.

Before proceeding, we must discuss Libya's Islamist movements. Since the 1980s, Libya has been home to a variety of terrorist groups linked to al-Qaeda in one form or another, such as the Libyan Islamic Fighting Group (LIFG) and parts of al-Qaeda in the Islamic Maghreb (AQIM). Indeed, in the year after Qaddafi's fall, the latter, having received a large supply of weapons, threatened Mali before the French intervention in January 2013 pushed them back. They are only bit players, though, as many of the conservative Islamists eschew violence and most resemble the Muslim Brotherhood. Even groups who have committed terrorist acts against international targets do not necessarily belong to AQ or IS. This is the case of Ansar al-Sharia, the group behind the September 11, 2012, Benghazi attacks that left U.S. ambassador J. Christopher Stevens dead.

Elections and the Plunge into Civil War

From the outside, there were reasons to believe that Libya could sustain the gains made after Qaddafi's death. The parliamentary elections in June 2012 were seen as a positive, as they would create the first national government legitimized through elections. Moreover, around 60 percent of the population voted, a rate many established democracies envy. This, however, assumed that a national identity existed within Libya that would allow a government to form. Before the elections, there were already disputes between the more conservative east and the more secular west. The government that emerged was weak, hobbled, and still unable to work with a competent bureaucracy capable of wresting the guns away from the armed groups operating throughout Libya. The divisions within postwar Libya are complex but roughly divide the country between nationalists based in the east and conservatives aligned with rebels out in the west.

These deep divides appeared in the General National Congress (GNC). One of the primary issues for the new government was the Libyan equivalent of de-Baathification. Islamists wishing a clean break with Qaddafi's government wanted to pass a law that barred any individual who had worked for Qaddafi from government for at least a decade. Unfortunately, such a legislative move would weaken the human capital available for the bureaucracy. Despite grousing from key elites, this law passed, which angered many in the country. In addition, the close personal ties between Islamists and the various rebel groups raised concerns about deeply entrenched graft and corruption. On top of all this, the government was unable to establish the rule of law. Indeed, many nationalists, secular businesspeople, religious minorities, tourists, and figures tied to the incipient Libyan military were targeted in acts of terror by the various militias and rebel groups nominally linked to the GNC.

This uneasy status quo lasted for another eighteen months, until May 2014. Signs of the eventual civil war were evident for some time. In October 2013, there was a failed coup attempt against Prime Minister Ali Zeidan by individuals linked to conservative Islamist elements within the GNC. On February 14, 2014, General Khalifa Haftar—a nationalist who once served under Qaddafi until he defected following Qaddafi's ill-fated incursion into Chad in the 1980s—attempted a coup against the GNC and failed. He launched another coup in May 2014, beginning in Benghazi and later moving elsewhere in the country, that targeted the evermore conservative and entrenched Islamists in the GNC. This move, known as Operation Dignity, sought to remove groups like Ansar al-Sharia from their positions as security providers and to force the GNC to agree to the creation of a house of representatives. On May 18, rebels under the Dignity aegis stormed Tripoli and dissolved the GNC. Libya held parliamentary elections again on June 25, with the Islamists losing badly. Seeing the writing on the wall and wary of the rise to power of an individual previously linked to Qaddafi, rebel groups from the town of Misrata and militias linked to the GNC responded by launching Operation Dawn. The parties that won the June 25 elections fled to the eastern town of Tobruk and created a new parliamentary body called the Council of Deputies (COD), which was recognized internationally. In contrast, the Islamists created their own body called the General National Council (GNC), which was supposed to be a successor of the original General National Council formed earlier. It is at this point when Libya fell into its second civil war and became a failed state.

It is important to note that religious cleavages do not necessarily divide these two coalitions. As Daveed Gartenstein-Ross notes, various Islamist groups joined Operation Dignity, as they felt left out by the dominant Islamic powers in the GNC. In addition, regional and tribal rivalries and more personal feuds animated much of the conflict that followed, although the macro narrative was a convenient tool for unifying the various fighting groups. Moreover, regional actors, including Egypt, various NATO countries, Qatar, Turkey, and others, inserted themselves. Their reasons for joining include stabilization of an important country in North Africa, stymieing the spread of Islamist groups, and fighting terrorist groups. Places like Egypt, which has its own IS branch, and Tunisia are directly threatened by foreign fighters gaining experience in Libya and later returning home to wage jihad. Needless to say, the multitude of factions vying for control led to a spiraling of terrorism within the country with major international implications. Within this context, Islamic State managed to carve out an important islet for itself in eastern Libya.

Islamic State in Libya: One Actor Among Many

The litany of rebel groups in Libya who have engaged in terrorism are far too many to list, showcasing the scale of devastation the country has experienced. Because of its international focus, though, Islamic State has commandeered the most attention. Until now, Libya has been the group's most successful colonization effort outside of Iraq and Syria, posing a risk to Europe's southern core. Much like its holdings in the Levant, though, its grip is receding.

Just as in Iraq and Syria, the first signs of IS ambitions in the country appeared in early 2014, when foreign fighters began returning to the country.

These fighters had not been officially recognized by Abu Bakr al-Baghdadi but began organizing in the city of Derna, a hotbed for Salafist jihadists since before Qaddafi's death. According to some sources, IS may have emerged from a split between Ansar al-Sharia elements loyal to al-Qaeda and those inspired by IS. Regardless, by June of that year, these individuals had established the Islamic Youth Shura Council before receiving formal recognition as an IS affiliate in November. By the end of that year, IS had made inroads into Sirte, Qaddafi's hometown, and the capital of its Libya territory until December 2016. By the middle of 2015, there were an estimated four to five thousand IS militants in the country.

As was true in Yemen, IS exported its brutal ideology, tactics, and governing institutions. In all territories it held, it established a sharia court and tried forming a bureaucracy to enforce its rule. These measures helped bring some semblance of law and order, but they were combined with atrocities to terrorize the population further. In February 2015, it video-taped the execution of twenty-one Egyptian Coptic Christians, committed various suicide attacks in the country, and carried out various targeted assassinations as it sought to emphasize its control over Derna. These actions did not produce the results they had in the Levant. The difference from its other efforts is that Libya is not divided between Sunnis and Shiites, precluding the same genocidal sectarianism that characterized its expansions elsewhere. Instead, much of this violence seems focused on securing coastal towns that facilitate the movement of people from Europe and the Middle East to keep a steady pipeline of recruits. This approach allows it to secure oil, a major source of income for the group's activities across the world. In turn, after securing this beachhead, IS can exploit the shipping routes for arms across Africa and expand to other parts with significant Muslim populations, perhaps even joining its affiliates in Nigeria.

This strategy appeared capable of achieving Islamic State's efforts, but it began to implode by June 2015. Perhaps out of arrogance or out of sheer belief in the ability of its ideology to win over converts, IS failed to secure many alliances that would help protect its position in the long term. Its violence in Derna proved too much for other Islamists in the city after it murdered the leader of a local AQ affiliate. This infighting led to an alliance of convenience between the national army in Tobruk and AQ elements in Derna to uproot IS from the surrounding areas. Reportedly, the fighting against IS included foreign fighters from nearby Tunisia and Egypt, justifying the fears of the leaders of those countries.

Sirte was another example of hubris by IS. The city was quickly taken over, and the group brought its governing apparatus. This quickly translated to public executions for lawbreakers, strict control of the media, degradation of women's rights, an emphasis on religious activities, and a strict enforcement of sharia. An important factor enabling IS dominion was the acquiescence of Qaddafi's tribe, which became disempowered following his death. This reservoir of goodwill evaporated quickly, as the group's capriciousness created a terrible humanitarian crisis within the city. In May 2016, the government in Tobruk, with international backing from France and the United States, launched an offensive against Sirte to liberate it. Brutal fighting followed over the next seven months, before IS lost control in December 2016, depriving it of its last major holding in Libya.

Out of all the efforts by IS to expand, the situation in Libya most closely approximated the conditions in the Levant, given the insecurity and the lack of any capable governing authority. Its expansion was ultimately blunted and reversed within two and a half years, correlating almost neatly with Islamic State's fortune in Iraq and Syria. Making sense of Libya's mosaic civil war is difficult, but two overarching factors explain why IS could not expand further. First, IS made little effort to adapt its ideology to local conditions, essentially importing a state governance model created to dominate Iraq and Syria, and did little to moderate and win over other Islamist groups that could have provided it with support. Second, Libya's marketplace of terrorism was already crowded when IS entered, and the group's early victories created a bandwagon effect among its rivals to unite and fight IS. Of course, IS still has fighters in Libya, and given a change in circumstances, it could hypothetically create another province. For the time being, this seems unlikely.

What's Next for Libya's Islamists?

Losing Sirte is a major blow for IS, but the group is resilient and will likely find new ways to enmesh itself in the ongoing civil war. It will certainly be part of the so-called virtual caliphate that will follow now that IS has lost its grip over Mosul and Raqqa and will draw recruits for fighting in other parts of North Africa and Europe. Failing that, it might strike an alliance with other Salafist jihadist groups and merge with them to help push out the nationalist government in Tobruk. There have already been signs of IS and AQ cooperating in Libya at the tactical level, and as the fortunes of the different groups shift, this might become more of a necessity.

Globally, a bigger problem is al-Qaeda in the Islamic Maghreb (AQIM). Although not discussed extensively in this book, AQIM has spent the last few years investing in its state-building functions within Libya. It has made strategic alliances, has started providing social services in areas where it maintains influence, and has sought to moderate its ideology to persuade others to join its cause, much like Jabhat al-Nusra did in Syria. Avoiding sectarianism and ethnic divisions, AQIM is poised to capitalize on the long-term instability in Libya and to become the paramount Islamist group uniting the disparate tribes and coalitions fighting against the nationalists. The group is also wise in seeking not to provoke too much American aggression, as it fears this would be critical in rolling back its advances, as was the case for IS in Sirte.

If AQIM does manage to assert territorial dominion and create a burgeoning state, this would pose a major security challenge for Europe and the United States. Until now, it has not renounced AQ's ideology or its emphasis on attacking the "far enemy" for propaganda reasons and on dissuading the international community from supporting moderate local governments opposed to its mission.

AFGHANISTAN: A LEGACY OF FAILED STATE RECONSTRUCTION

Afghanistan has been at the forefront of the global terrorist threat since the Soviets invaded the country. The fighting drew thousands of foreign fighters, including Osama bin Laden, and became the birthplace of al-Qaeda. After the Soviets' defeat by the collection of mujahedeen and Arab foreign fighters, Afghanistan fell into a state of civil war. Out of this chaos emerged the Taliban, who, with the support of Pakistan, quickly quelled the violence and conquered most of the country. Taliban (meaning "students") emerged from religious schools, or madrassas, in neighboring Pakistan. David Kilcullen attributes much of their success in the 1990s to their ability to impose the rule of law through the courts systems, which helped end the banditry in the country. The Taliban was the original Islamic State in many ways, but had a distinct South Asian flavor because of the importance of Deobandism, a religious movement arising in the nineteenth century similar to Wahhabism, and the importance of Pashtun tribal law (Pashtuns being the largest ethnic group in Afghanistan). Their harsh interpretation of sharia law led to widespread condemnation across the world.

In this environment, terrorism thrived. The Taliban did not participate directly in acts of terrorism, but it provided a safe haven for al-Qaeda and the assortment of groups associated with it. Apart from protection, it allowed all sorts of Salafist jihadist groups to establish training camps to commit plots abroad. It was here that AQ plotted 9/11. The American response to these attacks was catastrophic for the group, with the Taliban nearly defeated by the winter of 2001 and most of AQ's leadership hiding in Pakistan. The United States quickly deprioritized this conflict as it began preparing for the invasion of Iraq. Maintaining a token presence, and relying on NATO assets to rebuild the Afghan state and its security forces, the United States allowed the Taliban sufficient space to rebuild and to wage an insurgency that greatly stymied state-building efforts there.

Afghanistan from 2002 to 2009: Reconstruction and Resurgence

Providing a history of the Taliban and associated terrorist elements after the American invasion is challenging because of the confusion associated with defining the Taliban. As David Kilcullen explains, local conflict in Afghanistan is mainly driven by tribal politics masquerading as the Taliban. While the movement started by the late Mullah Omar has continued operating, Kilcullen instead argues that it should be regarded as an alliance between Pashtun tribes seeking to dominate the Pashtun regions of Afghanistan and Pakistan, although these dynamics have changed a bit with the emergence of IS as of 2015.

In December 2001, the UN implemented the Bonn Agreement, which created an interim government framework for the country and set a timeline for the writing of a new constitution and eventual elections. This resulted in Hamid Karzai's election as leader of the transition government in 2002 and later president in 2004. In 2002 and 2003, the United States continued focusing on AQ and Taliban targets, but these were secondary efforts relative to the ongoing Iraq War. During this time, the priority for the international community was rebuilding the country. More than two decades of war had devastated its infrastructure and its economy, and the international community recognized it was imperative to rebuild to prevent the resurgence of the Taliban. Another major priority was developing the Afghan National Army (ANA) and its police forces to help consolidate the security and stability of the country and eventually allow for Afghanistan to regain its sovereignty. Joseph Collins notes that given the weakness of the Taliban and other insurgent elements, the international community was able to make progress in repaving roads, improving the country's health care and educational systems, and capacitating parts of the local government.

Ultimately, these efforts failed in preventing a resurgence of violence. The move toward democratization, while a net positive in many regards, was poorly resourced for the scale of effort necessary. Afghanistan never had a history of centralized government, but it has always had a consensus-building body in the form of jirgas, which acted as a form of local democratic governance that could operate nationally with the government in Kabul. Unfortunately, this system was fragmented after twenty years of war, and most villages, disconnected from the outside world, had reason to distrust the Bonn Agreement. Moreover, the Taliban remained a threat, meaning that locals were wary of committing fully without having sufficient protection. Any effort at creating a national Afghan government palatable to the various ethnic groups would require a simultaneous bottom-up and top-down approach to state-building.

This level of effort demanded greater coordination and unity of effort than what the international community expected. Joseph Collins notes that, wanting to provide tangible and visible support, many international donors circumvented the Afghan government and worked with local nongovernmental organizations, depriving it of much-needed resources. This plagued the training of the country's security forces as well. The entities tasked with building and arming the military and the police changed over the years, creating inconsistencies in this arena. This state-building effort, done on an ad hoc basis, delayed the ability of the police and the military to act autonomously and undermined their overall quality. Corruption was also a pernicious challenge. With billions of dollars flowing into the country, it was hard to keep track of where it was going, leading to embezzlement, fraud, and waste. All this occurred in a country with immense broken geography littered with pockets of isolated communities. Not surprisingly, the government in Kabul struggled to expand its presence outside of key urban areas, leading to an uneven state-building that ceded primacy to local tribal politics.

This situation gave political space for the Taliban and other insurgent elements to rebuild. After the United States routed it, the Taliban moved its headquarters to Pakistan and spent the years between 2002 and 2005 organizing. It did commit a few incursions, but only in 2005 did it initiate the large-scale insurgency that has plagued Afghanistan for the last decade. Because there was only a token military force and the Karzai government lacked sufficient resources, the Taliban quickly began shadow government operations in most of the country. With drug money and donations from al-Qaeda, the Taliban and its allies—Gulbuddin Hekmatyar's organization and the Haqqani Network—started rolling back the progress made over the preceding years. The Taliban also counted on a major base of support in western Pakistan through the local Taliban branch.

Joseph Collins explains that much of the success of the insurgency came from its increased deadliness owing to learning and borrowing tactics used by al-Qaeda in Iraq. The number of suicide bombings increased, and outright acts of terror became commonplace. Beheadings were recorded, publicized, and disseminated over cell phones, and roads became dangerous as improvised explosive devices (IEDs) were deployed across the country. The insurgency also hacked away at the Afghan security forces piecemeal, attacking and killing many police officers. According to counterinsurgency (COIN) theory, police officers play a critical role in developing community ties to win hearts and minds, establishing the rule of law, and generating intelligence through local connections. Because the police lacked sufficient funding, training, and protection from the international community and the ANA, the Taliban took over large swaths of territory. More important, this violence targeted mainly civilians, with a UN report estimating that civilians were victims of 76 percent of the violence.

The United States was aware of this, but Iraq was the bigger challenge at the time. Nonetheless, by the end of his administration, President Bush laid the groundwork for a civilian surge to help with the state-building process in Afghanistan. He refused to commit ground troops because he recognized that his successor would have to own the war.

The Afghan Surge and Village Reconstruction

President Obama campaigned on ending the Iraq War and dedicating the necessary resources to the Afghan theater. In his first months in office, he asked his administration to provide an assessment of the situation on the ground and a new strategy. In March 2009, he moved an additional twenty-one thousand troops in the country to shore up the troop presence. After a year of debate, President Obama settled on a COIN strategy that required an additional thirty thousand U.S. soldiers and ten thousand troops provided by NATO allies, focused on defeating AQ and the Taliban and strengthening the Afghan government. He also increased the number of civilians working in the country and increased aid directed at Afghanistan and Pakistan. This was only an eighteen-month process, however. He stipulated that by July 2011, he would begin withdrawing troops from the country, with the goal of ending the American war effort there by the close of 2014, allowing Afghanistan to act as a sovereign nation again.

The increased troop count of around 140,000 soldiers from the United States and other NATO countries augmenting the Afghan security forces allowed for a rollback of the Taliban in many places. Unfortunately, given the weakness of the Afghan central government, building upon these gains was difficult. Areas that were cleared would soon revert to Taliban control. This pressure, though, proved valuable in terms of buying the Afghan government time to clean up the corruption plaguing it and also allowing the United States and its allies to train the military and the police forces.

The United States did innovate tactically and operationally to help reconnect remote villages with the national government. Using a platform called village stability operations (VSO), the United States began deploying special operations forces (SOF) to remote villages to provide security. SOF in turn would also engage in other projects to win the trust of the elders and ultimately the community. After securing the area, SOF would begin training local militias drawn from the village, with the idea being that the locals would have more of a buy-in to defend their communities than the Afghan army, which drew people from across the country. Furthermore, locals would have a better understanding of the human terrain, with more intimate knowledge of who supported the Taliban and other insurgents, creating an intelligence network that could be disseminated to the Afghan military. This platform would also create opportunity for civilians from Kabul to begin reconstruction efforts and begin making overtures to connect disparate communities to the central government. Like other efforts in Afghanistan, this was largely under-resourced and produced mixed results. Many of the trainees maintained dual allegiances or would switch sides after the international community handed over control to the Afghan government.

President Obama also began pressuring the Pakistani government to cooperate more in its counterterrorism efforts. It has always been an open secret that Pakistan supports the Taliban and other terrorist elements because of its own geopolitical concerns dealing with India and because of its desire to maintain a friendly government in Kabul. Pakistan is concerned about Indian investments in Afghanistan, worrying that these might create another unfriendly government to its west. It has also used terrorist proxies to provoke India, something best exemplified by the 2008 Mumbai attacks, which were linked back to Pakistan's Inter-Services Intelligence (ISI). Indeed, this latter entity is perhaps the biggest abettor of terrorism in Afghanistan. ISI has been accused of providing training and support to the Taliban and other extremists, and it is also believed that it knew where Osama bin Laden was hiding in Abbottabad and most likely gave him protection. Using both carrot and stick, President Obama hoped to induce the Pakistani government to cooperate more and cease supporting its domestic extremists, especially as many began attacking the Pakistani state itself.

These efforts also saw an increased use of U.S. drone strikes in Pakistan's tribal areas along the border with Afghanistan. Not surprisingly, these attacks resulted in the deaths of many members of al-Qaeda's senior leadership and key figures in the Taliban. It also resulted in numerous civilian deaths, which inflamed public opinion against the United States. These continued, though, with tacit approval by the Pakistani government, demonstrating the double games Pakistan played.

Mullah Omar's Death, the Emergence of IS, and Negotiations

The United States and NATO maintained a token force after the December 2014 withdrawal date, as it became obvious Afghanistan remained too weak to provide for its own security. In 2015, the Taliban advanced across the country, seizing large swaths of territory and even taking Kunduz. It also improved its ties with other insurgent groups in Central Asia, like the Islamic Movement of Uzbekistan. The Afghan military fought valiantly throughout 2015, but casualties mounted. Much of this, of course, was an effect of Afghanistan's perennial problem of continued weak and corrupt governance. Because the government was unable to win the loyalty of the tribes and lacked the resources to fund its police and army, the Taliban quickly supplanted Kabul's government. This was not helped by the disputed elections of 2014, which saw Afghanistan without a functioning government for several months.

While all this fighting was occurring, in the background, internal Taliban politics were affecting the insurgency. In July 2015, it emerged that the Taliban's leader, Mullah Omar, had died in August 2013 and that the Taliban had covered this up to prevent a fracturing of the movement. Indeed, this was occurring in the early months of 2014. There were reports of IS-linked fighters in Afghanistan and Pakistan. By September of that year, there were a large number of defections from the Taliban, and soon after, Abdul Rahim Muslim Dost emerged as the local leader of IS in Afghanistan. This led to even more defections and the arrival of foreign fighters, as well as greater use of terrorism against the civilian population in Afghanistan. IS sought to peel off Taliban support through its propaganda and wished to create the same sectarian strife it had accomplished in Iraq and Syria through attacks directed at Shiites.

These events quickly led to direct confrontations between IS and the Taliban and its allies, including al-Qaeda's central command in Pakistan. As was true of its efforts in other countries, IS struggled in generating much popular support because its strategy and tactics were seen as antithetical and abhorrent by the local tribes in both countries. As stated before, even though the Taliban holds an Islamist ideology, it really is a Pashtun-led insurgency in which membership is fluid, depending on if locals find it convenient to align themselves with the group. Therefore, in spite of its conservative outlook, the Taliban derives strength from respecting tribal laws and customs. More important, the current generation of Taliban fighters is different from the original cadre that emerged in the 1990s and is not as strict and orthodox as its forebears. This is not to say that they are not brutal, just that they have become more flexible.

IS did not think in these strategic terms and committed the same mistakes the organization made in other countries, assuming its government-in-a-box approach could be transplanted anywhere. By late 2015, its brutal violence managed to displace the Taliban in parts of eastern Afghanistan, but these positions were tenuous at best. The United States, Afghan security forces, and the Taliban began pushing IS from key positions, and by mid-2016, IS only held several villages. Much like its parent organization, this group is unlikely to continue much longer in its current state unless it changes its strategy and tactics.

The Taliban remains the most potent entity in Afghanistan. The government in Kabul remains weak and corrupt, and the international community has largely ignored the country since the rise of IS. Unsurprisingly, there have been efforts to negotiate with the Taliban to end the war, but this is unlikely to produce anything meaningful. Even with the withdrawal of the international community from the country, Afghanistan's economy is still heavily dependent on international donations to operate. The country lacks a strong tax base to continue arming and supporting its security forces, and at the time of this writing, the Trump administration seems to lack a plan for fighting the Taliban. In other words, given the weakness of its enemies, the Taliban need only to wait out the government in Kabul before it can initiate an offensive to end the war without having to make any more concessions.

This is the worst possible scenario for terrorism and also the most likely unless the United States and its allies change their strategy. The Taliban still retains a close alliance with al-Qaeda, and given the symbolism of Afghanistan and 9/11, the country can easily revert to being a base of operations for international terrorism. Moreover, the Taliban in the past has shown interest in committing attacks abroad. In 2008, Spanish authorities uncovered a plot, which was linked back to the Pakistani Taliban, to bomb the Barcelona subway system. And with the emergence of al-Qaeda's branch in the Indian subcontinent, there will likely be more terrorism in this region.

WHERE TO NEXT?

The conflicts discussed in this chapter share many similarities to Iraq and Syria. What is important to note, though, is that terrorism in all these places thrives because of the governments in place. This seems self-evident, but recognizing that these are political problems more than military problems helps reframe the nature of the threat and also provides insight into how terrorism might evolve into the future. All the groups discussed have likely internalized the lessons of Islamic State and have seen the dangers of being too brutal and too vociferous in declaring their agendas. They have also likely seen the value of adopting Jabhat Fateh al-Sham's gradualist approach in both winning popular support and not making them targets off Western governments.

Without adopting a political program for resolving their internal issues, all these countries will continue breeding terrorist organizations, and if reform is not adopted, any of these countries could easily cede large chunks of their territory to sovereign terrorist governments. The world public should not ignore them either. Their advance might not rally the world in the same manner as Islamic State, but as the case of Afghanistan in the 1990s shows, it is those places suffering prolonged upheaval and that people ignore that are most prone toward creating global chaos.

Of the countries discussed, the most fractured is presently Libya, providing ample opportunity for would-be jihadists to plot attacks across North Africa and southern Europe. The opportunity to take over the country is hard, though, because of the multitude of groups involved in the fighting. Afghanistan, unless the United States adopts a new strategy to prop up the government in Kabul, will likely fall to the Taliban. Even though it is not the same organization Mullah Omar created in the 1990s, it could easily revert toward providing a safe haven for groups like AQ. Yemen, though, will probably remain the most dangerous for the world. The humanitarian crisis there does not seem likely to abate, and AQAP is well positioned to stake territorial claim to a large part of the southern half of the country. Already the most dangerous al-Qaeda franchise before IS challenged it, AQAP will probably resume its previous role once it carves up the political space and begin plotting attacks outside of Yemen again.

11

TERRORISM IN EUROPE AND
IN THE UNITED STATES

EUROPE IS INCREASINGLY BECOMING AN IMPORTANT CENTER OF TER-
rorism, something the continent has experienced in the past. However, to
state that terrorism in Europe is mainly driven by Islamic terrorism would
be overstating the problem. Europol noted that in 2014, 201 terrorist plots
were attempted, with the vast majority of them being conducted by separatists, anarchists, and left-wing terrorists. In contrast, only two attacks
were tied to religion, the shooting at the Jewish Museum in Brussels and
a stabbing committed in Tours in December of that year. Nonetheless,
starting with the 2015 *Charlie Hebdo* shootings, Europe has become associated with a particularly violent and virulent strain of Islamic terrorism.
The November 2015 Paris attacks, the 2016 Brussels bombings, the 2016
Nice attack, the 2017 Manchester bombing, and the 2017 Barcelona attack are probably the most prominent examples because of the high casu-
alty rate, but there have been a fair number of lower-profile stabbings,
shootings, and attempted attacks by would-be terrorists.

The United States is not immune to continued Salafist jihadist threats
either, but the challenge there is not as severe. If anything, it is likely overplayed relative to the United States' domestic right-wing terrorism problem.
This, of course, is an artifact of the country's unique politics in relation to
guns, its history of race relations, and how it regulates speech. Unlike in

most European countries, expressing support for extremist or terrorist groups is not a crime. This allows for the distribution of material that would be prohibited in most other countries and gives political space for extremists of all types to share their views online.

THE LONE-WOLF PHENOMENON

Before beginning, it is worth discussing lone wolves. In 2008, an important academic debate broke out between Marc Sageman and Bruce Hoffman. Sageman argued that the most important terrorist threat came from the so-called lone wolves, or individuals who were self-radicalized and learned how to make explosives and execute terrorist attacks through instruction readily available in books or on the internet. This would increase, of course, with the proliferation of the internet, connecting disenchanted individuals with faraway communities virtually. The argument went that these self-radicalized individuals would make organizations like al-Qaeda redundant. Citing the evidence available at the time surrounding the July 2005 bombings in London and elsewhere in Europe, Sageman wrote about the coming "leaderless" jihad. Hoffman countered, citing the accumulating evidence surrounding the Madrid train bombings in 2004, the British investigation into the 2005 bombings, and investigations into a variety of successful and foiled plots across the world. In each of these cases, al-Qaeda's imprimatur was evident. Even though its role was much more covert, it provided training, financing, or guidance. Compared to plots that seemed to be entirely homegrown or carried out by lone wolves, the scale of their violence was much greater and much more ferocious.

In the decade since that debate, the idea that lone wolves are the most important terrorist threat has lost credibility. Yet it still remains a phenomenon worth exploring. Chapter 14 discusses the industry of terrorism, why organizations are better at committing acts of violence than individuals, but for now, it is worth mentioning that sometimes individuals get lucky. In the United States, one of the worst acts of terror was committed by Timothy McVeigh and Terry Nichols, but they seem to be the exception rather than the norm. Either way, individuals with access to high-powered weaponry can kill many people. The 2016 Orlando nightclub shooter seems to have become radicalized on his own and still managed to kill forty-nine people. In other words, although homegrown terrorists might not be the biggest threat, they are still capable of inflicting significant pain on their societies.

Why is lone-wolf terrorism so prevalent nowadays? Largely because of the ease of access to terrorist propaganda on the internet and the presence of weapons. Indeed, an important al-Qaeda ideologue, Abu Musab al-Suri, had advocated the importance of self-radicalization as early as 2004 and 2005, as AQ lost its base in Afghanistan. The value of his ideas is likely overblown by academics, as it was only one part of his teachings and not many jihadists seem to quote him, but the late leader of Islamic State's external operation, Abu Muhammad al-Adani advocated a similar strategy once it became evident that his organization was collapsing. Daniel Byman of Georgetown University explains that this tactic of necessity creates imitators, which other impressionable individuals can emulate, creating a problem that feeds upon itself.

Again, though, lone wolves are generally not as dangerous as terrorists with organizational backing or direction. Yet they are problematic in a subtler but perhaps more pernicious way. As Daniel Byman argues, lone-wolf attacks often generate more outward fear than the threat warrants. Nonetheless, opportune politicians often capitalize on these incidents to justify illiberal policies, such as Donald Trump's Muslim ban, which further alienates individuals at risk of radicalizing and becoming terrorists. In essence, while lone wolves will cause deaths, the greater risk is a society overreacting and pursuing strategies that undermine the values that define them. This is happening both in Europe and the United States.

THE FOREIGN FIGHTER FLOW

The current foreign fighter flow is historically unprecedented. It dwarfs both the number of fighters who traveled to Afghanistan in the 1980s and later to Iraq in the early 2000s. Estimates range from as little as 30,000 fighters to higher estimates of around 45,000. According to the International Centre for Counter-Terrorism (ICCT) in The Hague, as of April 2016, there were anywhere from 3,900 to 4,200 EU nationals fighting in Iraq and Syria. The majority of those fighters, approximately 2,830 foreign fighters, come from Belgium, France, Germany, and the United Kingdom. The ICCT also believes that around 30 percent of those fighters have returned and another 14 percent have died. Additionally, it believes that about 90 percent of the fighters originated from urban areas and that 83 percent are male. The Soufan Group notes that the majority of those that traveled from Europe had past criminal records. The American foreign fighter problem was not as big as of early 2016. Estimates by the U.S. government were that only around 250 citizens had attempted the journey, with around 150 actually making it. Interestingly enough, a sizable number of American fighters traveled to the region to fight against IS, either linking up with the Kurds or working with other groups based in Iraq.

The large number of fighters is partially an artifact of Islamic State's sophisticated information operations across social media. The Soufan Group has studied this problem at length and finds that social media creates the ground for persuading people to join, but generally is not the decisive factor. From their research, the same factors that lead to radicalization, meaning in-person social connection, matter much more in driving recruits. Those traveling are usually in their twenties and are individuals seeking a new life. Most travel with the intention of staying there and are unlikely to return either because they are killed or because they will want to continue fighting elsewhere. Of those that have returned, some have expressed disillusionment with Islamic State's violence.

With the collapse of IS, there is a greater worry of plots emanating from its members in Europe and the United States. In the early years, there was less concern because the skills of an insurgent are not necessarily the same as those of a terrorist. However, the various suicide bombings and plots in Western Europe have demonstrated that Islamic State has a sophisticated apparatus for plotting attacks in the West.

THE ISLAMIC STATE THREAT TO EUROPE

Europe has been a target for Islamic terrorism for generations, but only recently has the threat become so evident. In the 2000s, al-Qaeda successfully attacked Madrid and London, and individuals linked to it nearly pulled off stellar attacks elsewhere on the continent. The threat was largely uneven, though, affecting countries with emotional symbolism. The United Kingdom has been at the forefront of plots because of its association with United States and its history of colonialism in the Middle East. France has been a target for similar reasons, but IS also blames it for the breakup of the Ottoman Empire. Spain is a target because many extremists regard it as occupied Muslim territory that needs to be reclaimed. Belgium, the Netherlands, and Germany have been targets for plots as well, but with the exception of the murder of Theo van Gogh in 2004 in Amsterdam, there were few high-profile attacks before 2011 in those places.

The recent flow of foreign fighters has changed the calculus for the continent's security forces. Out of all the countries, the best prepared for the current threat were France, Spain, and the United Kingdom because of their long history of domestic terrorism; they therefore had legislation in place that enabled them to proactively tackle the problem. Even then, the number of plots has overwhelmed them, and they have been caught by surprise. For example, France had been tracking the individuals that executed the *Charlie Hebdo* shootings but lacked the resources to properly investigate them given the severity of other threats they had to manage. Likewise, the man who committed the Westminster attack in March 2017 was known to British security forces, but due to the fact that he was fifty-two, MI5 did not believe him to be a threat. These countries have been lucky because of the resources they have placed into fighting terrorism. Not all countries have the budget or the know-how for combating terrorism. Every country in Europe has had individuals travel to Iraq and Syria, and if any of these individuals return, these places might become targets for terrorism as well. Because of open borders, the difficulty of monitoring individuals traveling abroad to fight, and the fact that IS needs to get lucky only once to create havoc, Europol now regards the group to be the most significant terrorist threat to the continent.

While Europe as a whole is a target, Islamic State is focusing more on the countries involved in the U.S.-led anti-IS coalition. Europol explains that since 2014, when IS first declared the caliphate, it has transitioned toward the internationalization of its violence as a deterrent, hoping that such aggression will change the political calculus of Europe's domestic societies. Before 2015, most of its attacks were opportunistic and symbolic, designed to create the impression that IS was everywhere. This in turn helped draw more recruits and funding from abroad. With the pressure the organization feels in the Middle East, they hope that inspiring terrorism in the continent might reduce the operational tempo against them. There is some history to justify this stance. Following the 2004 Madrid train bombings, Spain withdrew from Iraq, but this is only an example with other contextual factors weakening the causal link.

What is interesting is that for many governments, the biggest concern is lone wolves. A Europol report from November 2016 notes that most plots in Europe seem to be linked to lone wolves inspired by Islamic State's ideology, but authorities have assumed this since the beginning even when evidence suggested the contrary. Take the case of Mehdi Nemmouche, the man who shot up the Jewish Museum of Belgium in 2014. The police in Brussels assumed he was acting on his own after arresting him, despite finding a video of him claiming responsibility with an IS flag behind him. Only later did they attribute the attack to IS after discovering he had traveled to Syria in 2013. Indeed, IS no longer needs would-be recruits to travel to the Middle East for indoctrination or training. An investigation published by *The New York Times* in March 2017 found that IS uses social media and encrypted communication platforms to radicalize individuals and help guide plots. Using programs like WhatsApp, Telegram, and Signal, IS can provide step-by-step instructions for target selection, weapon usage, and even operational command and control. In other words, modern technology is lowering the barriers to entry for would-be terrorists lacking knowledge or expertise. As such, what is likely happening is what Bruce Hoffman described in his debate with Marc Sageman a decade ago: there certainly are lone-wolf terrorists, but the most dangerous and most successful plots likely have some external influence in terms of guiding and plotting. Even then, many of the plots assumed to have been committed in a leaderless fashion might in the future be discovered to have had some external guidance, as was the case with Nemmouche.

Making the situation much murkier is that IS does have an external operations unit, the Emni. The group, which was run by Abu Muhammad al-Adnani, the former spokesperson for the group until recently, initially began as an internal police unit monitoring the behavior of its members. After 2013, the entity became charged with plotting attacks abroad. The Emni serves as both an intelligence and a commando unit. According to police reports, defectors, and members captured, it has been training foreign fighters and sending them back to their countries of origin. It also seems to be the key decision-making body within IS for when it comes to plots abroad. *The New York Times* notes that apparently there are branches for various continents and regions. The only place where the Emni does not recruit from is the United States because of the difficulties of smuggling people back into the country. Instead, as is explained later, IS finds it easier to radicalize individuals online and to convince them to buy guns, taking advantage of the country's lax regulatory framework for weapons.

The foreign fighters the Emni sends abroad might participate directly in attacks or they might serve as the command and control for plots. These individuals usually return and form sleeper cells, which can recruit more individuals who have never traveled to IS-held territory and task them with attacks. In this sense, IS has exported al-Qaeda's training camp model from Afghanistan and simply adapted it to the European security context. The training these individuals receive gives them insight for manufacturing bombs, as was the case with the airport attack in Brussels 2016, or selecting symbolic targets like the November 2015 Paris attacks. The Emni also serves as a logistics body, helping smuggle fighters back into Europe after they have received training.

This model has given IS tremendous results. The main figure coordinating the Paris attacks, Abdelhamid Abaaoud, had spent time in Syria in 2013 before returning to Europe sometime in 2014 or 2015. Belgian by birth, Abaaoud was implicated in ordering several successful and failed plots across Europe in 2014 and 2015. He apparently had been guiding Nemmouche when he targeted Brussels. Abaaoud later participated directly in the attacks in Paris, which involved a sophisticated level of expertise in terms of operational tempo and the use of explosives. The attacks involved the use of TATP, an explosive that is difficult to manufacture but is coveted by Islamists because it can be made from over-the-counter products. After setting these off near the Stade de France, which distracted local security forces, IS attacked the Bataclan theater and proceeded to kill more people.

The key thing about the Emni is that it recognizes the need for executing many low-intensity attacks to maintain its image. Recognizing the difficulty of pulling off attacks like the one in Paris, IS moved on to low-tech attacks, which are just as deadly and require less technical sophistication. Examples of this include the Bastille Day Nice attack, where a radicalized individual drove a truck and ran over people watching the parade, and the December 2016 Berlin Christmas market attack, which followed a similar approach. Other dangerous plots include the Westminster terror attack in March 2017 that saw Khalid Masood run over fifty people, killing five. Afterwards, he crashed his car and fatally stabbed a police officer before security forces finally shot him dead. At the time of this writing, no links have appeared connecting Masood to a bigger terrorist organization, but there are records that he sent encrypted messages over WhatsApp right before committing the attack, opening the possibility of some international connection. On April 20, 2017, three days before the first round of the French elections, a man named Karim Cheurfi opened fire against police officers and civilians at the Champs-Elysées, killing one and injuring three. Most likely timed to try to influence the French elections, the attack was later claimed by IS. Nonetheless, IS still continues to plot attacks using explosives, as evinced by the Ansbach suicide bombing in 2016, which thankfully only killed the bomber and no one else. More worrisome was the May 2017 bombing at the Manchester Arena, which resulted in the deaths of twenty-three people and over five hundred injured, mainly young girls, after the suicide attacker set off a nail bomb. British security forces remained silent while the investigation continued, but there were indications suggesting the attack was the work of a major terrorist group because the perpetrator, Salman Ramadan Abedi, had links to Libya, despite being born in the United Kingdom. Later, it turned out that he had acted alone but that his father had been a member of the Libyan Islamic Fighting Group (LIFG), a terrorist organization with links to al-Qaeda, which had formed to fight Muammar Qaddafi in Libya. Furthermore, it appears that he had been in contact with IS members in Libya.

Even in plots not directly ordered by IS, its influence is pervasive. This was the case with the August 2017 Barcelona attack. Following the low-tech model used with great effect in Nice, a man named Younes Abouyaaqoub drove a van through La Rambla, a street popular for pedestrians, in the Catalan city, killing 13 and injuring over 130 people. This was part of a larger plot by a cell with a connection to IS through a Salafist imam named Abdelbaki Es Satty. The cell originally sought to blow up a van full of TAPT, the explosive of choice for jihadist terrorists in Europe, somewhere in Barcelona. The attack fell apart when the men trying to manufacture the bombs, which likely included Es Satty, accidentally set off an explosion in their safehouse in the small town of Alcanar, killing Es Satty and another. Fearing their plot would unravel soon thereafter, the remaining members of the cell opted to use vehicular terrorism, first in Barcelona, and again in the town of Cambrils. In Cambrils, they ran into pedestrians, injuring several, before seeing their automobile flip over and proceeding to stab a woman to death after exiting the car. The attackers, wearing fake suicide vests, were shot dead by the police. Abouyaaqoub for his part was killed four days after the initial attack by police.

Es Satty, had a long history in jihadist circles. He was a recruiter for IS through his role as the imam of the town of Ripoll. Previously, he had been arrested for his ties to individuals belonging to an AQ affiliate that carried out several attacks in Morocco, including the 2003 Casablanca terrorist incident. In a previous stint in prison for drug trafficking, he also befriended one of the plotters of the 2004 Madrid train bombings, the worst terrorist incident in Spain's history. Es Satty's death makes it difficult to answer the exact nature of the IS connection. Nonetheless, as Spain's most prominent terrorism scholars, Fernando Reinares and Carola Garcia-Calvo, explain, at the time of the Barcelona attack, individuals like Es Satty were involved deeply in a continent-wide jihadist network that recruited and mobilized terrorists for Islamic State. In this sense, even if Es Satty was not a direct member of IS, his presence shows how deeply integrated its organizational structure is all over Europe.

More recently, IS has started turning back foreign fighters from Europe, as it recognizes its inevitable collapse. Instead, it is preparing them for future plots on the continent. IS is also taking advantage of the refugee crisis, hoping that the European public remains antagonistic toward them to validate IS propaganda and to deepen the social rift between Muslims and non-Muslims on the continent. Future attacks are likely to become more prominent, as many fighters from Europe begin returning to their home cities following the further losses the caliphate is currently experiencing. When the caliphate ceases to be a real entity and transitions into a virtual caliphate, the sleeper cells that the Emni sent abroad are bound to erupt once more.

THE TERRORISM THREAT IN THE UNITED STATES

Terrorism in the United States is more complex and has other dynamics at play than Islamism. According to the New America Foundation, the number of deaths caused by Salafist jihadist terrorism between 2005 and 2015 was 94.* During the same period, the number of deaths from guns was a staggering 301,797.† Ever since the Columbine massacre in 1999, the country has developed a worse reputation abroad for mass shootings than it has for terrorism, which, with the exception of 9/11, is exceedingly rare. This is not to say that Salafist jihadist terrorism is not a problem, but rather, it is often overblown into something bigger for political reasons. It is important to note, however, that part of the reason that only 94 people have died during this period is simultaneously a factor of the relative scope of the threat, the country's ability to integrate and assimilate its Muslim population, and because of the reforms undertaken by the United States since 2001 to prevent another 9/11. If American domestic security agencies ever become lax in regard to this problem, that number will be much higher.

So how does terrorism in America look? Since 9/11, the list of plots is quite extensive. These include the failed midair shoe bomb attempt by Richard Reid, a British national traveling to Miami in 2001, the 2008 Times Square bombing, which caused no fatalities, the Little Rock shooting in 2009 that killed one person, and Faisal Shahzad's failed Times Square bombing in 2010. Before 2014, when IS grew in stature, the deadliest and best-known attacks were the Fort Hood shooting in 2009 and the Boston Marathon bombing in 2013. In the former, Nidal Hasan, a U.S. Army psychiatrist, killed thirteen people and injured another thirty-two. In the latter, Dzhokhar and Tamerlan Tsarnaev placed pressure cooker bombs at the finish line of the marathon, killing three and injuring nearly three hundred people.

The nature of the threat has evolved quite a bit since 2014, but it has its antecedents in the jihadist threat from 2001 to 2013. After 9/11, AQ struggled in staging further mass-casualty attacks in the United States but found an avenue through the proliferation of online propaganda leading to an increased number of radicalized individuals in the United States. A few of the plots emerging from this era were carried out by so-called lone-wolf terrorists, discussed earlier, but many of them had an external element guiding, directing, or influencing the attacks. This is the lasting pernicious legacy

---

* Peter Berger, Albert Ford, Alyssa Sims, and David Sterman, "Terrorism in America after 9/11," New America, https://www.newamerica.org/in-depth/terrorism-in-america/

† Linda Qiu, "Fact-checking a comparison of gun deaths and terrorism deaths," PolitiFact, October 5, 2015, http://www.politifact.com/truth-o-meter/statements/2015/oct/05/viral-image/fact-checking -comparison-gun-deaths-and-terrorism-/

of Anwar al-Awlaki, who inspired Nidal Hasan. IS has adopted this model. A study done by Alexander Meleagrou-Hitchens and Seamus Hughes of George Washington University found that of thirty-eight IS-inspired plots between March 1, 2014, and March 1, 2017, eight of these had some direct connection to English-speaking IS operatives in Syria. This largely follows the model used by IS in Europe, except many of these individuals have not traveled to Iraq or Syria. Many did try, but when they found it difficult to go abroad, they decided to plot domestically. This was the case of Elton Simpson, one of the 2015 Garland, Texas, shooters. Prior to the attack, Simpson had attempted traveling to Somalia but was stopped by the FBI. Still committed to attacking, he reached out to IS operatives via Twitter, who guided and advised him to attack in May 2015.

Of course, those IS-directed plots are only about 20 percent of the Salafist-inspired attacks. The others were carried out by self-radicalized individuals, whose identification with IS may have been opportunistic and intended for shock value. This seems to be the case with the San Bernardino shooters in December 2015 and the Pulse nightclub attacker in June 2016. It is important to note, though, that this is the publicly available evidence. As often happens, as more evidence accumulates over the years, links to foreign groups might appear. For example, the Boston Marathon bombers initially appeared to be homegrown radicals who lucked out with instructions from the internet, most likely from Anwar al-Awlaki's *Inspire* magazine, but evidence indicates that the older brother was probably in contact with extremist organizations in Russia. The same happened with Faisal Shahzad, where evidence later revealed he had connections to the Taliban.

It is also worth mentioning that the majority of the perpetrators of these plots were either born in the United States or grew up there. The Fort Hood shooter, Nidal Hassan, one of the San Bernardino attackers, and the Pulse nightclub shooter were born in the United States, Faisal Shahzad had American citizenship, and the Boston bombers came to the United States as children. *The New York Times* attributes this to the disconnect between two competing identities for these individuals: the culture of their parents and their American culture. This is similar to the phenomenon in Europe as well, where the second generation seems to have a hard time reconciling its separate identity.

The curious thing about the United States is that Islamic terrorism gets most of the attention even though the U.S. faces an extremely potent right-wing terrorism threat. Most of these incidents are not labeled terrorism, however, because of how American law enforcement defines hate crimes and domestic terrorism. Taking a definition that approximates a more European reading of terrorism, the New America Foundation in June 2015, estimated the number of deaths caused by right-wing terrorism since 9/11 at fifty, a number that at the time was higher than jihadist terrorism. The numbers changed after the San Bernardino and Orlando attacks, but still underscore the potency of this phenomenon. The incidents that fall in this category include the Charleston church shooting, multiple police ambushes, and an attack against the Holocaust Memorial Museum in Washington in 2009. This tally excludes mass shootings like the Newtown massacre, the Virginia Tech killings, or Isla Vista killings, as these seemed to lack a political motive or any broader political aim to influence American politics or inspire fear among certain ethnic groups.

The plotters behind these attacks run the litany of hate groups from Christian militia members to anti-government entities. Christian extremists with parochial interests have not committed many acts of violence since 2001, except for the murder of George Tiller by anti-abortion activist Scott Roeder. The other groups are growing in prominence, however. In 2015, the Southern Poverty Law Center listed 892 different hate groups in the United States. This number has grown with the nomination and subsequent election of Donald Trump. Traditionally, most of these groups' violence has been directed toward ethnic minorities like Jews, African Americans, Hispanics, and Asian Americans, but more recently, hate crimes have been directed primarily at American Muslims.

According to FBI data, hate crimes in the United States showed a decline overall, but when examining the figures by religion, there was an upswing of violence toward Muslims. Examples abound. In September 2016, a man on a motorcycle started a fire at an Islamic cultural center near Orlando, while in August 2016, an imam was killed execution-style in New York City. At the time of this writing, the final statistics for 2017 are not available, but if press reports are accurate, they will likely document a general rise in hate crimes regardless of ethnicity or religious status. By late February, there had been more than one hundred reported bomb threats against Jewish institutions or acts of defacement of Jewish symbols, including cemeteries. February 2017 also saw the death of two Indian men by a man yelling, "Get out of my country!" in Kansas, most likely believing them to be Muslims. In May 2017, an alleged white supremacist named Sean C. Urbanski was charged with killing Richard W. Collins III, a young black man who had just finished university and had earned a commission in the U.S. Army. As of this writing, Urbanski has pled not guilty and has not been convicted of any crime, although authorities have charged him with a hate crime after discovering evidence on social media and on his phone that linked him to various hate groups, including a Facebook group called "Alt-Reich: Nation."

Indeed, many of these hate crimes have occurred in the context of the emergence of the so-called alt-right, which is not reassuring for the United States in the coming years. The alt-right was introduced earlier in this book but warrants more nuanced analysis because it has the potential to generate a potent strain of right-wing terrorism. The term dates back to the late 2000s when Richard Spencer, the president of the Washington-based white supremacist National Policy Institute think tank and the unofficial spokesperson for the movement, used it to describe a wing of American conservatism focused primarily on white identity politics and the preservation of what he called "Western civilization." The phrase gained mainstream usage during the 2016 presidential elections because many individuals associated with the alt-right started to openly support then candidate Trump. Prominent supporters included Richard Spencer, the chairman of Breitbart News, Steve Bannon, and the founder of the neo-Nazi Traditionalist Worker Party, Matthew Heimbach.

Taking cues from Donald Trump's more racially inflammatory remarks, such as calling Mexican immigrants rapists and arguing for a Muslim ban, the alt-right saw Trump's candidacy creating an environment to operate openly, and thereby became key influencers both in Trump's campaign and online discussions surrounding his candidacy. In the former case, Jeff Sessions, a perennial favorite of the alt-right because of his hardline views on immigration, became Trump's first attorney general. Similarly, Steve Bannon became a chief advisor to Trump, helped him frame his presidential campaign, and later his administration, in stark, nationalist tones. In addition, Stephen Miller, a close associate of Richard Spencer and one of Jeff Sessions's former legislative assistants, would go on to craft

Trump's Muslim ban in early 2017 and push for the end of DACA (Deferred Action for Childhood Arrivals).* Most Americans, however, became familiar with the alt-right because of its online activities. Platforms associated with the alt-right like Breitbart and Infowars played a large role in promoting content sympathetic to candidate Trump, becoming his most ardent supporters and the source of positive spin for his most controversial statements. Trump returned the favor, appearing in several interviews by contributors to these platforms, thus legitimizing both websites as viable news sources.

The alt-right falls on the extreme end of the left/right spectrum, but includes a few ideological quirks. Spencer has noted that it is a big-tent ideology that includes paleoconservative and libertarian followers of Ron Paul, anarcho-capitalists, theocrats, and fascists. In this grouping, there are also techno-libertarians, who argue that democracy and egalitarianism restrict technological progress because of the inherent biological differences among races and fantasize about the creation of a fascist state where technologists are free to invent and create without any state intervention. These variations distract from its inherent racism. All groups associated with the alt-right are bound together by the desire to resurrect European "blood and soil" notions of nationalism as well as by their pseudoscientific arguments about genetics and race to advocate white supremacy. Less extreme alt-righters, if there is such a thing, tend to couch their beliefs as being against "PC-culture," or political correctness, which they argue means speaking truth to power; in practice, this means being openly racist toward immigrants and minorities.

Key policy issues for the alt-right include restrictive immigration policies and regressive refugee settlement policies. Perhaps the only point of debate among the alt-right concerns the issue of "whiteness" and people of Jewish heritage. A small grouping of the alt-right tend to be less anti-Semitic than others, or claim that their anti-Semitism is nothing more than a joke. Stephen Miller, for example, is Jewish. Milo Yiannopoulos, another of the alt-right's more media-friendly avatars, is Jewish as well but has not hesitated to make jokes online about the Holocaust. Many, if not most, adhere to the German Nazi party line about Jews, with a substantial

---

* An executive order signed by President Obama designed to protect undocumented immigrants who had arrived at an early age from deportation and to enable them to work and study in the United States.

number being Holocaust deniers. Spencer, for his part, has said he is receptive to evidence that the Holocaust did not happen.

Another key feature of the alt-right is peddling of conspiracy theories. In much the same way that Richard Hofstadter described the far right in the 1960s in his essay "The Paranoid Style of American Politics," many in the alt-right view world events as driven by some dark actor intent on destroying Western civilization, with the white race as the ultimate victim. Not all conspiracies are alike. Some are somewhat benign, for instance those who believe that President Obama and the Democratic Party sought increased immigration to dilute the voting power of white Americans, thereby enabling the Democrats to consolidate power.

Others in the alt-right pushed the infamous "Pizzagate" conspiracy, which charged Democrats with running an underground pedophile ring in the basement of a pizza restaurant in D.C. More nefarious theories include the resurrection of anti-Semitic tropes involving "Jewish bankers" and financiers such as George Soros, who want to destroy democracy in the West, a further evolution of one of the worst hoaxes in history, *Protocols of the Elders of Zion*. The theory with the most receptive audience, and which undoubtedly motivates many of the alt-right, is the belief in a global effort to commit "white genocide"—that is, the elimination of the white race. Some, like Richard Spencer, do not necessarily advance this argument from a conspiratorial perspective but offer pseudoscientific racist reasoning that amounts to the same thing. According to this reading, whites in Europe and North America are inherently superior to other races but are losing their political dominance and their culture to immigrants and will someday become subservient, if not extinct, because of higher birthrates in the immigrant population.

While some conservative publications downplay these theories as the nonsense held by a fringe minority, they have the potential for real harm. In December 2016, shortly after Trump won the election, a man named Edgar Madison Welch attacked Comet Pizza in northern Washington, DC. after encountering the Pizzagate conspiracy theory online. He entered the restaurant during lunchtime and fired three times before realizing he was in error. Welch's visit was preceded by online harassment of the restaurant by those believing the conspiracy, which apparently included Trump's first national security advisor, Mike Flynn, who shared it on social media. No one was hurt in the incident, but it underscored the potency of conspiratorial thinking. There is sufficient historical precedence of conspiracy theories that incite people to act violently against minorities, as was the case in Nazi Germany, or today, with the Buddhist majority attacking the Rohingya in Mynamar.

The alt-right represents the rebirth of the country's most toxic, illiberal, and racist ideologies, but crafted to appeal to a younger generation. How the alt-right communicates is even different from its predecessors: it relies on online platforms such as Twitter or forums like Reddit, where the alt-right shares memes (or jokes, often laid over images) that convey their ideology in a supposed humorous fashion that allows alt-rights to claim they are only engaging in innocuous banter. And when people criticize alt-rights for their jokes, the common retort is that their critics are being politically correct and are too unsophisticated to understand their humor, and therefore warrant attacks in retaliation. This trolling often generates an online mob mentality where thousands harass prominent critics of the alt-right, and often occurs when leading alt-rightists identify prominent minorities in the media and attack them. Milo Yiannopoulos was permanently banned from Twitter after encouraging his followers online to harass Leslie Jones, an African-American comedian.

The alt-right relies on pseudoscientific arguments to gain legitimacy with their supporters and potential supporters. Derek Black, the son of Don Black (the founder of the infamous white supremacist online forum Stormfront and a former member of the Ku Klux Klan), explained in a profile appearing in *The Washington Post* how this has been a deliberate effort by alt-rights to give them plausible deniability of being labeled as racists. Some of the more public figures of the movement, like Richard Spencer and Milo Yiannopoulos, are known for dressing fashionably and speaking cogently before cameras; they are no longer the scary men marching with swastika tattoos screaming "Death to Jews." Rather, they appear as young millennials, educated at elite universities, drawing inspiration from debunked science and false philosophy to clothe their argument that the white race is on the verge of extinction.

With this extreme worldview, the alt-right can radicalize individuals into violence. Much like Salafists, the alt-right advocates a homogeneous society that absolutely rejects outsiders. The alt-right is much more extreme, however, because whereas Salafism castigates nonbelievers, the alt-right rejects billions on the basis of their physical attributes. The online platforms where these ideas find traction, such as Breitbart or Stormfront, ignore or censor any opposing view. The alt-right mind-set offers several solutions to what they see as the diminishing of the white race. Some are relatively benign, such as arguing for the end of nonwhite immigration into the United States. Others are more extreme, taking their cues from novels popular in these circles, like *The Turner Diaries*, which describes an America torn apart by race war. Adherents of this view tend to argue for more violent means.

At the time of this writing, there is no alt-right terrorist group, but there have been terrorist incidents by alt-rightists. In December 2017, William Edward Atchison shot up a high school in Aztec, New Mexico, killing himself and two students. Police searching his home for motives discovered he was active on numerous alt-right websites. In August 2017 in a Charlottesville, Virginia, James Alex Fields, an alt-right marcher protesting the removal of a statue of confederate general Robert E. Lee, drove his car into a group of counterprotestors, killing one and injuring nineteen others. These two attacks evoke the profile of lone-wolf terrorists, which many Americans associated with Islamic jihadist activities.

Worrisome too is the sense that Trump's presidency has legitimized and normalized many alt-right positions, inducting them into mainstream conservativism. He has resurrected the phrase "America First," a slogan popular with anti-Semites in the 1930s, and he has made many of the alt-right's policy preferences his own, starting with efforts to restrict immigration. After the Charlottesville incident, he famously argued that "both sides" bore responsibility for Heather Heyer's death, and at various points of his candidacy and presidency, he has hesitated to condemn white nationalists and supremacists. He has made many of the alt-right's ideas part of modern-day Republican orthodoxy. Though many Republicans will not buy into many of the alt-right's ideas, nevertheless, it would only take a small grouping of individuals to stumble upon its thinking, to radicalize, and then to take up arms.

Another source of right-wing terrorism comes from anti-government groups. Of the anti-government groups, the most prominent is the sovereign citizen movement, which portrays itself as a constitutionally originalist movement and rejects the current federal government, considering it illegitimate. Emerging in the 1970s, sovereign citizens have been implicated in a multitude of cop killings. In 2010, Joseph Kane killed two police officers in Memphis after a routine traffic stop. The ambush of Las Vegas police officers in April 2014 was committed by individuals linked to this organization. Another incident was the ambushing and killing of Christopher Smith, a deputy sheriff in Tallahassee in November 2014. Aside from attacking cops, the group is notorious for committing fraud to defame rivals or overwhelming local authorities with thousands of pages of paperwork to obstruct their ability to levy fines for mundane things like parking tickets. Structurally, sovereigns are decentralized, without any coordinated command or control, and only linked by a nominally shared ideology. In this regard, they are most representative of the lone-wolf phenomenon discussed earlier.

Sovereign citizens are only one strain of these groups. During the Obama administration, the Southern Poverty Law Center tracked close to 1,200 organizations of this type, with around 276 being armed militias. Anti-government organizations usually share a conspiratorial worldview that believes the federal government is working alongside the United Nations to deprive American citizens of their guns and property and to impose a world government. This mind-set created the panic in the summer of 2015 surrounding the American government's Jade Helm 15 exercise in various southwestern states, which many anti-government groups thought was a prelude to martial law and the confiscation of their weapons. In addition, these groups captured national attention with the Bundy standoff in 2014 that drew militia members from across the country to fight against perceived overreach by the federal government.

A 2012 study done by the Combating Terrorism Center (CTC) at West Point found some interesting trends related to right-wing terrorism. First, there tended to be an upswing of right-wing violence during election years and that an increasing number of attacks occurred in states with large minority populations. They also noted that this movement caused more casualties in the first decade of the 2000s than in the 1990s when excluding the Oklahoma City bombing. However, because most of these efforts are decentralized, the level of violence is not high enough to generate the same panic. Indeed, as Bruce Hoffman has noted, the concept of leaderless terrorist violence was first postulated by the American white supremacist movement in the 1980s. The reason for this was that it drew less scrutiny from federal authorities and made it harder for one arrest to break apart their perceived resistance.

TERRORISM GOING FORWARD?

Terrorism will continue being a problem for both Europe and the United States, but in different ways. Europe has strong laws against hate speech and seems to have regulated its right-wing terror problem for now. Left-wing extremism seems to have died with the Cold War, but these groups always have the possibility of emerging, depending on the context of local politics. Furthermore, until 2015, the biggest problem affecting the continent were separatist groups, which tend to be underreported relative to violence committed by Islamic terrorists. This latter data must be qualified by noting that this is for the whole of Europe and that individual countries experience terrorism differently. Going forward, Europe's proximity to the Middle East makes it an easy target for continued attacks by al-Qaeda and Islamic State. How this evolves will depend on the continent's policies toward refugees and if it deploys a framework for integration and assimilation. Further cooperation and intelligence sharing among security forces will undoubtedly help the continent move forward, but given the size of Europe and the strained budgets of its member states, it might not be able to pool enough resources to stop all attacks. On top of this, while it is easy for outside commentators from countries with unified security apparatuses to prescribe solutions for Europe, it is important to keep in mind that European security is a tapestry of various policies developed at varying societal levels, making harmonious negotiations and diplomacy a luxury. That it seems dedicated toward working to this goal is commendable.

The United States, in contrast, is blessed with two large oceans and two friendly neighbors to its north and south. This will slow the growth of its Muslim population, especially because the Obama and Trump administrations have proven to be quite stingy in accepting refugees from Iraq and Syria. As such, most terrorism threats to the U.S. will likely come from its domestic population. Regarding Islamic terrorism, the threat to the United States has certainly been exaggerated. In the period between

9/11 and 2016, more Americans were killed by right-wing American terrorists than by Muslim terrorists. In 2017, the United States experienced thirteen terrorist incidents. Only two of these can be attributed to jihadist violence—the October 2017 truck attack in lower Manhattan and the failed suicide terrorist attack in New York's Port Authority bus depot in December. The other eleven were committed by, or linked to, individuals from the far right.

A challenge confronting both Europe and the United States is allocating the necessary resources and properly analyzing the problem of terrorism. The nature of terrorism makes preventing every attack impossible unless governments start pulling resources away from other non-security-related programs. There will have to be cost-benefit analyses for these societies, as they must operate under conditions of constraint and scarcity. In an ideal world, where other challenges do not exist, all terrorism could be stopped. At the same time, while billions of dollars or euros could be spent to strengthen security at the cost of other important societal goods, such as education and health, these debates are often hard to have when grieving family members mourn the loss of their children, spouses, and friends. Of the two, it is likely that some European countries are better prepared for these discussions without devolving into demagoguery or inflating the problem more than necessary.

Countries such as the United Kingdom and Spain have a longer history of confronting terrorism and have developed a degree of resiliency that allows their societies to frame the problem in the right context. The United States, however, even with its long history of domestic terrorism—from left-wing radicals in the 1960s and 1970s (the Weather Underground), hate groups (the Ku Klux Klan and its many lynchings in the American South), and various right-wing terrorists starting in the 1980s—seems to lack such resiliency. One need only consider the effects of the 2013 Boston Marathon bombings, when two individuals caused the city to shut down and local officials to declare martial law, suspending the Constitution temporarily. The risk of terrorism, as discussed before, is not so much that terrorists will destroy a country but that it will cause societies to overreact and see them give up on their values in the name of security. Therefore, for Western societies, the seminal challenge is creating an effective and efficient counterterrorism policy that secures their domestic populations while at the same time not eroding the very values that define them as such:

the rule of law, civil liberties, social pluralism, inclusionary democratic institutions, public spaces with unfettered access for assembly purposes, due process.

The obstacle, of course, when it comes to this last point is developing a proper metric for counterterrorism. When security forces are doing their job well, their victories will never appear on the front pages of newspapers. In contrast, whenever an intelligence failure occurs or some completely unexpected terrorist incident happens, this captures the public's attention, and failures are broadcast globally. This is how it should be, because failure usually implies death, especially given the numerous instances where terrorism incidents occurred either due to the lack of imagination by counterterrorism entities, as was the case with Nemmouche in 2014, or because of strategic intelligence failures as with the May 2017 Manchester attacks. At the same time, terrorism will continue being a problem for society until time collapses upon itself just because of the inherent entropy and randomness of the universe. This is not meant to justify security lapses but rather to suggest the importance of a more robust societal understanding of the threat posed by terrorism and, similarly, the value of defining success in counterterrorism in more concrete terms than the abstract and nigh impossible goal of preventing terrorism forevermore.

PART 3

Reflections on Terrorism

12

THE CULTURE OF MODERN
TERRORISM

GENERAL HISTORIES OF TERRORISM ARE OF INTEREST BECAUSE THEY
give a causal explanation for the state of the world, but much like a hearty
soup with no flavor, they shed little light on the intangible factors that
played a role in these developments. If the story of modern terrorism is
politics or, more specifically, the failure of governance, then it is worth
considering the factors at play behind those politics. For as Aristotle explained some twenty-four hundred years ago, humans are political animals
that must interact with each other to form societies with laws to regulate
behavior. How do humans accomplish this? By developing a shared language, creating art and music, and developing a culture that subcon-
sciously dictates what is right and wrong. This is to say that history is but
only one aspect of understanding terrorism. Philip Bobbitt said it best when
he wrote that the "perception of cause and effect—history—is the distinc-
tive element in the ceaseless, restless dynamic by means of which strategy
and law live out their necessary relationship . . . and it is the self-portrayal
of a society that enables it to know its own identity." Whether people wish
to acknowledge it or not, terrorist groups are societies unto themselves
with their own codes, culture, argot, and history that explain the strategies
they use and the rules they choose to follow. IS is not just a product of Assad's
brutality, and neither were the anarchists in tsarist Russia in the 1800s.

Islamic terrorism owes much of its ideological understanding to developments in Egypt at the end of the nineteenth century, when a number of Islamic thinkers, such as Mohammed Abdu and Rashid Rida, who were to have considerable influence on the following two generations, appeared on the scene. They were true believers but at the same time could be considered reformers. They had considerable influence on Hassan al-Banna, the founder of the Muslim Brotherhood in Ismailia, Egypt, in 1928. Al-Banna wanted to educate a new generation in the spirit of the original teaching of the Prophet. But he was a reformer. His movement was not only concerned with religious preaching but also did a great deal of social work, which made it very popular in Egypt and was also present in some other countries. The Muslim Brotherhood became a major political force, probably at times the organization with the largest membership in the country. It did not, most of the time, strive to attain political power but intended to exert great pressure on the government in power in the spirit of their religious beliefs. This led them into almost permanent conflict with the authorities. During much of the time of its existence, it was banned and many of its leading figures were imprisoned.

The Muslim Brotherhood did not preach terrorism, but since it could not achieve its goals legally and was for long periods pushed underground, part of the movement (particularly the younger generation) became more and more radical. Virtually all terrorist movements in Egypt and some other countries had originally been part of the Brotherhood and subsequently have left it because its elderly leadership was too tame for their taste. This is true, for instance, in regard to the group that killed Anwar al-Sadat. Before that, though, they had been among the initiators of the great fire in Cairo (January 1952), which destroyed part of the capital city. The Brotherhood also participated in political assassinations, which were frequent in Egypt in the 1930s and 1940s. It is interesting that the targets of these operations were normally not the British overlords who controlled the country at the time. Instead, it was fellow Egyptians. Among the victims of these assassinations were several prime ministers, such as Mahmoud El Nokrashy Pasha, but also the founder and head of the Muslim Brotherhood, Hassan al-Banna. They were not the only reformist organization that engaged in terrorism. The Egyptian monarchy came to an end with the rebellion of the senior officers in 1952. Some of the officers had belonged to Misr al-Fatat (Young Egypt), a fascist organization of sorts

that on the whole had not engaged in terrorism but had believed in achieving its goals by peaceful means. This movement brought into power Ga-
mal Abdel Nasser, the great Arab nationalist who promised a new way of
life for Arabs across the world after dominion by the Ottoman Turks and,
later, the British and French empires. However, the Muslim Brotherhood
did not fare well under the rule of Nasser. It was again banned, its leaders
were imprisoned, and more than a few were executed, such as Sayyid Qutb
(1966), one of the most radical and influential thinkers of Islamism in our
time. His writings, a centerpiece for al-Qaeda's and IS's ideology, has inspired most Islamic radicals since the 1980s. What is curious about him is
that a prolonged visit to the United States had in no way affected his views
but made him more radical in his rejection of the West and modernism,
and this seems at play in contemporary terrorist movements as well. What
is important about the Muslim Brotherhood is that it provided the language
and a foundational story for how to attempt to reform societies. Hamas, for
example, emerged in the Arab regions of Israel and Gaza, where, not too
successfully, it has been the ruling force in recent years.

A movement similar to the Muslim Brotherhood, the Gama'at Al-
Islamiyya, emerged in British India and later in Pakistan and played a
similar role to it in South Asia. It also had influence in some other countries, such as Afghanistan and Indonesia. Gama'at did not directly sponsor
terrorism but prepared the field for a variety of terrorist groups, which appeared in recent decades. Its leader and chief ideologist was Abul A'la
Maududi (1903–1979). He was not initially against the partition of India,
but subsequently joined the camp of those favoring it. He was in constant
conflict with a movement of nationalist separatists headed by Muhammad
Ali Jinnah, who had a considerable influence on the Islamists in Asia (especially in Afghanistan). He believed in political activity and intended to
influence the leadership of the Muslim community. He believed that politics was an inseparable part of the Islamic faith. As he saw it, Muslims
were not just a religious community group but rather one based on a certain theory or ideology with allegiance to a single leader, obedience, and
discipline. As mentioned earlier, this movement did not initially favor terrorism, but in the course of time, it came to support a variety of terrorist
movements in Asia and the Middle East. Thousands of its members joined
groups of jihadist fighters in several Asian countries.

Again, though, the preceding is but cause and effect. How can we explain the rise of movements like the Muslim Brotherhood and Gama'a Al-Islamiyya, and the current wave of Islamism in general? There is no simple explanation for the genesis of religious movements like Christianity and why Jesus appeared at a certain time and place; the same is true for Muhammad and Islam. However, the resurgence of Islam seems to have certain obvious causes.

A few centuries after the time of Muhammad, Islam was a powerful religion that produced a high culture both in Baghdad and in Spain. At this time, much of Europe was shrouded in darkness, and its culture was clearly inferior to that of this golden age of Islam. In later centuries, the Ottoman Empire became the leading force, and the sultan also held the position of caliph. The Ottoman Empire stretched from northern Africa to most of the Middle East and, with the fall of Constantinople in 1453, it destroyed the Byzantine Empire and took over most of its territories (including most of the Balkans). But then the tide turned. The Ottoman Empire came under strong pressure from several sides. However, the internal crisis of the Ottoman Empire was the decisive factor for the decline of Islam's golden age. This crisis was a result of a variety of factors, including the weakness of most of the sultans (some of them were mentally defective) and the absence of a middle class in the empire, which could have served as a pillar of the system. Economically, too, the country was quite backward compared with Europe, which grew richer, partly as a result of acquiring colonies. From the early nineteenth century, Russia became a powerful enemy of Turkey. Gradually, the Balkan states acquired independence from Constantinople. Turkey became the "sick man" of international politics.

This process reached its nadir in the early twentieth century, as Turkey was on the losing side of the First World War. England took over Egypt, the Italians were now the masters in Tripoli, and (according to Sykes-Picot) France was now the master in Syria and Lebanon. Iraq also became part of the British Empire. What remained was Kemalist Turkey. After the Second World War, the West became weaker, and most of the Arab states became independent. The increasing importance of oil and cars made some of these countries very rich, but the majority were left behind. Culturally, the Muslim world was unimportant. In brief, the Muslim world was in a sad state despite the fact that most of it had become independent.

It was against this background of backwardness that the wave of Islamism, beginning in the late twentieth century, should be explained. The Islamists wanted their world to once again play an important role in world politics and also in world culture.

IS AND THE NATURE OF EVIL

With the resurgence of Islamism has come a change in how victims of their terrorism are regarded or viewed. In the history of terrorism, it has been the norm that terrorists try to eliminate their enemies, but an element of cruelty was usually not involved. This has changed markedly with IS, a group that has been most successful of all in utilizing social media and symbolism, often beheading its enemies, who wear orange jumpsuits similar to those worn by the prisoners of Guantánamo Bay. Some terrorist groups, especially in the nineteenth century, took great care not to hurt people who, in their eyes, were innocent. There is a famous play by Albert Camus about an incident in which a Russian terrorist decided not to kill a high dignitary because he appeared on the scene together with his family, and there was a danger that the family too would be killed. The terrorist decided against the attack despite endangering his own life by doing so. This play was based on a true happening, and it was apparently not the only one of its kind.

The behavior of the twentieth century was not essentially different. There are few reports on acts of great cruelty committed. Until the early 1980s, Brian Jenkins's famous precept that terrorists wanted many people watching and not many dead held true. With a few exceptions, terrorists did not prioritize mass-casualty attacks and did everything they could to avoid them. The IRA noticeably tried its hardest to moderate its violence for fear of losing the support of its base in Northern Ireland. These, of course, were secular movements who wanted popular support for their political aims. Even the Irgun found itself regretting the high number of civilian deaths caused by the bombing of the King David Hotel, while still acknowledging the positive effect the explosion had on its cause. This began to change at the end of the twentieth century, when some terrorist groups started to kill indiscriminately by trying to explode aircrafts, bomb supermarkets, or attack other places where many people congregated.

Whether it was Hezbollah's pioneering use of suicide bombings, Aum Shinrikyo releasing toxic gas in Tokyo's subway system, or Timothy McVeigh's attack in Oklahoma, the norms of terrorists shifted.

However, with the appearance of IS, yet another age dawned. There is no need to discuss in detail the kinds of atrocities committed, because they have been fully documented and IS does not deny them. To give but a few examples, crucifixion or rape of young girls, graphic beheading videos, the stoning of women who allegedly commit adultery, abuse and enslavement of the Yazidis, and desecration of Christian and Yazidi religious sites. Groups that commit such acts are located not only in the Middle East but also in other Asian and African countries.

The question then arises as to why these acts are committed and how to explain them. Is the aim to frighten their enemies, or should one look for deeper reasons? This in turn leads us to the issue of evil. The essence of evil has been difficult to understand for most of us today, who were taught that real evil does not exist. It has been rightly noted that people living in the Middle Ages would have found it easier to understand; they would have regarded such evildoers as emissaries of Satan. It is also true that Europe, from the days of the Inquisition to the period of the last burning of witches, is by no means free of acts of individual and collective atrocities. But with the eighteenth century, there has been a profound change, and this seems to be the reason for the difficulties that contemporaries have believing in the existence of evil in other parts of the world, even today. There is, for instance, the belief (even among criminologists) that mass murderers killing their victims in a particularly cruel way must be the victims of childhood neglect, undeserved punishment at an early age, or some other social circumstances.

There is much reason to assume that more profound issues are involved. To understand these is not easy, but a recent article in the IS journal *Dabiq* is of considerable interest and relevance. (Dabiq is a small town in northern Syria in which the final decisive battle between Muslims and their enemies is to take place. It is also the name of the IS periodical.) The article is called "Why We Hate You & Why We Fight You":

1. We hate you, first and foremost, because you are disbelievers, you reject the oneness of Allah—whether you realize it or not—by making partners for Him in worship, you blaspheme against Him,

claiming that he has a son, you fabricate lies against His prophets and messengers, and you indulge in all manner of devilish practices. It is for this reason that we are commanded to openly declare our hatred for you and our enmity towards you. There has already been for you an excellent example in Abraham and those with him, when they said to their people, "Indeed we are disassociated from you and from whatever you worship other than Allah. We have rejected you, and there has arisen, between us and you, enmity and hatred forever until you believe in Allah alone" (Al-Mumtahanah 4). Furthermore, just as your disbelief is the primary reason we hate you, your disbelief is the primary reason we fight you, as we have been commanded to fight the disbelievers until they submit to the authority of Islam, either by becoming Muslim, or by paying juzyah—for those afforded this option—and living in humiliation under the rule of the Muslims. Thus, even if you were to stop fighting us, your best-case scenario in a state of war would be that we would suspend our attacks against you. If we deemed it necessary—in order to focus on the closer and more immediate threats, before eventually resuming our campaigns against you. Apart from the option of a temporary truce, this is the only likely scenario that would bring you fleeting respite from our attacks. So in the end, you cannot bring an indefinite halt to our war against you. At most, you could only delay it temporarily. "And fight them until there is not fitnah (paganism) and (until) the religion, all of it, is for Allah" (Al-Baqarah 193).

2. We hate you because your secular, liberal societies permit the very things that Allah has prohibited while banning many of the things He has permitted, a matter that doesn't concern you because you separate between religion and state, thereby granting supreme authority to your whims and desires via the legislators you vote into power. In doing so you desire to rob Allah of His right to be obeyed and you wish to usurp that right for yourselves. "Legislation is not but for Allah" (Yusuf 40). Your secular liberalism has led you to tolerate and even support "gay rights," to allow alcohol, drugs, fornication, gambling, and usury to become widespread, and to encourage the people to mock those who denounce these filthy sins and vices. As such, we wage war against you to

stop you from spreading your disbelief and debauchery—your secularism and nationalism, your perverted liberal values, your Christianity and atheism—and all the depravity and corruption they entail. You've made it your mission to "liberate" Muslim societies; we've made it our mission to fight off your influence and protect mankind from your misguided concepts and your deviant way of life.

3. In the case of the atheist fringe, we hate you and wage war against you because you disbelieve in the existence of your Lord and Creator. You witness the extraordinarily complex makeup of created beings, and the astonishing and inexplicably precise physical laws that govern the entire universe, but insist that they all came about through randomness and that one should be faulted, mocked, and ostracized for recognizing that the astonishing signs we witness day after day are the creation of the Wise, All-Knowing Creator and not the result of accidental occurrence. "Or were they created by nothing, or were they the creators (of themselves)?" (AtTur 35). Your disbelief in your Creator further leads you to deny the Day of Judgment, claiming that "you only live once." "Those who disbelieve have claimed that they will never be resurrected. Say, 'Yes, by my Lord, you will surely be resurrected; then you will surely be informed of what you did. And that, for Allah, is easy'" (At-Taghabun 7).

4. We hate you for your crimes against Islam and wage war against you to punish you for your transgressions against our religion. As long as your subjects continue to mock our faith, insult the prophets of Allah—including Noah, Abraham, Moses, Jesus, and Muhammad—burn the Qur'an, and openly vilify the laws of the Shari'ah, we will continue to retaliate, not with slogans and placards, but with bullets and knives.

5. We hate you for your crimes against the Muslims; your drones and fighter jets bomb, kill, and maim our people around the world, and your puppets in the usurped lands of the Muslims oppress, torture, and wage war against anyone who calls to the truth. As such, we fight you to stop you from killing our men, women, and children, to liberate those of them whom you imprison and torture, and to take revenge for the countless Muslims who've suffered as a result of your deeds.

6. We hate you for invading our lands and fight you to repel you and drive you out. As long as there is an inch of territory left for us to reclaim, jihad will continue to be a personal obligation.*

Such hysterical outpourings are rare, perhaps even unprecedented, in the history of terrorism. How to explain them? They have occurred in a civilization that was once among the leading in the world, but it has no humanist tradition and did not experience an Enlightenment. Voltaire wrote a play about Muhammad in which he noted his fanaticism, but this was not really the main point in his critique, which drew into doubt whether Muhammad had really been a true prophet. In fact, what Muhammad preached (even though it included the idea of a holy war) was not remotely as fanatical as the present-day propaganda of the radical Islamists. This again leads us to the issue of evil, normally dealt with by theologians and psychologists. They usually focus their research on very ancient periods in the history of mankind. More recently, as pointed out early on, a tendency has emerged to deny (or at least to doubt) the existence of evil. Freud, especially in his exchange with Einstein, was more realistic in this respect than some of his followers. Reading the preceding, though, makes one wonder about the ontology of evil. These are individuals motivated by religious motives to use violence. There have been religious movements in the past, but even they found it necessary to control their violence. As recently as 2013 al-Qaeda was chastising its members for excessive violence and atrocities.

The preceding at least gives some justification for why IS acted the way it did. What of the atrocities committed by IS? The question of evil is intimately linked to them. Warfare in the age of the Qur'an and the Hadith was not exactly gentle, but atrocities were not common. This is true for subsequent ages, but it is also true that in Medieval Europe, there was an injunction usually observed. This was called Treuga Dei, according to which clergymen were not to be killed, nor were women, children, and nonfighting individuals in general. Later warfare became rougher, especially in the Thirty Years' War, and the Swedes under Gustavus Adolphus were known for occasional brutality. For years to come, children in central Europe were frightened after they misbehaved because their parents

* Islamic State. "Why We Hate You & Why We Fight You." *Dabiq* 15: 30–33 accessed at https://clarionproject.org/factsheets-files/islamic-state-magazine-dabiq-fifteen-breaking-the-cross.pdf.

told them, "The Swedes are coming." In our age, atrocities have frequently occurred in countries such as Cambodia but particularly in the continent of Africa. This refers to the mutilation of the Tutsis with machetes and the cutting of their Achilles tendons, as well as the rape of women and girls. Some of these committing atrocities were Christians—at least nominally. Others were Muslims. The crimes committed in Rwanda have been documented in long reports by the United Nations. They refer to fighting in the Central African Republic; such mutilation sometimes occurred after the rape and included mutilation of the vagina with machetes, knives, sharpened sticks, boiling water, and acid. Sexual violence against men included mutilation of the genitals, which were then displayed as trophies.

But the leaders of IS and those who joined their ranks were on a somewhat higher social and cultural level. How to explain the atrocities committed by IS is a matter of policy. As noted previously, their violence had a shock value meant to intimidate its rivals. It certainly delivered. During IS's rampage across northern Iraq in 2014, stories of Iraqi soldiers surrendering in the mistaken belief that surrendering would inspire leniency by IS were common. But this could by no means be the full explanation for IS's continued engagement in atrocities against minorities, such as the Yazidis, in the territories it had "liberated" for a time. Obviously, such action could only be carried out by individuals who took a certain joy in inflicting pain on their victims. It means that at least some of them were sadists or, as some observers have claimed, mentally disturbed. Other terrorist groups, including al-Qaeda, occasionally blamed IS for these outrages, which gave terrorism a bad name.

During the thirty-year period of the Troubles in Northern Ireland, there was much indignation about the IRA's attacks. Irish atrocities were relatively mild. They killed people, but never in a grisly, sacrificial manner like Islamic State. They would shoot individuals in the kneecap, making it impossible for their victims to physically work for the rest of their lives. The atrocities committed by IS are obviously of a different color and character and have broken all taboos. In the last decade, only Assad's relentless use of chemical bombs and his death camps are comparable. Again, though, this should be viewed in the context of evil and its broader meaning. Is there any utilitarian function behind such systemic elimination of life or in mutilations, beheadings, or other acts of extreme violence

THE CULTURE OF MODERN TERRORISM | 189

besides inspiring fear? Not all deaths are publicized or disseminated as propaganda.

This feeds into a broader problem concerning the members of IS. The reality is that the organization is collapsing and will likely degenerate to a traditional terrorist organization. Many of its members will move on to other fighting grounds, and some will try to return to their home countries. After being exposed to such inhumane treatment of others, most will likely continue acting in such a barbarous manner unless they receive help from a psychologist. This is now part of the broader IS culture that will be repeated as an example of practices that worked and gave results. Again, atrocities occur even by the most enlightened nations, but that is why the global community revised the Geneva Conventions in 1949 following World War II. The idea was that warfare is sometimes necessary, but when the fighting ended, people would have to return to their societies and reintegrate, and so attempting to curtail excesses and atrocities would help protect people's sanity. These bids to protect people's sanity are not part of IS's socialization program. To use the findings of the Stanford psychologist Philip Zimbardo, these individuals have been empowered and ordered to commit the vilest of acts, and nothing has been done to reduce it. In part, most likely, it is because it makes them even more committed to the cause, making it harder for them to break out. This concept is explored further in a following chapter.

JIHAD COOL

The effectiveness of IS propaganda has been often analyzed, and its sophistication has been frequently exaggerated. It is true, as a report by ABC put it, "IS propaganda expertly uses hip-hop music, video games and even children to successfully recruit young people to their violent cause."* According to a spokesman from the Justice Department, "what they are trying to do is to convince young people to go slaughter civilians in a vicious war." Their publications have been described as slick as well as sophisticated, but in fact, the actual content of their messages is primitive. Some

---

* Jack Cloherty, Pierre Thomas, Jack Date, and Mike Levine, "ISIS Propaganda Machine Is Sophisticated and Prolific, US Officials Say," ABC News, accessed December 26, 2017, http://abcnews.go.com/International/isis-propaganda-machine-sophisticated-prolific-us-officials/story?id=30888982.

have even called this kind of approach "strategic." However, it is precisely this kind of primitive propaganda that appeals to the public, which IS intends to reach. IS probably never heard of Adolf Hitler (let alone Gustave Le Bon or other commentators on mass psychology) and never read *Mein Kampf*. But they practice what Hitler and others have said about propaganda. To be effective, it has to be short and concentrate on some essential points, and it must be repetitive. It is a frequent mistake to believe that a statement once made will be remembered by the public. It has to be repeated time and time again. Another commentator, writing about "cyber-Jihad," also claims that IS is strategic in recruiting young men and women throughout the world using internet sites, worldwide magazines, and most social media tools, including Facebook, Twitter, Instagram, and ASKfm. All this is true, but it does not mention the simple, primitive character of the messages.

The impact of social media on the radicalization of young Muslims has been widely commented upon and need not be discussed here in great detail. Of equal and even greater importance are the songs and hymns of IS and similar groups, as they are part of the group's culture and play a role in normalizing or facilitating evil and atrocities. They are called *nasheeds* in Arabic. Similar to songs in America, *nasheeds* often convey messages of hope and love but can also be full of malice and spite. People have been singing, in all probability, since time immemorial. There have always been love songs and sad songs; people have sung while working and at leisure. There has been singing while wandering and playing games, but there have also been aggressive songs when going into battle and when fighting. The IS *nasheeds* belong to this category; they convey a message following the Dawa ("mission"). The message is that only terrorism will prevail; the battle will continue until everyone will embrace Islam. Music plays an important part because it conveys togetherness, comradeship, and fraternity. Why is it successful? This leads us to the general question concerning the reasons young people are responsive to this kind of message. This will be discussed elsewhere, but jihadism cool is certainly influenced by Western hip-hop culture.

The fact that music is used by extreme Islamists should be considered because, according to a long tradition, music is bad and should not be practiced. It is, according to Ibn Taymiyyah, like alcohol to the sword, and alcohol is of course taboo. For a long time, it has been the unanimous belief of Islamic scholars that Muhammad thought musical instruments sinful. Hanzala Ibn Abi Amir, a companion of Muhammad, has made it known that he had heard the prophets say, "From among my followers, there will be some people who will consider illegal sexual intercourse, the wearing of silk [forbidden in the Qur'an], the drinking of alcoholic drinks, and the use of musical instruments as unlawful." Most subsequent Muslim scholars have declared that every type of music and musical instruments is *haram* ("forbidden"). Modern Islamic scholars have been somewhat more liberal, but certainly not the more Orthodox among them. This negative attitude has continued to the present day, and many Islamic theologians are very critical in this respect, just as they oppose soccer and similar games because they distract Muslims from their religious duties. The creators of these harmful *nasheeds* have composed their songs entirely a cappella, as per tradition. The feedback from the songs posted online is rather worrisome; young adults frequently share the opinion of how beautiful the song is, and it is not uncommon for these listeners to admit, whether joking or not, that they feel ready to commit violent acts against Americans.

The use of these *nasheeds* as an educational and propagandistic means is further evidence that the jihadists are by no means the most pious of Muslims. They observe, of course, the most important orders of the Qur'an (and also taboos) but in many respects have their own interpretations, ignoring tradition. Many of them have tried to circumvent the traditional taboo by producing songs without musical accompaniment. It could be argued that while these recitations do belong to the realm of music, they certainly do not belong to the realm of beautiful music, as commonly understood. Many of their *nasheeds*, which are intended for Western ears, are mere cacophony with texts that could equally have appeared in speeches by preachers or in newspapers of their movement. However, they correspond to a certain mind-set, which explains their enormous success. The first jihadist *nasheeds* appeared in the 1970s and 1980s. Palestinian political songs were heard even earlier, but their content was nationalist rather than Islamist.

Since then, there have been literally thousands of such *nasheeds*, and even IS has its own anthem. It begins with the words "My Umma, dawn has appeared." Other leading *nasheeds* proclaim, "The Islamic State has arisen by the blood of the righteous. The Islamic State has arisen by the jihad of the pious." Observers have noted that some of the songs are originals, but they are quite frequently traditional and familiar religious songs converted to odes of jihadism. Outsiders, like the present writers, could easily provide an example:

> O lions of the desert, O tigers of the city,
> Bravely, you march into the battle.
> The coward enemy retreats with fear,
> The final encounter is close by.
> If you die, it will be the death of martyrs
> For a Holy cause, etc., etc.

There is a fascinating similarity between these beliefs and secular movements that are convinced that the future belongs to them and that they will prevail all over the globe. One could refer to "L'Internationale," written by Eugène Edine Pottier, and its refrain, "C'est la lutte finale" (This is the final battle), which also says, "Let the international socialist movement be victorious all over the globe." There is a profound difference inasmuch as "L'Internationale" was sung by secular people whose ideas, at the time, were freedom and liberty. "L'Internationale" became the anthem of socialists and communist movements everywhere until the middle of the twentieth century.

The idea of a final victory also appeared in Nazi Germany, but hardly ever in Fascist Italy. Songs like "Wir Werden Weiter Marschieren" were frequently heard in Germany after 1933:

> We shall go on marching
> even if the whole world perishes.
> Today Germany is ours and tomorrow the whole world.

To appreciate their character, a few examples of the lyrics have to be given, such as for the song "Ya Dawlat al-Islam Nawariti al-Dunna" (O Islamic State, You Lit Up the Earth):

> O State al-Islam you lit up the earth . . . your sky graced us with
>   lots of blessings when you erected the religion, its smell

emerged that I enjoyed its perfumes so they prepared the light
of the Rahman Khilafa in the land of Iraq which won these
mercies.
So the brave ones out of our heroes and raised the bannered the
most true banners, a straightforward path.

Another such song deals with the issue of terrorism:

They're calling me a terrorist
Like they don't know who the terror is
When they put it on me, I tell them this
I'm all about peace and love
They're calling me a terrorist
Like they don't know who the terror is
Insulting my intelligence
Oh how these people judge . . .
It seems like the Rag-heads and Pakis are worrying your dad
But your dad's favorite food is curry and kebab
It's funny but it's sad how they make your mummy hurry with her
  bags
Rather read the Sun than study all the facts
Tell me, what's the bigger threat to human society
BAE Systems or homemade IEDs
Remote controlled drones, killing off human lives
Or man with homemade bomb committing suicide
I know you were terrified when you saw the towers fall
It's all terror but some forms are more powerful

Those interested in more examples of jihadi music are referred to the following artists and performers: Abu Talha al-Almani and Douglas McCain. Both of these men, now dead, were jihadists fighting for Islamic State, and both actually had their start as minor hip-hop artists in Germany and the United States respectively.

13

TERRORISM MISINTERPRETED

WHENEVER A NEW POLITICAL PHENOMENON APPEARS IN THE MEDIA, A variety of interpretations follow; some close to reality, some far-fetched or even totally wrong. It was relatively easy to understand the European terrorist groups of the late twentieth century; some were nationalists or separatists, while others belonged to the far left or extreme right. It has been far more difficult to understand the new terrorism—Islamic State and similar groups. They belong to another world, and their inspiration comes from other sources.

This refers specifically to IS and similar groups, which have appeared in recent years. Western students of Islam and the Arab world have been, on the whole, reluctant to deal with the subject. Why has this been the case? Why, among the many hundreds of books on the subject, are there very few written by Middle Eastern experts and students of Islam? This is a fascinating subject that deserves to be further investigated.

Parallels can be drawn to how people studied older political movements. When fascism first appeared on the European political scene, it was widely believed that it was in the old right-wing tradition even though Mussolini had been a socialist. The differences between German Nazism and Italian Fascism are considerable. Some European fascist movements were strongly religious, such as the Romanian Iron Guard; others were essentially anti-religious. They tolerated the churches because they had a considerable following, which the Nazi leadership would not want to antagonize. Others were convinced that fascism was populist in character. But populism can, with equal ease, turn to the left and to the right. The discussions about the essence of fascism continue to the present day. It will probably never end, because there is not one but a variety of fascisms. In a similar way, definitions of terrorism are difficult (probably impossible) because there is not one terrorism but a variety of terrorisms. They have certain things in common but are different in many ways.

It is this variety in terrorism that makes it difficult to try to forge a specific pronouncement to explain all terrorism. There has been a strong urge among political scientists to find a law, or laws, concerning jihadist terrorism. This would make it possible not only to interpret the phenomenon but also to predict to a certain extent its likely future. It could well be that the Laqueur law of the ecology of terrorism, dealing with the relationship between climate and the occurrence of terrorist operations, offers some certainty, but of how much use is it? It says that no terrorist actions have occurred in the Arctic, in Spitsbergen, the northern Siberian taiga, Alaska, Greenland, or, generally speaking, north of approximately 60-degree latitude. Whether this is a result of the fact that few people live in these regions or whether the cold weather acts as a depressant on suicide terrorists or militants in general is not certain; perhaps both these factors are involved. By and large, terrorist operations occur in temperate zones and occasionally in very hot regions. If Noël Coward, in his famous song "Mad Dogs and Englishmen," had been dealing with terrorism, he would have said that terrorists seldom go out in very hot climates of, say, forty-five degrees centigrade. But terrorist operations have also taken place in the hottest areas of the globe. These findings are undisputed, but their value for the understanding of terrorism is limited, as earlier stated, and contributes to the misinterpretation of the phenomenon.

The situation is further complicated by the tendency in the academic world to look for explanations by way of current fashionable theories in the fields of sociology and political science. These theories are not really meant to explain the terrorist phenomenon, but there is a temptation to try them out on any newly appearing phenomenon. Not all these theories are entirely wrong, but usually they are of only limited value. They often focus on the situation in one country but not in others or deal with one specific situation, ignoring many other similar situations.

One issue that has provoked a considerable amount of debate is the relationship between poverty and terrorism. Whether such disputes should have taken place is not entirely obvious, because the facts and figures seem to be self-evident. The poorest countries in the world, according to the World Bank and most other institutions, are the following:

> Central African Republic, the Democratic Republic of Congo, Burundi, Liberia, Niger, Malawi, Mozambique, Guinea, Eritrea, Madagascar, Togo, Guinea-Bissau, Comoros, Sierra Leone, Gambia, Burkina Faso, Haiti, Kiribati, Ethiopia, Rwanda, and Afghanistan.

Most of these countries have witnessed a great deal of violence, but terrorist operations as generally understood have not taken place in these countries (with the sole exception of Afghanistan), and yet there have been more than a few political commentators arguing that poverty is an important, if not the decisive, factor in the occurrence of terrorism. Jake Harriman writes in *The New York Times*, "Extreme poverty is the greatest humanitarian crisis of all time and a fundamental contributing factor to 21st century terrorism and insurgency [extreme poverty is defined by the World Bank as consuming $1.25 per day]." No one will dispute the first part of this statement, but the stress on poverty as the "fundamental contributing factor to . . . terrorism" seems to be not just dubious but plainly wrong in view of the facts just quoted. Mr. Harriman continues by saying, "I discovered that it is controversial to make this claim, so don't take my word for it." He brings as witness in support of his views Nobel Peace Prize laureate Archbishop Desmond Tutu, who said, "You can never win a war against terror as long as there are conditions in the world that make people desperate." Archbishop Tutu's service to humanity may be immense, but he is not a student of terrorism. According to all the known facts, the terrorists who were involved in 9/11 (or in most of the attacks in the Middle East and Muslim world) were angry, radicalized young people. They were not, however, desperate people motivated by the dismal social and economic conditions in the third world.

Contemporary Marxists have tried to contribute to current thinking about terrorism as well. David Maher and Andrew Thomson, in "Applying Marxism to Critical Terrorism Studies," tried to find a better understanding of terrorism through a historical materialism framework, bringing social relations and class into typical terrorism studies. But what does the insertion of the class factor explain? Almost all the leading figures, and all their followers, in present-day terrorist groups were not working class but middle class or lower-middle class. In their approach, contemporary Marxists are linking terrorism to capitalist development. The capitalist development in Europe and Asia, as well as in the Americas, may have caused a great many inequalities and great social injustice, but it is impossible to show that it caused significant terrorism. Furthermore, noncapitalist development did generate terrorism in the former Soviet Union (the Caucasus and in Central Asia) as well as in Western China (Uighurs). The authors of the article mentioned above conclude their review as follows:

An HM [historical materialism] lens provides a way to understand and explain terrorism and counter-terrorism as embedded within a wider set of dynamic and changing social relations.

Importantly, such a framework acknowledges the marriage of the political and economic spheres, and how this can provide critical insights into terrorism.

As we have argued, HM can be used to unveil valuable insights into the links between terrorism and capitalist development.

Marx and Engels, on the whole, took a dim view of terrorism in their lifetimes. There were certain exceptions, including some sympathetic comments by Marx on the Irish Fenians and comments by Engels in his later years on terrorism in Russia. There is a world of difference between these theories and the realities of al-Qaeda and IS. They do not explain the emergence of contemporary terrorism, such as manifested by IS and similar Islamist groups. For this reason, virtually no attention has been paid to the Marxist approach.

We shall return to the issue of economic distress and terrorism when dealing with the "critical terrorism studies," which enjoyed a certain amount of attention and notoriety in Britain in recent years. Before delving into that, though, it is worth noting that there has been a great deal of discussion about the relationship between terrorism and level of education. In this respect, there is much difference between the terrorist groups of the second half of the twentieth century and the movements motivated by religious fanaticism. Among the former, there were many university students who dropped out, but the question arises, what does a university education mean? Does it mean a deep immersion in the achievements of Western culture or a preoccupation with currently fashionable theories? In the great majority of cases, it meant the latter, with the half educated leading the quarter educated.

In the case of separatist terrorist movements, the lower classes in society are usually more broadly represented, but they still require some sort of leadership. Terrorism is not an easy business. Bomb manufacturing and organizing terrorist groups to operate successfully require some sort of intelligence, or else most terrorists would be failed lone wolves. This has always been the case with terrorist movements, as they have always depended on violent ideologues with certain worldviews to lead and to frame strategy. This seems to hold true for the members of IS, and it has proven advantageous to the group's recruitment activities. Many of them may be graduates of technical colleges (no offense intended), but their knowledge of and belief in true culture is nonexistent. Even their knowledge of their own religion is superficial. They do not know culture, and they do not want to know it. Their interests lie in various group sports and jihadist pop music. Yet their leader has a doctorate in Islamic theology, and the organization from which it separated included among its ranks doctors and engineers. But does this automatically imply causality? The question whether a deeper immersion in higher culture would have acted as an antidote to terrorism is, of course, an open one. Those who committed the 9/11 attacks were educated in Western universities and had spent time abroad. There are, however, many millions of individuals with similar backgrounds who never felt a need to commit violence to advance their political causes. The neurological and psychological pathways leading to radicalization are many, and they require more investigation to give a proper accounting of how this process works, beyond noting the evident correlation.

Moving beyond radicalization, others have postulated new theories to explain why terrorism happens. One of the recent theories on the emergence of terrorism was pronounced by a political scientist, Robert Pape, head of the Chicago Project on Security and Terrorism (CPOST) program dealing with, among other subjects, the explosion of global suicide terrorism. According to Professor Pape, his research through the years on suicide attacks shows that they almost always occur when a military invasion had taken place. "From 1980–2003, suicide terrorism was relatively rare," but "from 2004–2009, there were 1,833 suicide strikes—92 percent aimed at American targets." This approach is as unconvincing as many others of recent years. A look at the world map of terrorist operations shows that in some places, increases in terrorism were indeed caused by foreign invasion, but in most cases, they were not. Nor is it clear why invasion should have brought about a dramatic increase in suicide terrorism and not in other forms of resistance. Neither does he offer an explanation for instances where suicide terrorism does not occur during times of invasion. Most of his research is built off his earlier work from 2003, "The Logic of Suicide Terrorism," where he also used a loose definition of the word *invasion*. In that piece, most of his examples came from Sri Lanka and the LTTE. It is a stretch to argue, though, that the Sinhalese and the Tamils were fighting each other because an invasion had occurred. The basic facts about the spread of terrorism, following military invasion, have been known at least since Napoleonic times (guerrillas and terrorism in Spain and Russia, the operations of Denis Davydov) and have never been in dispute. But in most historical instances, there has been an emergence of terrorist movements without any relationship with foreign military invasions and rarely with suicide terrorism.

Of the many interpretations of terrorism that emerge in recent years, one of the strangest and most wondrous is the critical theory of terrorism school, which found a home at the Aberystwyth University in Wales and had some supporters elsewhere in England. It draws its inspiration from the Frankfurt School, which came into being in Weimar Germany in the 1920s. Its founder and best-known proponents were Max Horkheimer and Theodor Adorno respectively; Herbert Marcuse and Franz Neumann also belonged to it. According to a recent article entitled "Why a Forgotten 1930s Critique of Capitalism Is Back in Fashion," there is a revival in connection with contemporary terrorism. This formulation is quite inaccurate, for the "critique" goes back to the 1920s, and it had a strong revival in postwar Germany (as well as in America) in the 1960s and 1970s. The argument posits that since then, the fashion has largely faded. Nothing could be further from the truth. The Frankfurt School was also influenced by psychoanalysis, and during the Second World War, when most of its members were in the United States, it produced its major work, *The Authoritarian*. The Frankfurt School was embraced by members of the student revolt of the 1970s. Its main interest was in the impact of capitalism on contemporary culture; Adorno's interest was predominantly in contemporary music. The members of the Frankfurt School were critical of capitalism and most "official" ideologies. The notion of "emancipation" and "liberation" (*befreiung*) played a dominant role in the thinking of the Frankfurt School. The leading thinker of the Germany-based critical theories was philosopher-sociologist Jürgen Habermas, whose main interest was in the field of sociology.

The Frankfurt School's ideas were in no way concerned with terrorism, its motives and aims. The idea that it could in any way help to understand terrorism was far-fetched, to put it gently. Some of the members of this school commented on and analyzed Nazism and its rule. Best known was Franz Neumann's *Behemoth*, which attempted to explain Hitler's policy, mainly his deference to the economic interest of the ruling class in Germany. This was a profoundly mistaken approach, but Neumann's book was widely accepted as authoritative for many years. Of extreme absurdity were Neumann's views of Nazi anti-Semitism, which he again attempted to explain as motivated by economic interest. It is only fair to add that the views of Neumann (who died in a car accident in Switzerland in the 1950s) were not entirely accepted by other members of the school. In later years, the school split in connection with his attitude toward the students' revolt. Marcuse became a hero of this movement, whereas Adorno was ridiculed, and his life was probably shortened by attacks against him. Horkheimer became deeply pessimistic toward the end of his life, moving far from his earlier beliefs.

It is a long, long way from *Das Kapital* to the Qur'an, from the Frankfurt School believing in the ideals of the Enlightenment, and the ideology of an Islamic State movement as pronounced by Caliph Ibrahim (Abu Bakr al-Baghdadi) and al-Zawahiri. Critical studies have undertaken to bridge the two camps. It is a quixotic enterprise and deserves to be ridiculed rather than analyzed and commented on in detail. According to a variety of statements, critical studies believe that the contemporary study of terrorism takes place in a particular kind of political context. It has generated a vast number of political activities, it uses powerful emotions, and it has become a cultural taboo, an object of pure hatred as well as admiration. Critical studies also argue that terrorism has often been overplayed and has become a negative ideograph of Western identity, making self-reflected probing research (such as practiced by the "critical students") difficult.

Against this background, critical studies intended to present a truly detached objective alternative. The editors of critical studies believe in such an approach; in their view, all research on terrorism is in need of greater self-reflection as both a general attitude toward terrorism-related research and a strategic attempt to provoke debate. These are high-minded principles, but what do they mean in practice, when shorn of the academic phraseology? They wish to articulate a new approach based on the left-wing negation of official government policies and the traditional approach toward terrorism's motives and aims. However, all serious research in the past has been "critical," and that one group would have a monopoly of criticism seems far-fetched and impertinent. Take one of the obvious issues: whether terrorism has ever been justified. The obvious answer is clear: no one ever denied that the assassination of someone like Hitler before the Second World War would have saved the lives of millions of people and prevented an enormous amount of suffering and damage. World literature is replete with praises for the murder of tyrants. In the Middle Ages, elaborate ideological defenses of tyrannicides were published, such as by the Spaniard Juan de Mariana and John of Salisbury. The former, a Jesuit theologian, wrote a book called *On the King and the Royal Institution*, where he described the relationship between a monarch and his or her subjects, using scholastic logic to explain how and when a monarch could claim power and what was the position's authority. In a controversial chapter toward the end, Mariana argued that the seizure of power by force of arms justified the removal of that person from power, either legally or through violence. This argument was still quite controversial more than a decade later, when King Henry IV of France was assassinated by the Catholic fanatic François Ravaillac in 1610. John of Salisbury, for his part, was a twelfth-century English scholar who wrote extensively on the prerogatives of a king. Describing how a king was a head of state that acted with moderation, restraint, and through the rule of law, he contrasted this figure with a tyrant, who abused power. Much like Mariana, John of Salisbury thought that such abuse provided sufficient justification

202 | THE FUTURE OF TERRORISM

for tyrannicide. No one has ever claimed that all terrorism was unjustified. The idea and the claims of the critical theorists are therefore ahistorical.

As many see it, Noam Chomsky is the godfather of this school of critical theorists. He is a very distinguished linguist, but his knowledge of history and politics is limited (as his past views have usually been utterly wrong). Chomsky is an anarchist; he believes that what a state is doing must be a priori wrong, for a state is based on compulsion and on imposing certain laws on the citizens, thus limiting their freedom. But in our age, a world without government is unthinkable; normal activities would come to a standstill in no time. Most of the believers in the critical theories probably do not go as far as Chomsky, but as far as terrorism is concerned, their opposition to "orthodox" or "traditional" views on terrorism seems to rest on the belief that terrorists are more often right than wrong, as opposed to governments in their attitudes and actions toward terrorism. Critical theorists have been criticized by other academics for overemphasizing the discourse, but the meaning is not made entirely clear. However, it is not necessary to devote much thought and space to the views of a school, in which most of its tenets are clearly foolish. Some of their views may be correct but, as has been pointed out earlier on, they are obvious and undisputed.

The criticisms of the critical studies school are far more aimed at counterterrorism than the terrorist movements. It is perfectly true that some of the practitioners of counterterrorism have come up with dubious ideas. This speaks, for instance, to the French theorists following their experiences in Vietnam and Algeria. However (inasmuch as terrorist movements are concerned today), the belief that the operations of Baader-Meinhof or the Italian Red Brigades were justified is difficult to maintain. But once we come to deal with the cutthroats of IS and al-Qaeda, justification becomes impossible for even the staunchest followers of critical studies. Their beliefs are deeply reactionary, their bestial activities (such as the deliberately cool killing) are impossible to justify from any point of view, let alone from believers in humanist ideals. Critical theory faces obstacles that cannot be ignored, and it comes therefore as no surprise that their influence has markedly declined in recent years.

The critical studies of terrorism have many complaints concerning the traditional school of thinking. They claim, for instance, that "objective social science" is a hegemonic project that is far from being objective and operates in the service of existing power structures. The research of these "objective" scholars is frequently used to legitimize coercive interventions in the developing world. Another complaint concerns the focusing of the traditional school on terrorism on nonstate actors. They argue that "state terrorism" is far more dangerous and has created many more victims. Perhaps this is true, but it fails to acknowledge the point that there are international laws that exist to negate this behavior in the first place. State terrorism is considered a war crime or a crime against humanity that may warrant international intervention. Many terrorists, of course, act with impunity. This attempt to eradicate the differences between these two kinds of terrorism goes back a long way, and it was the main tenet of Chomsky and his followers.

Yet another complaint concerns the alleged ethnocentrism of the traditional school. This complaint is largely imaginary. Far from singling out one specific ethnic group, there have been frequent attempts in recent years to ignore or to quantify the true origin of terrorist fighters; in one recent case, one such individual was described as Norwegian, because he was holding the nationality of that country. As far as the current terrorism is concerned, the issue at stake is not the nationality of terrorist groups or individuals. There is no denying that Chinese are among them, as well as Nigerians and a great number of other nationalities. The issue, of course, happens to be Islamism, and the general picture in this context is absolutely clear. It was by no means clear thirty or sixty years ago. But in the attempt to deny the fact that, in the contemporary world, Islamism has a virtual monopoly on violence of this kind is deliberately misleading for political reasons. For these reasons the critical studies are facing (at the present time) not just a great struggle but an impossible one. For the critical student of terrorism, the traditional school is based on a series of virulent myths, half truths, and contested claims, all biased toward Western state priorities. Returning to the above discussion about poverty, critical theorists argue that many of the contemporary terrorists are poor, starving, and exploited people, the product of the evil capitalist system. This theory has the advantage of leading to the belief that once the system has been changed, terrorism is bound to disappear. However, all other considerations (apart from the prospects that the countries in which terrorism is most violent will reach a per capita income similar to that of Kuwait or Qatar or Luxembourg or Liechtenstein) are unfortunately unreal. Thus, to summarize, the school of critical studies is nothing but a heavily politicized enterprise, whereas the traditional school includes or included elements that are indeed the product of political prejudice. These are infinitely less frequent and less pronounced than the former; in brief, they deserve to be ridiculed rather than be taken seriously and be the subject of lengthy reputation. What should be subject to further investigation is how a school spreading manifest absurdities could gain a certain amount of influence in the academic world, at least for some time.

TERRORISM AND THE PSYCHIATRISTS

Psychologists, psychiatrists, and sociopsychologists observe and sometimes study the terrorists. There is no unanimity and there are lots of kinds of terrorists, and the same goes for psychiatrists. Some of their contributions are valuable; others are far-fetched or even nonsensical. They come to different conclusions; often research is influenced by the political views of the author. The "radical" left maintain that the roots of jihadist terrorism lie in the historical crimes and injustices of the West. They consider that terror is a logical reaction fueled by Muslim anger and vengeance. Westernized jihadists, far from rejecting the civilized norms and ideals proclaimed by the West, are in fact alienated from a West that excludes, demeans, and harasses Muslims. Instead of using the rhetoric of Marxism from the nineteenth or twentieth centuries, terrorists justify their violence with the language of Islam. In contrast to this view, even when jihadists use the Qur'an to define their struggle, their justifications for violence are primary secular and grievance-based. Half of the human bombs in Lebanon were perpetrated by secular organizations.

Traditional psychologists agree that there are three types of terrorists: criminals, crazies, and crusaders. Further, terrorists can be divided into three basic groups: leaders, volunteers, and forcible recruits. Leaders exhibit a sense of grandiosity, infallibility, and mission. Religion is not necessarily a factor. For example, bin Laden was preoccupied with doctrinal purity, while al-Zawahiri is more interested in power itself. With volunteers, a sociopath is welcome, but psychopathy is not necessary; most are not crazy in the sense of having psychotic disorders but rather are intensely loyal to their leader and the collective group. Borderline mental illness may contribute to violent extremism when combined with emotional trauma, substance abuse, and an extremist narrative. Volunteers, being the largest group of jihadists, share many common characteristics: the need for a leader (father figure); the desire to belong to a group; feelings of anger, alienation, and disenchantment; empathy with perceived victims of social injustice. They often have friends or family sympathetic to the cause and experience no ethical barriers against engaging in violence. Also important is the feeling, shared with gang members and dissidents or other nonviolent opposition groups, that joining a movement offers social and psychological rewards such as adventure, camaraderie, and a heightened sense of identity.

Forcible recruits are trained in discipline and cruelty. They often undergo training similar to that of army recruits or prisoners: dehumanization, subjugation, and resocialization in the new environment. Wahhabi jihadists stress the separation from family and original group allegiance, to be replaced by the allegiance to a higher goal—Allah or the caliphate. Often, allegiance must be proved by killing a family member. Recent data shows that suicide attackers are not often the criminal, illiterate, or poor but from largely secular and educated middle classes.

14

ECONOMIC EXPLANATIONS
OF TERRORISM

FOR MANY YEARS, TERRORISM WAS STUDIED PRIMARILY BY HISTORIANS, political scientists, and psychologists. These fields came with their own subject-matter biases and found their analyses proscribed by the methodological limits of their ontological character, but they provided the first wellspring of knowledge for the academic study of terrorism. Historians gave a full accounting of terrorism as a tactic—which, when combined within a strategic framework, could have the necessary operational tempo to change history, with the assassination of Archduke Franz Ferdinand being only one of many examples. Psychologists were the first to acknowledge that terrorists were not necessarily mentally deficient and that many terrorists throughout history seemed quite normal and stable. Political scientists, especially those studying comparative politics, looked for structural features that made all types of political violence, including terrorism, possible, whether this was weakness in government or the generation of grievances by capricious autocratic governments. More important, academia maintained the study of terrorism as something worth researching when most military studies focused on conventional conflict. In other words, academia has always been quite forceful in establishing that terrorism is something that can alter the world and should be studied.

Nonetheless, academic silos and the overarching character of the Cold War precluded a robust accounting of the phenomenon divorced from instinctual or moralized prejudgments. Even once the study of terrorism became more prevalent toward the end of the 1960s, the conventional wisdom emphasized irrationality, religiosity, and ideology to explain terrorism, with one infamous book in the 1980s arguing that all global terrorism was a conspiracy by the USSR to destabilize the West. This created a myopic understanding of terrorism and the danger it posed. Indeed, until 9/11, many individuals of the structural realist school of international relations, which analyze great power dynamics exclusively at the state level, tended to regard terrorism as a strategic nuisance that did not amount to a threat capable of changing the world, despite the historical record suggesting otherwise. Just like the organizational firewalls that precluded American intelligence agencies from cooperating with one another until the early 2000s, this balkanization of terrorism academically had a pernicious effect, as it prevented cross-pollination and the ability to innovate the field.

This started to change in the 1990s. Although quantitative and statistical research methods had been ubiquitous in certain social science disciplines since the early twentieth century, only in the early 1990s did scholars attempt to study terrorism from an empirical and quantitative perspective, beginning with Martha Crenshaw's landmark research into when the use of terrorism becomes a logical choice by nonstate actors, challenging the status quo. An increasing number of social scientists soon realized that it was possible to study terrorist violence using statistical methods culled from the physical sciences. An increasing number of these scholars came from economics.

Economists specialize in understanding how people make decisions under conditions of scarcity. Normally understood to mean money and resources, economics is applicable to virtually any situation where decisions must be made involving trade-offs. Terrorist groups, like other violent actors, make trade-offs when it comes to strategies, tactics, targets, and resources. In addition, because such groups are organizations manned by normal people, individual motivators for violence are legion but generally follow a rational path.

Applying economics to terrorism has proven innovative and fruitful in a few key regards. First, the empirical research done by these scholars has helped disentangle Islam from the perspective as the main driver of terrorism. As discussed in other parts of this book, as far as indicators go, being Muslim is no more of an indicator that someone will become a terrorist than belonging to other religions. Besides the cases of Aum Shinrikyo, the Japanese death cult behind the Tokyo sarin attacks, or the secular and atheistic Tamil Tigers, examples of other religious groups being led to violence are numerous. Whether it is American white nationalists deploying an overtly Christian rhetoric to justify racial violence or Jewish extremists opposed to a two-state solution in Israel, any religion or ideology that proffers simple solutions to complex problems is bound to provide sufficient justification for violence.

Second, using economics has divorced terrorism from normative and moral debates about the validity of its use as a tactic and has instead focused on its innate rationality. As Martha Crenshaw noted many years ago, given that terror groups must maintain an internal coherence through shared values, "terrorism is seen collectively as a logical means to advance desired ends." From her analysis, it emerges that the use of targeted violence to inspire fear generally results when power disparity exists between a nonstate actor and a government, individuals have attempted various other approaches such as guerrilla-cum-military action or democratic activism, the group cannot attract sufficient followers to transform into a viable insurgency, and there is an opportunity to attack. If terrorism is thought of as a rational choice from a selection of bad options, it helps explain more broadly the structural factors at play for terrorism to be deemed a viable tactic and, more important, how to prevent them from occurring. Again, this further helps detangle terrorism from the association with purely Islamic causation and helps universalize the study to explain violence for all generations.

These two reasons are not the only value given by economists studying terrorism, but they certainly help push the field forward. This section therefore gives a nonexhaustive overview of how economics has influenced the modern study of terrorism. The purpose of this chapter is to provide analytical support toward the hypothesis guiding this book, largely that Islamic State has come to define the nature of terrorism for the foreseeable future. The optimistic component of this chapter is that terrorism is a tactic with vulnerabilities that can be acted upon, suggesting a path forward for countries experiencing protracted terror campaigns.

TERRORIST ORGANIZATIONS AS INDUSTRIAL ACTIVITY

In the 1970s and 1980s, terrorists had a degree of romanticism akin to that of rock stars. With their balaclavas and their rebellious images, terrorists lived globe-trotter lifestyles, with many having unfettered access to drugs, alcohol, and sex. Certainly this has changed, especially with the rise of more religious and seemingly pious groups, but when individuals become professional terrorists, meaning they derive their livelihood from this trade, they still enjoy social benefits not available to normal folk. At the heart of this image is the conceit that an individual has the ability to foment change on a grand scale either through violence or by inspiring others to follow in his or her footsteps. The problem with this image is that it is false and impractical. Rarely do terror plots ever succeed without some sort of sustenance from a larger organization. The terrorists of the 1970s and 1980s often depended on external support, either through donations, through state support from countries like Iran or Libya, or via fundraising activities, as was the case with the Irish Republican Army and the money collected from the Irish American community during the Troubles. In the case of lone wolves, without an extensive infrastructure for disseminating an ideology and tactical guidance, they would be even less successful.

For terrorism to be a viable tactic, there needs to be an industrial effort behind the planning, recruiting, training, procurement of supplies, and actual execution. This reality means that in many ways, groups like IS and AQ fall within the bounds of Ronald Coase's theory of the firm. Coase's theory, at its most basic level, argues that pricing in open markets rarely takes into account such transaction costs as information costs, trade, and enforcement of contracts that inflate the costs of trade. Coase argues that an entrepreneur who could organize a firm could reduce these costs. For example, in an open-market system, each transaction, whether in the form of directions or allocation of profits, would require many simple contracts that add a price in terms of time. By contrast, internalizing this mechanism allows firms to establish one-off complex managerial arrangements that reduce the necessary level of bargaining, thereby reducing the costs.

Terrorist organizations have an incentive for organizing along these lines for the reasons outlined above, with the added caveat that they manufacture political violence. This line of study has been useful in informing how terrorist organizations operate and what their weaknesses are, and it is best exemplified in the work of Jacob Shapiro of Princeton. Shapiro argues that unlike traditional firms, terrorists must contend with the fact that their business is not legally sanctioned. This adds an additional cost that normal firms do not have to worry about: the importance of secrecy as they move toward command and control, and various decisions taken by a group are often determined by the pressure they feel in both domains. If terrorists are violent ideologues bent on changing the world, when they organize into a group, they must have some strategic purpose and a tactical idea on how to accomplish this goal.

Shapiro takes this idea into a very practical domain. If a group's ideology is to create carnage and remains indiscriminate in its targeting, then command and control matter little. The only thing that matters is slaughter. This is seen in cases when terrorist groups want to create bloodshed for the sake of bloodshed, as this damages a government's legitimacy and the perspective that it can provide security. In contrast, if a group has a specific agenda for the policy changes it seeks, violence is modulated and requires greater coordination. Like all firms, the ability to choose targets and to advance a vision requires experience, talent, and learning. Leaders of terrorist groups are unlikely to contribute to plots directly, because they must live for another day and continue coordinating other similar attacks. They must therefore delegate this responsibility to foot soldiers, who may not be as talented or might have joined a violent group for the sake of committing violence, and lack perspective about committing too much violence. This, of course, means bureaucracy, which oftentimes means creating regular methods of dispatching orders through means that create extensive paper trails. Electronic communication, for example, is easily traceable, while orders via couriers might identify where a leader is hiding. Depending on the pressure leaders are facing, communication might falter, enervating its ability to control behavior of groups. Shapiro explains that this translates into tangible group behavior. If a group is treated as a unitary actor and counterterrorism policies focus exclusively on leadership, then lower-level personnel might find themselves unconstrained and act more violently. Of course, efforts to conceal behavior depend on whether terrorists have safe havens and the strength of the government they are fighting.

This also appears in the question of finance. Groups relying on secrecy must still fund plots, but the question becomes how you transmit money without exposing the makeup of an organization while assuring that the funds are used correctly. Normal firms use audits and the threat of legal sanctions to prevent fraud. Terrorist organizations can of course use violence to coerce behavior, but this would require a means of monitoring personnel more directly. This is not a luxury most terrorist groups have, and if foot soldiers and middle managers have an incentive to cheat, they most likely will. Evidence collected by the United States in areas controlled by al-Qaeda in Iraq during the surge support this conclusion. American soldiers found USB drives with Excel sheets documenting payments made by AQ to foot soldiers. Per Shapiro, the person crunching the numbers for AQ realized the organization was making payments to nonexistent soldiers and their families. This was only one among many documents recovered by coalition forces, which revealed the organization's structure, reflecting the inherent risk of bureaucratization for organizations that require secrecy to survive.

The implications of this research are many when it comes to counterterrorism, but for the purpose of this book, they help in removing the mystical cloak that accompanies many terrorists. Rather than seemingly unified rational organizations capable of committing wanton acts of violence, these groups suffer from the same problems other human institutions experience. One of the most telling cases of this dilemma came in late 2014, when Islamic State found itself struggling in creating health policy in Mosul. Unlike its counterparts in Raqqa, IS leadership in Mosul found itself overwhelmed in trying to provide health care services to a city of nearly a million while also enacting the group's vision. At this point, the United States and its allies had begun its bombing campaign, weakening communication networks between both cities and also limiting how effectively the group used its funds. With such a perilous circumstance, IS started suffering the challenge of governance while maintaining secrecy. Governing improperly would alienate the population and would turn them against it, but that would require more bureaucracy than it could manage.

WHY IS TERRORISM EFFECTIVE?: THE CLUB GOODS THEORY

Why do seemingly rational people join terrorist organizations? Because they feel they benefit from participation. That answer seems self-evident, but it is worth exploring. Joining groups like Islamic State or al-Qaeda involves the exchange of one's autonomy for membership in a group. The profiles of terrorists outlined elsewhere in this book noted that terrorists, both contemporary and historical, have always shown a high degree of intelligence and normality from a psychological perspective. Yet as high-functioning individuals aware of perceived injustices in their home countries or places where they might have an emotional attachment, such as their heritage countries, they also often feel disgust toward the status quo. These ideas are likely shared by many people in society, but very few are willing to delve into them deeply or, more important, try to act upon them.

Ron Wintrobe has written on this subject, arguing that for many individuals, joining terrorist organizations is a way of finding the solidarity they felt missing within nonextremist groups. These groups might not only share the individual's values, validating his or her beliefs, but also provide solutions. Using the concept of individual utility curves, Wintrobe theorizes that as individuals give up more of their autonomy in exchange for solidarity, they tend to align their beliefs even closer with the leaders of an organization. As time passes, the desire for more solidarity requires even more sacrifices to maintain allegiance with a group, encouraging the individual to act more extreme.

Building off this idea, Eli Berman and others have found that this type of sacrifice is critical in preventing defections, which enables deadlier attacks. When individuals join extremist organizations, the loss of autonomy usually involves some sort of sacrifice. The typical examples are religious groups that sanction behavior not seen as pious or that require some sort of bodily alteration to signal a person's commitment to a cause, such as circumcision in Jewish communities. Berman gives the example of poor Afghans spending years studying at madrassas, learning skills that are not necessarily transferrable to higher-paying jobs but makes them attractive to the Taliban as recruits. Another illustrative case is Palestinians who go to jail for supporting Hamas. This type of sacrifice serves a few functions. One, it separates individuals from the mainstream society, making it harder for them to reintegrate or for society to accept them. Two, much like Wintrobe argues, these types of sacrifices also change a person's utility function, bringing them closer in line with a terrorist organization's vision. Three, it helps weed out individuals who are not as committed to the values of a group, bringing in recruits that are less likely to defect. According to Berman, it is this latter point that makes certain groups deadlier than others: preventing defections. People that defect not only threaten specific plots but might also reveal to the authorities the organizational structure of a terrorist group. Preventing this type of behavior is critical for the long-term success of groups like al-Qaeda and Islamic State.

Berman takes this a step further and argues that the most successful terrorist groups also provide benefits exclusively to its members. These can be social services, monetary payments, or guarantees that an organization will provide for a member's family if they happen to die in combat. Examples of this type of behavior are rife throughout contemporary history. Jabhat al-Nusra and al-Qaeda in the Arabian Peninsula both engaged in this behavior to win over recruits in Syria and Yemen, respectively. The Taliban managed to take over large swaths of Afghanistan in part because of its ability to impose the rule of law and allow for markets to function. In all these cases, these groups demanded that individuals adhere to the group's values to receive these benefits, further strengthening the bond of solidarity individuals feel.

Looking beyond individual rationality, when a person adopts an organization's values, his or her worldview alters. Taking into account the club goods model for terrorism, what emerges is a rational explanation for the acts of terror but also for why suicide bombings seem rational. If terrorists tend to be more educated and psychologically normal, when they join an organization, they are aligning their moral system to that of a group, which from the outside seems abnormal. Once these values are completely internalized, terrorist behavior no longer takes on a selfish characteristic, especially if the group engages in social services to a community. Rather, terrorism becomes an altruistic action intended to benefit coconspirators or to advance a political cause the individual believes to be just. Therefore, it is more likely that individuals engage in suicide terrorism not because they believe they will be rewarded in the afterlife but because they feel their actions will benefit their compatriots, their friends, their nations, or their families.

TERRORISM AS THEATER AND THE MACRO/MICRO DIVIDE WITHIN CONFLICTS

There are two final ideas, not exclusive to economics, that are worth exploring for their explanatory and descriptive power in relation to modern political violence. First is the idea of terrorism as theater, a concept that dates back to the earliest terrorists in the eighteenth and nineteenth centuries and their idea of propaganda of the deed. The second is the narrative divide between the macro and micro conflicts that arise in all political violence.

Early on in this book, it was noted that a universally accepted definition of terrorism was nearly impossible because of how contested the term is by both practitioners and scholars. Nonetheless, if one operates from the belief that terrorism is a violent tactic designed to inspire fear to effect political change, then terrorism depends on a broader audience for the ensuing fear to be able to change the political calculus of a society. Bruce Hoffman has contrasted the fear that terrorism inspires from that of a mugger. A mugger might threaten violence with a gun to compel a person to give up his or her wallet, but the threat is short term and directed exclusively at the individual being mugged. In contrast, the violence threatened by an act of terrorism has a larger audience in mind and involves a gripping spectacle, which keeps people watching and affects their own calculus.

There is an economic logic to this violence. As Tyler Cowen explains, spectacular acts like 9/11 not only inspire fear but serve as cultural touchstones that create a rally-around-the-flag effect that helps cement identities. Such overt violence, with its ability to shock, is demonstrative of a group's ability and helps draw recruits and donations. Those wanting to become terrorists wish to be associated with the most effective and deadly terror groups, and these wishes create a sorting effect among terrorist organizations. More important, people supporting a terrorist group want to see more spectacular acts and are encouraged to donate money to see more such events. Terrorism as theater is then another way to argue that terrorist groups engage in image curation to help generate capital investment. Al-Qaeda, for example, became known for committing mass-casualty attacks with multiple targets across the world. Islamic State has yet to commit a plot on the scale of 9/11, but it has released dozens of videos depicting beheadings, crucifixions, mutilations, and other cruel punishments. More important, it declared the caliphate, which trumped many of AQ's accomplishments. These are but different approaches to the same goal: inspiring would-be recruits and generating funding.

If terrorism as theater is a form of institutional branding, it only affects the behavior of a group if it is viewed as a monolith. For individuals joining terrorist groups, theatrics allow them to act with the legitimacy of a brand that comes with political underpinnings viewed as morally acceptable by a member's community of origin. In this sense, understanding the macro and micro narrative divide elucidates other more nuanced reasons for why people become terrorists.

Throughout history, chroniclers of violence have noted that there is often an overarching theme that explains conflict, but at the more localized level, this is more often a pretext for taking up arms rather than the primary cause. When war breaks out, the general atmosphere of organized chaos makes behavior like settling scores, seeking revenge, and handling other kinds of personal disputes permissible, as long as they are couched in terms that are politically palatable to a broader community. David Kilcullen notes that in contemporary conflicts, the definition of what constitutes a member of the Taliban shifts routinely as villages and tribes change their allegiance depending on what benefit they might obtain. Similarly, Stathis Kalyvas has documented hundreds of examples of this phenomenon from conflicts as diverse as the American and Spanish Civil Wars and various insurgencies.

This happens frequently with terrorists. Fernando Reinares, in his seminal study on the 2004 Madrid train bombings, notes that al-Qaeda used Spain's involvement in the Iraq War as a moral justification for the attacks. In reality, though, the plot was first conceived in the weeks following 9/11 by members of Spain's al-Qaeda cell for reasons unrelated to Iraq. Shortly after the attacks in New York and Washington, Spanish authorities discovered that the AQ cell in Madrid had collaborated with the Hamburg network that crashed the airliners into the World Trade Center and the Pentagon. Cognizant of the severity of these revelations, they apprehended most of the members of this cell, seeking to dismantle it. Spanish authorities failed to arrest all the members, though. One in particular managed to flee to Pakistan and began plotting the attacks in December 2001 as an act of revenge against Spanish society. Afterward, this individual, Amer Azizi, traveled to the headquarters of al-Qaeda's central command and convinced the group's leadership to support his plans. By 2003, with the war in Iraq ongoing, the impending attack was incorporated into AQ's global strategy and messaging, giving the eventual attack a political and moral legitimacy normally not afforded to acts committed solely because of vengeance. When the attack occurred in March 2004, it coincided with the country's elections and helped tip the vote toward the leftist socialist party, leading to Spain's withdrawal from Iraq a few weeks later. In the popular discourse, the attacks were a direct reaction to Spain's involvement in the war, but rarely are the private motivations of the attackers discussed.

This phenomenon holds true in virtually all locations where terrorism is present. In Afghanistan, Libya, and Yemen, individuals and groups strategically align themselves with terrorist groups, adopting their messaging and cause, both to receive support and to justify their violence. Of course, this violence might be motivated for reasons as simple as access to resources or drunken disputes that escalated into blood feuds. Lone-wolf terrorists also exhibit the same behavior. When these individuals commit attacks, even if they have never interacted with members of a large organization, they often seek to align their violence with the political messaging of groups and movements like AQ, IS, or the alt-right because of the moral cover it provides. The 2016 Orlando nightclub shooter showcased this behavior, attempting to align his own unstable behavior with the seemingly superior motives presented by IS.

THE ECONOMICS OF TERRORISM

The four ideas discussed in this section barely scratch the surface of the contribution of economics to the study of terrorism, but they give a foundation for understanding terrorism as a phenomenon divorced from religion and the mistaken notion of irrationality. Throughout this book, it has been argued that terrorism is a strategic activity committed by weaker nonstate actors to change the world. Oftentimes, this is lost in discussion, as people focus on its outcomes—death and fear—and never consider the thought process behind it. While it is easy to treat it as a black box activity and focus only on the results, doing so makes terrorists seem preternaturally evil, when in reality they are as human as anyone else. This might be unsettling, but returning them to a human-centric perspective shows how constrained and limited they are.

As such, if economics is the study of decision-making under conditions of scarcity, then its theories are applicable to terrorists, as they must also react and respond to limitations. Consider IS. The reason it so befuddles and induces fear is because of how industriously it kills and turns those deaths into propaganda consumed by viewers across the globe. The segmentation that occurs at every level of the group—from a leadership that gives strategic guidance, to organizational branches charged with administering social services and training recruits, to the creation of middle managers to regulate a bureaucracy—underpinned its ability to assert that it was creating a state. This, however, occurred when the Iraqi and Syrian governments were weak, giving the group freedom to build and organize. Since their activities are not protected by the rule of law and are not something desired by most people, as soon as a competent government could pressure it, the organization began falling apart, and with it vanished the notions of creating a state.

Its comparative advantage right now, relative to rival groups, is that it has an efficient public relations machine that has helped maintain its brand even as it loses territory in various theaters. In the meantime, it has lost most of the middle managers that helped it assert control in Iraq and Syria, and it has lost the thousands of troops necessary for implementing its policies. It has certainly tried rebuilding its cadres, but these individuals lack the experience of the early cohorts, who cut their teeth fighting the American-led coalition during the Iraq War and later when IS stormed across northern Iraq. Its legitimacy still depends on the creation and maintenance of the caliphate, yet it must seek to do this even as its ability to provide social services diminishes, and even as its propaganda increasingly fails to match reality. If terrorism is theater, then IS is being exposed as wanting by the Iraqi military and its foreign supporters, thus changing the calculus for would-be recruits and for donors watching from abroad. Indeed, with a resurgent al-Qaeda slowly winning over fighters and providing social services in various continents, the next wave of jihadists will have more market options for its violence.

It is important to remember, however, that this is only one narrative about IS. It still remains quite influential with its base and the lone wolves in Europe who consume its propaganda. Even within individual theaters, there are variations of IS that affect its behavior. In Syria, it is both part of the rebel groups fighting Assad and the dominant power in the city of Raqqa. Elsewhere, IS fights AQ for supremacy as the leading jihadist group in Yemen and Afghanistan, but finds itself collaborating with AQ in Libya in a nationalist struggle cloaked in the language of religion. In fact, among those using its brand are thrill-seekers, formal criminals seeking redemption through jihad, tribal leaders wishing to advance the interests of their people, cause-fighters seeking access to arms, and people drawn to violence by circumstance and not by choice.

This is to say, terrorism is a much more complex and fraught subject than popularly thought. At the same time, it is a form of political violence constrained by human rules, making terrorists just as fallible as regular people. While this is not to underestimate the lethality of terrorists, it also provides an alternative paradigm for understanding organizations like AQ, IS, or any other violent group.

15

RELIGIOUS VIOLENCE
AND TERRORISM

ANY DISCUSSION OF THE CURRENT PROBLEMS CONCERNING TERRORISM, sooner or later, comes up against two crucial issues: How important is terrorism, and how is it going to end? We shall deal with the former issue later. As far as the end of terrorism is concerned, present writings have been mainly concerned with traditional terrorist movements but not the present contenders. However, the end of Baader-Meinhof, the Italian Red Brigades, or even the IRA and the Basques terrorists are of little help for the present threat, which is based on a wave of religious extremism. Such cases have been infrequent in recent history outside Islam.

All comments in this respect are bound to be speculative. I could imagine, to take an optimistic view, a letter written in forty years' time by Ibrahim al-Bakr in Raqqa, who fought in Syria in his younger years and later became a deputy governor of Raqqa district, to his friend, Mahmoud Ghazal, a businessman in Port Said, Egypt, who also fought in the ranks of IS at the time:

Ya achi fi ma'aarkat [My brother in battle],

In my sleepless nights, I often think back to the great days of our youth. Those were the days that were long gone when we were fighting for a great cause. We often sinned and failed. I frequently ask myself, why did we fail? . . . What are the reasons for our setback, why did we not succeed to a greater extent? It now seems to be clear to me that the main mistake was the idea "Al-Islam howa el haal" [Islam is the answer]. I believe now that the Prophet of blessed memory would never have agreed to a slogan like this, nor would have al-Boukhari or any of those close to the Prophet. It was a catchy slogan, presented by a group of elderly leaders of the Brotherhood, but they were altogether out of touch with the modern world. How could "Islam is the answer" be of relevance in a digital world. How could it be an answer to problems of modern medicine and technology affecting society to mention just a few of the problems involved?

We should have been far more modest and restricted ourselves to religious issues, to the strict observation of what our holy book says. We should not have tried to encompass everything everywhere. What was the result of our enthusiasm and overeagerness? We attracted a few intellectuals, such as Qutb and some of the middle class, but mainly the poor and the down-and-out, who were the great majority in our demonstrations. Our fighters were from many countries. We did not find a common language. Look at the people who came from far away to help us. We attracted the young, who became militants and like both of us, hurried to the battlefield of their times. Those fighters were products of the West. But our appeal remained very limited because it soon appeared that we did not have the answer to all issues. The great majority of our brothers and sisters all over the globe did not join us. Some of them may have had certain sympathies, but by and large, they were either involved in internal rivalries and struggles or preferred a quiet life and making a living for their families.

The cardinal mistake was that we forgot that our communities were divided on many issues. And so were the fighters that came to join us.

The idea to establish a new caliphate was a harebrained scheme. There had been no caliphate since the 1920s, and what existed at the time was no more than a shadowy institution of no great importance. True, the states that emerged in the Arab world were largely artificial; it is now a hundred years since Sykes-Picot. But once separate and autonomous states emerged, there also emerged vested interests who wanted these new countries to continue to exist. I do not think that there was any way to overcome this development and to establish again one unified Muslim state any time after the downfall of the Ottoman Empire.

Our faith, the faith of Islam, is spread all over the world. What we should not nurture are illusions. What do Muslims in Indonesia have in common with those in Nigeria, for example? Time has taken its toll. By now even Muslims in India have little in common with those in Pakistan, even though India and Pakistan once were one country until the partition in 1947.

Look back and remember the young people who came from the West to join us in our holy struggle. They were full of enthusiasm in the beginning, but how much of it lasted? These young people resented certain features of life in their homelands. But they are products of Western civilization. They wanted adventure, and they got some of it, but after that, their enthusiasm and militancy declined, and they either returned home or became a major problem for us. And yet I am not pessimistic. We have a good chance of success, not because of our bombs and weapons but because of our women—the future. We will be the majority in many countries around the world. The ways of providence are unforeseeable.

I do not know, my brother and comrade, whether you fully agree with my ideas, but in any case, I wish you well in your enterprises even though the oil business is not what it used to be, what with all these recent inventions. You see, times change, and we, whether we want it or not, have to change with them. I hope your family is well, and I am sure your children will be successful in whatever they are doing.

This kind of scenario presents the optimistic view—namely, the decline of the influence of IS and al-Qaeda. However, it is also true that religiously inspired fighting and terrorism have lasted much longer than groups like the European terrorists of the 1980s, which were based on strange and usually half-crazy secular political ideas. How long have fighting groups lasted based on deep religious belief and religious fanaticism? To find some guidance in this respect, one needs to go back into history. It is difficult to imagine a military victory of IS or al-Qaeda, but they may succeed in deepening internal divisions in Western countries in which Muslims constitute a significant minority. This has happened to a certain extent in France, and it may happen in other European countries; it is less likely in the United States, a country constituted of a variety of minorities.

The three best-known examples of religious groups using terrorism and being defeated are the Jewish zealots in the Roman province of Judea, the Shiite Assassins cult, which formed in Persia around the time of the First Crusade, and the Thuggee cult in India. The first was crushed by the Romans during the destruction of Jerusalem, but managed to inflict terror through the province for nearly seventy years, as they opposed Roman rule. The Assassins, for their part, lasted some three hundred years and managed to kill numerous heads of state, as they opposed the Seljuk Empire and created their own state. Only a Mongolian invasion managed to subdue this religiously inspired group of killers, but its legacy continues. Similarly, the Thuggee cult formed at some period before 1350 and lasted until the nineteenth century, when the British destroyed the cult. According to sources, these individuals worshipped the Hindu goddess Kali and killed in a ritualistic fashion to honor her. The extent to which this is true is debatable, given the prevalence of Muslims in their ranks, but nonetheless, they were known for having a strict of set of rules governing whom and how they could kill. The duration of their existence has led estimates of those they killed to range from half a million people to as many as two million. The records for these groups are sparse, but at least they give a mental map of how long religiously inspired violence can last. The reason for their collapse seems to have been the overwhelming power of better organized fighting forces, which could also impose the rule of law.

To find examples of fighting groups, after the age of crusades inspired by militant religions, one still has to go back at least a few centuries. One example would be Oliver Cromwell, a member of Parliament and a military commander who eventually emerged as the leader of the party called the Roundheads. He was a chief commander of the New Model Army, which in its fighting, particularly in Ireland, used fairly brutal methods. He became a hero to some and an abomination to others. He is well remembered, even today; Vladimir Putin on a recent occasion compared himself and the actions of contemporary Russia to Cromwell and his campaigns.

Another more fitting example are the Hussite Wars, occurring about two centuries before (1419–1434). Jan Hus, not well known in the Anglo-speaking world, was a forerunner of Protestantism. He was a Bohemian priest and head of Prague's Charles University, one of the earliest in Europe, existing to this day. Hus did not accept the authority of the Roman Catholic Church, and his followers were fighting the Catholics mainly in Bohemia. It was essentially a war between priests and their followers. The issues at stake are no longer of great interest; they concern, for instance, the question of whether the obligation of the faithful was to receive communion in both kinds—bread and wine—the doctrine of Utraquism, and so on. The Hussite camp was divided into several factions, but it was fighting with great fervor, and as a result, what was later to become Czechoslovakia became predominantly Protestant territory. Hus was burned at the stake as a dangerous heretic. Yet another interesting case that deserves to be studied concerns the rebellion of the Anabaptists led by John of Leiden in the city of Münster, Germany. These events took place in 1534 and lasted altogether one year. In the instances of Cromwell and his following in Britain and Jan Hus, the military operations ended with the death of the leader. However, the consequences were far-reaching.

For a closer phenomenon that could teach us about the duration of violent religious explosions, one has to go back to the Muslims and the appearance of a variety of Mahdis, beginning in the eighth century with King Ṣāliḥ ibn Ṭarīf of the Berghouata in modern-day Morocco. The term *Mahdi* does not appear in the Qur'an but emerged soon after. It means "one called to provide guidance to the pious," but Mahdism as remembered today concerns mainly colonial wars against the British in the nineteenth century. The best recalled today is the Mahdist War (1881–1899) in the Sudan, which included the assassination of General Charles Gordon. This has been the subject of books and movies, but how much light this sheds on current events remains doubtful. There certainly was a great deal of religious fanaticism involved but not much terrorism as we understand it today. It lasted a long time, but eventually the enthusiasm ran out. Some of the followers returned to private life, while others went into politics. This has frequently been the course of events both in the Muslim world and elsewhere: realizing that the armed struggle and terrorism led them nowhere, the militants chose politics. This was the case in Europe in recent decades, but will it also take place in Asia and Africa?

But do events that took place in the nineteenth century help us to understand the current situation? The imperialist West that once acted with determination and without scruples has disappeared, and the aim now is to hit extremists in their homelands. But even more important is the aim to gain predominance in the countries under Muslim rule or in which Muslims are well represented. This makes the Middle East and various Asian and African countries major battlefields with occasional attacks in Europe and America. Such operations by individuals or little groups have become particularly likely with the return of jihadists from the battlefield in which they are fighting.

Among this backdrop of battlefields, the other scenario one has to deal with is the possibility that an extremist Islamist group will be able to obtain weapons of mass destruction. Up until now, the past has served as a referential guide for explaining interesting features of the current terrorist threat. As discussed in other parts of this book, religious terrorists are the actors most likely to use nuclear weapons if they get access to them. This may be difficult today but will probably be much easier in the not-too-distant future. Until now, the threat of terrorism has seemed prolonged, unlikely to end, but unlikely to cause the collapse of the Western world. Nuclear weapons would change this calculus and add a hitherto unknown dimension to how terrorism ends. What if members of such a group explode a nuclear device in a Western city and threaten more such attacks? In this case, there will be overwhelming popular pressure in Western countries to use extreme measures. Muslim communities in the West may be outlawed or expelled unless they will exhibit a great readiness to capture the perpetrators and their supporters. Massive nuclear strikes against the countries in which weapons of mass destruction were produced by the terrorists are more than likely. Needless to say, in such a situation, traditional liberties will be severely curtailed or altogether abolished in the West.

This possibility cannot, unfortunately, be excluded. If terrorist groups will not engage in such actions, it is always possible that some ultraradicals (or madmen) will do so. With technological progress, a very few people can cause enormous havoc. It would be very difficult if not impossible to establish within a short time whether the perpetrators were indeed members of a terrorist group and acted on its behalf or whether these actions were carried out by lone madmen. There have been similar incidents by individuals in the recent past, though weapons of mass destruction were not involved. It is impossible to predict how Western governments would react in such situations.

SUICIDE TERRORISM

Suicide terrorism has attracted enormous interest and has been given much publicity, but it has been frequently misinterpreted. Many historians of terrorism date its contemporary form back to 1983, but another date in the early 1980s could be chosen with equal justice. Suicide missions have become frequent in our age, but they go back far in history. It appears in the Bible with the story of Sampson bringing down the temple in Gaza. It was common practice in Sparta; in the words of a poet, "They give away their life as the law demanded." It was practiced in ancient Rome and in the Middle Ages, and by the Shiite Assassins in the eleventh century, who attacked mainly Crusaders but also fellow Muslims who were considered enemies.

The early Christian martyrs were certainly not terrorists, but they knew that their mission was an extremely dangerous one and more likely than not that their mission would lead to their capture and death. Soldiers and civilians engaging in suicide missions can be found in the history of every nation. They were glorified in the works of leading writers of the time. An interesting example appears in *Konrad Wallenrod* (1828), a poem by the Polish writer Adam Mickiewicz. He wrote:

> *I deceived you, from Granada*
> *I brought you the plague*
> *"For my kiss breathed venom in ye.*
> *And the plague shall lay you low. . . ."*
> *Laughed, and died; his eyes yet open.*

In this case, the hero is a Muslim from Granada by the name of Al-Mansur carrying the pestilence into the enemy Christian camp—perhaps the first known case of biological warfare in literature. Mickiewicz later regretted this poem, which had become very popular, but did not succeed in buying up all the circulating copies. However, in another poem—"Reduta Ordona," he wrote:

> *God said "become,"—God "die" will also say.*
> *When faith and freedom runs away from human,*
> *When tyranny and pride embrace the earth*
> *Like Moskals surrounded Ordon's Reduta—*

God will punish the tribe of crime-poisoned winners
And God will blow up this earth, like Ordon did with his Reduta.

Mickiewicz returned to the same theme, but this second time the hero was a Pole while the enemies were the Russians.

In the schools of pre–World War II Germany, one could sometimes find the following inscription by Horace: *Dulce et decorum est pro patria mori* (It is sweet and honorable to die for one's country.) There is also, for instance, the story of Arnold Winkelried in Swiss history, who sacrificed himself to enable his comrades to make progress in battle. There are many other examples. The best known who are closer to our time are the Japanese kamikaze. More than 3,800 of them died in attacks mainly against American targets. Most of them were pilots, but kamikaze attacks were also carried out in the navy and in land warfare. The suicide concept goes far back into Japanese history; it was expected that the samurai would give their lives for the emperor. There are no reliable statistics as to the total number of kamikaze attacks committed by the various branches of the Japanese military; it could well amount to 10,000 or even more.

Contemporary acts of suicide terrorism are more spread out. For comparison's sake, according to the Chicago Project on Security and Terrorism (CPOST), the number of suicide terrorist attacks is in the neighborhood of 5,430 just for the period from 1990 to 2015. Further obstructing the data, evidence shows suicide attacks before 1990 are rarer. Suicide missions in World War II, as in previous wars, were by no means committed only in Japan. The Soviets had their Alexander Matrosov, who had sacrificed himself in order to save his comrades in arms. They were frequent in the air forces of both sides of the Second World War, especially in the early years of the war, when the equipment on the planes was not yet very sophisticated and the range of the planes was limited. True, most of these missions were committed in a military framework, but the motivation was the same as that of individuals.

As pointed out earlier on, many, if not most, of the rebels and terrorists up to the nineteenth century were "suicidal." Since the primitive weapons in their hands such as knives and pistols were so short-range, they knew that they were bound to be caught (and the punishment used to be certain death). In brief, suicide missions have been committed all throughout history, out of a variety of motives and in a variety of countries and cultures.

There has been some research by psychologists concerning the motivation of individuals who completed suicide missions. Some have drawn the conclusion that those who organized these missions chose emotionally unstable candidates with what psychologists defined as a weak ego. This may be true in some cases but not in others. Others have pointed to the attraction of the famous seventy virgins who would be at the disposal of "martyrs" in heaven. Since those who committed suicide missions can no longer be interviewed, the results of this kind of research has to be considered with measured caution.

Since the 1970s, psychologists and psychiatrists have written extensively about terrorists and their motives. For instance, Luis de la Corte Ibáñez states in "The Social Psychology of Suicide Terrorism":

> According to several authors, social psychology is the scientific study of the way in which people's thoughts, feelings, and behaviors are influenced by other people (Aronson, 1999). The phenomenon of social influence is at the very heart of social psychology. Sometimes this influence happens in a non-deliberated or non-direct way. But other times individuals and groups deliberately try to change another person's behavior. There are a variety of tactics that people apply to influence other people. Terrorism involves the use of force or violence in order to instill fear as a means of coercing individuals or groups to change their political or social positions which means that social influence is the ultimate goal of terrorism. Obviously we could say the same about suicide terrorism.

It should be recorded, however, that such comments by psychologists and psychiatrists all refer to the terrorism of the last century. The authors were not familiar with jihadist terrorism, which was to become the dominating form in the decades thereafter. In contrast, those that have studied the phenomenon up close in more recent decades have shown that jihadist suicide terrorists are not deranged, mentally challenged, or acting irrationally. This subject has been discussed before in a preceding chapter concerning economics and the study of terrorism. Needless to say, prejudging suicide terrorists as fanatics disregards what makes them lethal and underestimates their capacity to attack. This discussion must be placed within the context of singular events that have forced national reactions like Hezbollah's suicide bombing attack against the Marine barracks in Beirut, which greatly altered America's foreign policy toward Lebanon. This section, if anything, is to remind the general audience that throughout history, suicide attacks have been regarded as noble, rational, and worthy, even if the result was the same.

REFUGEES

Of the hundreds of thousands of refugees from the Middle East and Afghanistan, as well as other Muslim countries, the overwhelming majority have wanted nothing but a quiet and better life. IS and allied groups no doubt use the opportunity to infiltrate some of their militants, but these are a minority. However, to what extent have the Muslim communities helped the authorities in Europe and the United States, forewarning them of planned terrorist operations? There has been a recent such case in Germany, and in all probability, there have been more such cases of which we have not heard. But the evidence is not overwhelming. What of the younger generations? Like thousands of the young generations of Muslim communities in other American and European countries, Pakistanis in Britain, North Africans in France, and Turks in Germany, will the integration of the refugee communities be more successful than that of other Muslim communities in the past? It is possible that the refugees will provide a new stimulus (economic, social, and cultural) in their new countries, but this is not very likely in the short run. On the other hand, there is increasing hostility on the part of the local communities. In some places, there have been open attacks, as well as the ejection of the newcomers, who were considered a threat to the traditional character of these countries. Some of the influx has to be viewed against the background of British and French imperialism; having been the masters of colonial empires, the immigration of colonials may have been inevitable.

Elsewhere, the willingness to accept refugees was undoubtedly based on guilty memories and shame about their behavior and reluctance to accept refugees in past ages, especially before and during the Second World War. Be that as it may, the politicians willing to accept the stream of refugees disregarded two essential factors. First, according to the available evidence, nearly half were not political refugees but were "economic" refugees in search of better incomes and living conditions. Other parts of the globe such as the Americas or Australia have been traditionally welcoming of immigration, at least until fifty or a hundred years ago. But they were in fact depending on some measure of immigration. This, however, has not been the case of densely populated Europe, which furthermore has not yet overcome the repercussions of the economic crisis of 2008 (and which suffered from substantial unemployment). Second, the politicians willing to accept these refugees did not fully realize the political reaction that this was bound to generate. All over Europe, the right wing, and especially parties of the extreme right, have been greatly strengthened as a result of these political miscalculations, and democratic parties have declined. This has been particularly noticeable in France, but also to a considerable extent in Germany, Britain, Greece, the Balkans, and probably also in Italy and Scandinavia. It is difficult to understand even in hindsight how this reaction was not foreseen, and it is impossible to predict how far-reaching its effects are yet to go.

We witness, at present, strange developments in the United States, Britain, and many European countries. The Middle East seems to be afflicted by a permanent crisis, and the situation in Africa is unlikely to improve soon. Europe has been declining for a long time, and if this continues, it may become little more than a museum of an erstwhile great culture. However, the reputation of IS may also suffer for having given terrorism a bad name.

Terrorism will continue as long as there are territorial and separatist conflicts, as long as there are ideological or religious movements with aims spanning the whole globe. They will probably not continue with the same intensity, but there will always be a fanatical fringe believing that violence alone will help to attain their goal. There is an interesting historical parallel—the fate of the Roman Empire. The Romans had managed to absorb and acculturate various foreign nations, but failed at the time of the Hun invasion. Why this was the case is a matter of debate to this very day.

16

TERRORISM: THE FUTURE

ANY PREDICTION ABOUT WHEN THE PRESENT WAVE OF TERRORISM WILL
end is necessarily speculative. This for the simple reason that a variety of
factors are involved; for instance: the strength or weakness of Western and
other governments, or the appearance or absence of a charismatic leader
who could lead the present wave in various directions. It could well happen
that the present wave spearheaded by IS and allied groups will recognize,
after a number of years and after additional setbacks, that their policy of establishing a caliphate was mistaken. The historical caliphate has not been
accepted by a majority of Muslims for a long time (after it came to an end
and the Ottoman Empire no longer existed). New states developed, and
with these states came vested interests. To overcome these interests today
will be difficult, if not impossible. Iraq and Syria could possibly unite at a
future date, but it is unlikely that other Islamic states from Indonesia to
Nigeria will ever constitute a true Ummah even in a spiritual sense.

Some observers predict that IS and similar such groups are now on the
retreat and will try to find a new base in the countryside, having failed in
the cities. In other words, they will attempt to transform themselves into a
guerrilla movement. But this seems doubtful for a number of reasons. IS
was and is essentially an urban organization. What was possible in China
at the time of Mao cannot be repeated in the Middle East or Africa.

The history of terrorist movements shows that in our time almost all fail. Walther Rathenau, the Jewish foreign minister of Germany, was killed in 1922, but German foreign policy remained the same. Matthias Erzberger, a politician belonging to the center party in Germany who had voiced pacifist opinions, was killed by far-right extremists without any political effect. Engelbert Dollfuss, the Austrian chancellor, was killed in 1934, but Austria continued to exist, at least for a few years. King Alexander I of Yugoslavia and the French foreign minister Louis Barthou were killed in Marseille in 1934, but it had no political effect whatsoever. Several American presidents were killed, but it had no impact on American policy. Even in the Arab world, political murder had no effect—for instance, the killing of Hassan al-Banna or the murder of King Abdullah in Jerusalem. One could think of an assassination that was tried but did not succeed: the murder of Adolf Hitler before 1939. But for Hitler, there would not have been, in all probability, the Second World War. No other Nazi leader—including, for instance, Hermann Göring or Rudolf Hess—had the same ambitions as Hitler, the same relentless madness, the same courage, the same popular appeal to go to war. True, they wanted Germany to expand, but not at the price of a world war. The Second World War, needless to say, caused enormous devastation and many millions of victims. The Second World War was also the cause of many disasters in the years after, as it caused the decline of Europe. It is possible that Europe today would not be in the sorry state it is but for the Second World War. There were several attempts to kill Mussolini that failed, but it is unlikely that Italian Fascism would have collapsed as a result. Gandhi was killed, but it had no effect on Indian policy.

True, there was another exception. The First World War was triggered by an assassination, but the rivalries and tensions between the major European powers were such that the war was already highly likely. The list could be prolonged. While the killing of a dictator in a fascist state can indeed make a great difference, this seems not to be the case in a democracy or even an authoritarian regime. There has been one major European country in which a leading politician was not killed—namely, Great Britain. A British prime minister was assassinated in 1812, but the motive was personal, not political.

If we go back in history, it emerges that separatist terrorist movements tend to last longer than terrorist groups motivated by ideology. A good example is the Irish IRA, which can be traced back under different names to the late eighteenth century—more than two hundred years. But it's also true that the Irish national movement for many years engaged in political activity rather than violent struggle. All this does not of course mean that political violence has been and will be of no importance. But there are many kinds of such violence: war, civil war, guerilla warfare, and so on. And compared with them, terrorism is certainly of much lesser importance. IS seems to have realized that killing the leader of a democratic country would not make any difference, and for this reason, its attacks have always been directed mainly against civilians uninvolved in politics. The mission of IS is not, however, concerned with territory but with people. IS wants all mankind to embrace the only true religion; others will be eliminated or, in the best case, relegated to second- or third-class citizens having to pay a special tax for their unbelief. The history of terrorist groups shows that those with realistic, limited aims had a chance of some success. Those who intended to change the world profoundly did, as a rule, fail.

Issues concerning the end of terrorist groups have been occasionally studied, but these studies almost always concern earlier terrorist movements. The issue of IS is different, inasmuch as it is part of the Islamist wave that started some thirty years ago. How long did similar such waves in the past last? Some, like the various Mahdism phenomena, were a short duration and ended with the death of the leader. Others, like Salafism, lasted a very long time and, in fact, are in various ways still active today. The Muslim Brotherhood was founded in the 1920s, but even though underground, it is still active today. However, the Muslim Brotherhood, like other offshoots of Salafism or Islamism, turned to political activity, and the same may happen to present-day Islamist groups. In all likelihood, there will always be an ultraradical group believing that violence alone will bring them closer to their goal. As stated earlier, much depends on the attitudes of Western governments, the Russian government, and the Chinese and other Asian governments.

One of the reasons to not to be too sanguine about the future of IS is the fact that extreme Islamist groups have always had a tendency to split. We know from documents obtained that there were considerable differences of opinion even within the top leadership of al-Qaeda. Osama bin Laden was quite critical of some of the views and the strategies of his former deputy, Abu Musab al-Zarqawi; he thought that the measures taken against Muslim dissidents were too harsh, and some of his religious views were not in line with traditional Islamic orthodoxy. Some of the leaders of other Islamic groups, including those who appointed themselves caliphs, were far from generating acceptance; they had no standing as ideological guides outside the small groups they were heading. An Islamic leader recognized by most or all people belonging to that camp has not yet arisen, and even if he should arise, it is more than likely that he will not be recognized by all.

One possibility, indeed likelihood, which is frequently ignored, is the reemergence of Islamism in Russia. Until about 2015, it seemed that Moscow had the situation under control, and the majority of the local Muslim establishments seemed to have been perfectly content under Russian rule. But this is no longer the case. This refers in particular to Dagestan—a small republic in the northern Caucasus with about three million. Dagestan was never quite "pacified" from a Russian point of view, but during the last year, fighting in this region has become far more intense. Traditionally, the contest was among Sufism and groups close to al-Qaeda, but of late, IS seems to have grown in influence (establishing a Caucasus Emirate, or Wilayat Qawqaz), and there is a more or less "open struggle" between the Islamic State and al-Qaeda. The number of victims in this struggle may amount to several thousand (exact figures not being available). If the fighting were to remain limited to Dagestan, these developments may not fester into major importance. But it could very well be that the progress of IS could spill into neighboring regions in which Muslim communities constitute a significant segment of the population. According to reports from Tajikistan in Central Asia, there have been numerous arrests in 2015 and 2016 of Muslim preachers accused of extremist sermons and propaganda.

Little mention has been made so far about jihadist operations in Russia. Is this likely to change in the future? IS cannot afford to neglect the substantial Muslim community in Russia (quite apart from the Caucasian situation and the Central Asian republics). The situation is further complicated as the result of growing Chinese influence and power in this part of the world. The attitude of the Russian government toward IS has been difficult to understand. When al-Zawahiri visited Dagestan in 1996, he was first arrested and later released. He may have assured the Kremlin that his organization (al-Qaeda) would never attack any Russian targets, only American ones. But the Russians rightly, at least from their point of view, may not have given such a statement their full trust. While this assurance may have been well intended, it is not at all clear whether the leadership of al-Qaeda (or IS, at that) is in full control of the actions of their various organizations in various parts of the world. This goes, above all, for those Islamist fighting groups inside Russia and the Caucasus. The Russian foreign minister has called IS a terrorist organization and announced proudly that only the Russian intervention in Syria had saved the country from falling into the hands of the terrorists. But Russian military intervention, especially by the Russian Air Force, has far more often been directed against the *enemies* of IS than against the IS organization itself (Russian policy makers seem to believe that there are basic differences between IS and al-Qaeda). Whether such a policy can be sustained indefinitely and whether it will eventually serve Russian interests best is not at all certain. But at the present time, Putin and his advisors seem to be convinced that, by and large, IS and the other jihadist organizations are determined to inflict damage above all on America and at best try to refrain from attacking Russian targets. But it is not at all clear how long this will last.

Let us return to our starting point—the issue of IS ideology, its intensity and rootedness. Which are the motives of the IS campaign of recent years and also of like-minded terrorist groups? It has been pointed out earlier on that our knowledge in this respect is by no means absolutely clear. The assumption that the main motive is religious extremism is of course correct, but it is also an oversimplification. Islamism does play a central role, but it is by no means the only factor involved. Nationalist and separatist interests do play an important role into interests of clans and various national groups, as well as the interests of individuals and social strata. It has also been stressed that while IS and similar such groups obey the main commandments of Islam, they have their own ways of interpreting them and, if need be, find interpretations of their own. The history of these groups in recent decades shows that nationalist motives were quite often involved and that the beginnings of terrorist campaigns were in the secular camp.

The same is true with regard to other Islamist militant or terrorist groups in recent decades. An obvious example is the Chechen movement, which had its roots in secular circles and only later on became an extremist religious group. To what extent the present rulers of Chechnya are indeed fanatical Islamists is a moot point. Another example is presented by the political developments in Pakistan. Originally, the idea of a division of India and the establishment of a separate Muslim state occurred in secular circles headed by Ali Jinnah. Only following the coup carried out by the Pakistani army in 1977 did Islamism become the official state ideology.

The jihadist terrorist groups are, at present, retreating. But in all likelihood they will be able to cause a considerable amount of mischief and political turbulence given the weakness of the Middle Eastern and African governments for years to come. At present, the United States and Europe are considered the main enemies. But America is far away from the Middle East, while Russia and China are immediate neighbors. Given these geographic circumstances, the end of the present terrorist wave may not be that near even if the identities of the main enemies change.

LESSONS FROM THE CURRENT WAVE OF TERRORISM

Whenever the current wave of terrorism ends, no matter how distant that day might seem, there will be a remarkable corpus of literature for terrorists in the future to study. If this book cannot predict the end of the current wave, it should at least give some thought to what it implies for future terrorist organizations. To begin, Islamic State's terror is largely remarkable for how derivative it is compared to other terrorist organizations. Its violence, its tactics, its operations, and its strategy all originate from some other source that is not internal to the group, and hardly reflect a breakthrough in originality. Even its interpretation of Islamic eschatology is not unique and comes from well-trodden sources exploited by other jihadist groups or from radical extremists dating back centuries. Yet despite sharing its traits with innumerable entities throughout history, both religious and secular, something about the group has made it the new standard-bearer and symbol of the potency nonviolent actors have when it comes to committing atrocities. Whereas for the first decade of the twenty-first century, the referential act was al-Qaeda's attack against the United States on September 11, 2001, now the most symbolic images are of beheadings and wholesale massacres committed in a systemic fashion by individuals wearing black masks. This is not to underplay the attacks on 9/11, as they remain the deadliest single act of terrorism ever, and their role in shaping history will be discussed and dissected for generations to come. Viscerally, though, there is something quite horrifying about the notion of an organization adopting cognitive and institutional procedures and processes for

236 | THE FUTURE OF TERRORISM

the annihilation of entire groups of people individually instead of relying on uncontrolled explosions, while at the same time using these same organizational methods to govern and conquer territory. If Islamic State's violence is not unique in approach, it certainly seems to have increased the gradient of palatable violence by nonstate actors and what seems possible.

The latter point is the most crucial. For many years, al-Qaeda spoke of creating a caliphate and re-creating the system of government that existed during the Prophet's time. This was outlined in Saif al-Adel's so-called Seven Phases of the Base.* IS subverted AQ's plan and simply did what seemed unthinkable or at least what seemed to be the eternal hope and promise of all jihadist organizations. Even as IS collapses, its borders recede, and its grip on territory diminishes, true believers now have a model that they can hope to achieve and acquire, because it has been done. Not only did IS conquer and vanquish, it reformulated laws according to sharia, experimented in monetary policy by creating and introducing its own currency, learned taxation policy and means of acquiring these funds, debated the question of health care policy in modern times, conceived and implemented a system of courts that people respected, and imposed something akin to the rule of law over a territory the size of the United Kingdom. These achievements, although easy to list on paper, require an advanced bureaucracy that can acquire information, disseminate it among senior- and mid-level managers, maintain sufficient legitimacy to deter cheating or defection, and have an enforcement mechanism to turn ideas into laws and policies. Not only that, but with innovations in information technology, there is likely paperwork to document all this so that it can be exported and adapted into future scenarios.

There is context to IS and its success, and it is worth discussing before continuing. As explored in the historical portions of this book, the group's success owes to failures in governance. In Libya, Iraq, Syria, and Afghanistan, it took advantage of poorly governed areas and exported its government-in-a-box model to these places, ingraining itself rapidly and quickly into local populations. If Assad had not been so brutal, or if al-Maliki had been more conciliatory toward Sunnis, IS would probably still be analyzed within the constellation of the various jihadist organizations with ties to al-Qaeda. However, poor governance has been an issue for millennia across the world, and

---

* Bill Roggio, "The Seven Phases of the Base," FDD's Long War Journal, August 15, 2005, https://www.longwarjournal.org/archives/2005/08/the seven phase.php.

yet within the context of the nation-state, rarely has there been a nonstate actor that has so vividly left its mark on the question of sovereignty. Despite the fact that the Islamic State is a learning organization that appropriated what worked from the Irgun, the IRA, the Red Army Faction, the Tupamaros, and others, only it has been able to subvert the question of statehood and sovereignty and reformat it for its own purpose. In this regard, then, it offers lessons—which, if adapted to peculiar contexts and circumstances, can be applied anywhere where governance is a problem.

What are its truths? Broadly speaking, it is that terrorism can work, but usually not in isolation. It has the most success when conducted as part of protracted campaigns to influence hearts and minds and conquer territory, while consolidating these advances with a bureaucracy. This echoes the above discussion about whether terrorism works and the difficulty of disentangling it from other political violence occurring. This seems self-evident, but only until recently has a group successfully implemented this strategy. The Taliban ruled an Islamic emirate but lacked an appealing message that would attract the same wave of recruits as the Islamic State. It also lacked a sophisticated state apparatus beyond courts to improve the quality of life for its citizens, meaning it was not a long-term model, for it could not deliver to its citizens. The direct predecessor of IS, al-Qaeda in Iraq, also governed but did so too violently, and it ended up isolating its base. In contrast, Islamic State always maintained agency when it progressed, both provoking and proactively building a program that appealed to the people it governed and also individuals across the globe that bought into its message. There are hard limits to this lesson, though. This state-building project could only occur when there was no viable state to stymie its efforts, and it started to recede the moment concerted air strikes and massing of forces began uprooting IS from its strongholds.

Al-Qaeda has internalized these lessons and is engaged in ambitious state-building projects across the world from South Asia to North Africa. In the places this gradualist approach is working, the conspicuous common element is the absence of government. Eventually, AQ will be positioned to absorb IS and to expand its own caliphate project. There are already signs of tactical cooperation between IS and AQ in parts of Libya, the Levant, and others, and over time, this process will gain steam. Assuming it does not provoke a response by the West, these failed states where AQ asserts itself will become the base of operations for future plots, much like Afghanistan and Sudan in the 1990s.

WHEN TERRORISM PREVAILS?

The world of 2018 looks markedly different from the world of August 2001, and in large measure, this is because of the success of terrorist groups in staging massive plots. If IS and al-Qaeda have developed strategies that work, does this mean terrorism is destined to prevail? The reality is that the current wave of terrorism should be understood within the context of its structure and its time. While IS might represent an existentialist threat to Iraq, it only plays that role because of mishaps from Iraq's central government. For the West, the threat is far less because, as has been explained elsewhere, terrorism is unlikely to ever destroy a society—unless a group acquires weapons of mass destruction. To emphasize this point, IS, for all its industrial might, lacks the capacity of a modern state to mobilize people and resources for an all-out onslaught akin to the Mongol hordes. At most, it can inspire fear globally, but it cannot defeat modern militaries. Terrorism has prevailed in the past, but not because terrorists vanquished their foes with car bombs or with assassinations. They succeeded when governments overreacted or when there was not a government *to* react, making a terrorist group the entity best positioned to govern and impose laws. This seems contradictory, but those earth-shattering moments always ceded agency to other actors and could have been prevented. The case of the Irgun in Palestine and the FLN were discussed briefly in a previous chapter. It is worth focusing on two more examples.

Archduke Franz Ferdinand's assassination is often touted as the quintessential terrorist plot that changed history. Indeed, his death provoked the mobilization of forces across Europe and led to the First World War, but the reasons for that conflict were more complex and strategic than terrorism alone. It was European overreaction within the tinderbox of an arms race and hegemonic competition that set off the war. Ferdinand's death was but a pretext for the various parties to take up arms. Perhaps, in a modern context, with more regularized diplomatic interactions and confidence-building measures, war could have been stopped. That was impossible, though, as this was the age before the League of Nations, and efforts to build norms against aggression had not been codified forcefully into international law. Contrast this era to the Cold War, where nuclear annihilation was a globally persistent threat, forcing the rival powers to engage in confidence-building measures to reduce tension. While strategic mishaps occurred, the constant communication between the United States and the Soviet Union helped create a sense of stability lacking otherwise.

A more contemporary example is 9/11. American life changed dramatically following these attacks. Al-Qaeda killed thousands, caused untold amounts of material damage to the U.S. economy, and forced the United States to change its laws to better fight terrorism. It also led the United States to enter Afghanistan and for it to usher in the global war on terror. To what extent was AQ directly responsible for this, though, aside from the death and destruction? Part of AQ's goal was to incite an American invasion and to enmesh the United States in a protracted guerrilla war that would bankrupt its economy, forcing it to withdraw its support for the apostate governments in the Middle East, specifically Saudi Arabia. Only then would AQ be able to declare a caliphate. While history might seem to validate this strategy, it is worth analyzing how the invasion occurred.

In 2001, the United States did not become enmeshed in a large-scale war in Afghanistan due to strategic decisions taken by the Bush administration. Instead of toppling the Taliban government and routing AQ in 2001 with conventional forces, the United States relied on a small contingency of special operations forces (SOF) working in tandem with the Afghan Northern Alliance, the main opposition to the Taliban, and supported by airpower. This light-footprint approach was maintained after the invasion because the threat environment was limited. Furthermore, because NATO activated Article 5 as a show of solidarity with the United States, once the main fighting concluded, the invasion of Afghanistan quickly transitioned into a state-building project under the purview of the United Nations. In other words, this was not the protracted insurgency-cum–guerrilla war that AQ predicted. It did transform into one down the road, but only once the international governance project failed to deliver on its promises, creating the political space for the Taliban to reemerge.

The war AQ wanted did occur in Iraq for reasons unrelated to 9/11, even though the Bush administration often used it as a justification. Indeed, news reports from the era suggest that the Bush administration had been planning to invade Iraq long before the attacks in New York and Washington. Even if one assumes that 9/11 was the direct cause for the invasion, given how tenuous the links were between Saddam Hussein and AQ, this war should be seen purely as an overreaction from a government failing to analyze the situation strategically. Nonetheless, this war created the conditions for IS to emerge. This is to say that this war, regardless of the motivations behind it, was one of choice and not of necessity, and the evils that followed it come in large measures from decisions taken by the U.S. government, not strictly from AQ's brilliance. At any point before March 2003, the United States and its coalition partners could have decided not to invade Iraq, and history likely would have been different.

Going back even further, what enabled 9/11 in the first place was the fact that the global community ignored Afghanistan. By 1996, when the Taliban was ascendant, the UN was raising alarms to the human rights abuses being committed, and American intelligence was well aware of al-Qaeda's ambitions and that it was hiding in the country. It was also well known that AQ had built training camps in Afghanistan for future terrorists, many of whom were participating in the conflicts in Chechnya and in the former Yugoslavia. Whereas the activities after 9/11 were an overreaction and later an issue of governance, the conditions beforehand were that of inaction and also failure of governance.

Viewing terrorist groups in this fashion changes how they are perceived from that of a potent fighting force to that of a parasite or disease, which is avoidable if addressed with the proper treatment in a proactive manner. The goal is not to be reactive and to fall into political imbroglios that cause more trouble than necessary. In this sense, it is reminiscent of David Kilcullen's argument for how insurgents emerge during conflicts. In his book *The Accidental Guerrilla*, Kilcullen explains that normally, insurgent groups first enter contested regions to establish support bases through propaganda and the assumption of shadow-government functions, such as the provision of security or justice. Generally, these groups fail to integrate completely into local society, as their ideology is typically alien to local customs and traditions. The degree of institutionalization depends on the compatibility with societal norms, meaning rejection might occur if their doctrine is too extreme. After gaining local sympathy, the organization spreads to other contested regions using the same approach. As these regions lack a strong government presence, the government typically remains aloof to these developments until the insurgent group's network base becomes too entrenched to uproot. When governments finally do intervene, Kilcullen notes, they often resort to heavy-handed tactics that indiscriminately target the whole of society, leading to a rejection of governmental presence vis-à-vis the insurgency, increasing its support and its ranks. As this is an epidemiological model, Kilcullen argues that the insurgency will continue to spread to all areas that a government attempts to inoculate it with the wrong remedy.

This model can be applied to the contemporary state of terrorism as well. It is not so much that terrorism can always be stopped, but with proactive policies rooted in empirically based analysis, the threat can be contained, and its overall damage can be limited. As a parasite, terrorism thrives when political and social milieus create palatable and hospitable environments; it depends on weak states and governments, because chaos begets chaos. Reacting chaotically only feeds the problem more.

SO WHAT ABOUT THIS CURRENT WAVE OF TERRORISM?

The common theme is that terrorism works either when international norms fail to rein in an overreaction by a major power like the United States, or when governance does not exist in a particular country or territory. So what are the implications of this?

First is the importance of maintaining the terrorism threat in perspective. Governments across the world should do their utmost to protect their citizens from terrorism, but within the framework of the rule of law. The imprimatur of legitimacy begins with a government's ability to provide security to its population. The other part of the covenant between the individual and the state, though, is the protection of those values that define a society by upholding the rule of law. There is a tendency by states to overreact and begin loosening protection for civil rights and civil liberties when the question centers on security from terrorism. The United States experienced this with legislation passed in the wake of 9/11 that curtailed certain freedoms in the name of fighting terrorism. Actions such as these, where a government purposefully violates the values that define it to fight terrorism, perversely accomplish the goals of groups like AQ or IS and delegitimize the state. Furthermore, while AQ or IS can kill people, they are not invaders with nuclear weapons. Maintaining this perspective and building in this determination not to overreact goes a long way toward containing the damage terrorists can accomplish.

This is more true in the international arena. Not every incident demands an immediate and forceful response that reshapes a political order. History has demonstrated how a particular war of choices sparked by terrorism can easily metastasize into something bigger and worse. The stakes are especially high in Iraq and Syria due to the involvement of Russia and Iran. Miscalculation by any major power trying to fight IS or Jabhat al-Nusra might provoke a global catastrophe greater than anything occurring right now just by the misuse of violence. Similarly, in the future, upholding the international norm of nonaggression will go a long way in preventing wars like the American invasion of Iraq or the Soviet occupation of Afghanistan, both of which spawned the most dangerous terrorist groups currently in existence.

In terms of the significance of IS and AQ, if this new state-building approach to spreading terrorism is an evolution of the present wave, it is such only because the international community has not done enough to impose governance in war-torn regions. Rather than generating worry, this should create cautious optimism about the threat posed by IS and AQ. These organizations both arose in the context of failed states and depend on this form of political oxygen for their survival and success. When having to fight a modern military, they fail. They win, though, if they are able to provide a political alternative in places ruled by capricious dictators or lacking the rule of law.

In other words, terrorism is not an exogenous feature of the modern nation-state but rather a symptom of bad governance. Indeed, the entire point of terrorism is to challenge the foundations and legitimacy of governments. When terrorists attack to generate fear, they do so hoping that it reverberates throughout society and that society will overreact. When there is no government to speak of, much like a disease, terrorists spread and take advantage of the safe havens to plot ways to expand their activities. IS succeeded because al-Maliki did not know how to govern and because Assad is a nasty and brutish man. Al-Qaeda in the Arabian Peninsula is deadly because the ongoing civil war means that there is no such thing as governance in Yemen's southern half. And al-Qaeda gained legitimacy when the United States invaded Iraq, as this action seemed to validate its propaganda of a war between the West and Islam.

This changes both how terrorism ought to be understood and the appropriate responses. Certainly, military might is important for removing threats without endangering a country's own population, but this can go only so far. Indeed, this issue is not even one of reducing poverty but, quite genuinely, how the global community regulates itself and its member states. As noted previously, the link between poverty and terrorism is weak, but the link between failed states and terrorism is quite high. As long as it is seen as a viable alternative to perceived injustices, then it will be a tactic that intelligent and willing individuals will use to advance their goals. Addressing these concerns in war-torn regions will reduce the likelihood that plots will be committed against stable countries.

Admittedly, bad governance is not the only vector for terrorism. As noted in an earlier section of this book, many contemporary terrorists do become radicals in stable Western countries and are from well-off families. These individuals probably adopt these ideas through the exposure to Salafist communities, which preach a rigid and exclusionary interpretation of Islam, or by reading online propaganda. If these individuals decide to commit violence, though, and are not given proper training, they will not be as effective. Granted, opportunistic individuals will follow the examples of the London Bridge or Nice attackers and use rudimentary weapons to kill people, but the scale of damage is much less than coordinated plots using explosives, guns, and urban guerrilla tactics. For all the instruction provided by *Inspire, Dabiq, Rumiyah*, or any other terrorist magazine, the deadliest attacks occur if individuals receive training and guidance—hence the importance of the training camps run by IS and AQ in Afghanistan, Yemen, Syria, Iraq, and other places that turn raw recruits in professional terrorists. This is corroborated by data. While there has been an increase in the last decade of terrorist plots in Europe, this began only after the onset of the conflict in Syria in 2011. Similarly, the last major spasm of attacks in Europe began in 2004, following the onset of the conflicts in Iraq. The reason, of course, is that many young individuals traveled to these war zones, received training and instruction from hardened fighters, and returned to their home countries to attack.

To summarize, although this current wave of terrorism might seem terrifying, it is a problem that can be managed. Admittedly, this is easier said than done. State-building is expensive, requires a long-term commitment by the international community, and demands buy-in from locals. If the international community acts proactively rather than reactively, however, it is a problem that can be stopped before it begins. Ultimately, though, the best defense against terrorism is the rule of law domestically and internationally, and that should be the priority. IS was successful in Iraq because there was neither.

It has been this book's thesis that terrorism is not an existentialist threat because of the inferior military capability terrorists normally possess short of their acquiring weapons of mass destruction. In the face of things, even monumental attacks like 9/11 are never going to destroy the United States or its constitutional order. There is an important caveat to all this. A state's response to terrorism, on the other hand, can pose an existentialist threat to itself. The United States is not the only country guilty of formulating improper responses to the problem of terrorism. During the Troubles, the British government developed a punitive and draconian anti-terrorism program that allowed British security forces to engage in torture against perceived IRA sympathizers, actions that only begat more terrorism. This was dramatized in the movie *In the Name of the Father*, which told the story of Gerry Conlon, one of the innocent Irishmen accused of bombing two Guildford pubs. Gerry Conlon, in his biography, explained that in their anger to mete out state punishment in a very Foucauldian manner, the British police tortured him and extracted a false confession out of him and imprisoned him for fifteen years. Conlon, not part of the IRA, became a martyr and a symbol of British oppression in Northern Ireland. In the course of prosecuting a counterterrorism campaign, the United Kingdom surrendered any claims to moral legitimacy and became equal to the IRA, who was violating the rule of law. This occurred in the very country that gave birth to such important liberal thinkers as John Locke, Edmund Burke, John Stuart Mill, and countless others.

When innocent people die in the name of some abstract political cause, it is normal to seek out vengeance, especially when there are methods for registering political opposition and dissent. However, as history has demonstrated repeatedly, most times this is ineffective or self-defeating. The case of France in Algeria is the stuff of legends, but a similar story can be told in cases not discussed in this book: the Peruvian military against the Shining Path, the British against the Mau Mau in Kenya, and even Spain in fighting ETA. Well-ordered democratic societies should avoid this punitive antediluvian temptation both because it generates blowback and because it is anathema to their existential values. Terrorism will likely never end, but its worst effects can absolutely be mitigated.

EPILOGUE: TERRORISM UNDER PRESIDENT TRUMP

THIS BOOK HAS ATTEMPTED TO PROVIDE PREDICTIONS ABOUT GENERAL trends about terrorism, but it has avoided specifics. General trends are observable and should remain constant for some time unless something major occurs, but individualized predictions are likely to be disproven quickly, requiring humility on the part of the writers. Yet the election of Donald Trump is a structural feature that will affect terrorism for the near term, and quite possibly for generations, if he is successful in passing key legislation, such as his several attempts to ban Muslim immigration to the United States, or if for some reason he plays a major role in fracturing the European Union. At the time of this writing, he has already done the former and he has made overtures to the latter. As dangerous as speculating can be, a few macro-scale trends are emerging.

Whereas most policies Trump might pursue will have a temporal lag in regard to their influence, the one direct policy that will affect the problem immediately is his relationship with President Vladimir Putin of Russia. Trump's election coincided with the fall of Aleppo in December 2016 and changed American policy toward the conflict. In the final months of his administration, President Obama sought a diplomatic solution to the conflict in Syria, hoping to push Assad out and depriving Islamic terrorists of the necessary political oxygen to win local support. By that point, this seemed moot. Russia's decisive intervention in November 2015 had undeniably rescued Assad from defeat, and with that, the regime had less incentive for negotiating or contemplating an exit plan. Although the United States and its allies were reluctant to confront Russia and Assad militarily, they could still question the moral legitimacy of any military outcome while still providing covert support to the moderate Syrian rebels. This has changed. President Trump campaigned on improving ties with Russia and even talked about cooperating with Putin on counterterrorism in Syria. Without this political pressure, Assad will remain a beacon for Islamic terrorists, all the while being unable to control the majority of Syria. This likely means the insurgency will continue, but also that groups like Jabhat Fateh al-Sham and IS will have ample territory to build training camps and to plot international attacks.

What about Trump's strategy for combating terrorism? He campaigned on a largely nationalistic and overtly Islamophobic platform, and at one point, he claimed to have a secret strategy for defeating IS. He has been quite adamant that fighting modern terrorism involves calling it *radical Islamic terrorism*, in essence downplaying the threat posed by other strands of nonstate violence. His administration tried outlining its vision in its 2017 *National Security Strategy*. It involved traditional counterterrorism principles pursued by Trump's predecessors, such as combating online radicalization and financiers. The document also discussed pressuring Pakistan to cease its support of terrorist groups, and countering Iranian meddling in the Middle East. Interestingly, the document does not mention *radical Islamic terrorism*, nor does it truly explain Trump's approach to counterterrorism. Nevertheless, there are a few developments indicative of what his administration intends in the coming years.

First, he is loosening Obama-era regulations concerning violence toward civilians and giving the Pentagon greater leeway to authorize attacks in undeclared war zones. Obama's policies, although criticized as overly limiting and cautious, were intended to reduce blowback from years of drone strikes in Yemen and Pakistan and to soften America's image after the Iraq War. The hope was that fewer civilian casualties would undercut the propaganda value of potential military actions against terrorist groups. Trump's second big step was promoting a more muscular military presence in places like Syria and Yemen. In March 2017, various news outlets leaked a plan to increase the number of ground forces deployed to Syria to help with the fight against Islamic State in Raqqa, but this is far from an invasion or occupation of territory. Other planks of this plan involve continued bombing and cutting Islamic State funding. Regarding Afghanistan, President Trump has not articulated a strategy, although his generals have requested an increase in the number of troops deployed to that theater. In early April 2017, he garnered international attention after authorizing the use of a GBU-43, nicknamed the "Mother of All Bombs," or MOAB, against IS targets in Afghanistan. The use of the MOAB, the most powerful nonnuclear bomb in America's arsenal, had tactical coherence. It destroyed a vast network of tunnels where IS was hiding and hoarding weapons and supplies. Whether this marks a change in policy is uncertain, but it did have an impressive psychological effect on the global public.

The one thing that is certain, as it has been a trend since 2001, is that American special operations forces (SOF) will see an increase in the number of troops, although the feasibility of this is questionable, given the cost and time required to properly train more special operators. More covert operations will occur to fight terrorism in a larger quantity. For all their skills in fighting and combating terrorists, their deployment should give one pause. An overreliance on SOF means that the government sees them as a panacea, without thinking through the fatigue they might suffer, how costly it is to train them, or how the present lack of oversight over most of these units affects their performance. The country became aware of these risks in the fall of 2017. In October, reports emerged that four SOF members and four soldiers from Niger were killed in an ambush by an IS affiliate. In November, a report emerged of an incident where two Navy SEALs killed a Green Beret in June 2017 after he threatened to inform their superiors they were stealing money. These incidents, though disparate in nature, shed light on the vulnerability of these units to both overuse and misuse.

Whether these moves make the world safer from terrorism is debatable. Certainly there will be more dead terrorists, but in very honest terms, this seems like a continuation of President Obama's kinetic counterterrorism efforts, but with more aggression. To his credit, President Trump has had some important successes. Under his watch, coalition forces retook Mosul, Raqqa, and other cities critical to IS's caliphate project. Yet what these policies do not do is find a way to cut off the political oxygen that keeps terrorism alive, which was the other component of Obama's strategy for fighting IS. With Trump's proposed budget cuts toward international diplomatic

248 | THE FUTURE OF TERRORISM

efforts and in aid across the world, countries will find themselves strapped for resources and more vulnerable to being overwhelmed by terrorists. This is to say that Trump's counterterrorism policy is in essence an overreliance on tactical tools to avoid investing in the necessary resources to formulate a strategy with a clear endgame for terrorism.

The other ways that Trump can affect the nature of terrorism are more abstract, making their consequences difficult to pin down if they ever come together, and that is largely through his rhetoric. Much of Trump's electoral success occurred by normalizing behavior that before would have been considered unethical or anathema to any politician running for office in a major Western country. From his vocal distrust of Latin American immigrants and Muslims, he has created a climate where certain strains of American society feel empowered to act against these groups. This was covered at length before when discussing the prominence of right-wing terrorist organizations domestically and the rise of hate groups since he won the election. It is worrisome, though, that the United States appears so reactive to any act of violence committed by individuals with Middle Eastern names, with large sections of the country immediately up in arms the moment news breaks out. Contrast this with how inured its society appears when stories about mass shooters appear and the relative death toll of each. From an outsider's perspective, there seems to be a problem of unbalanced expectations and major threat inflation.

If he manages to turn any of his rhetoric into policy, things will become more problematic. His attempts in January and March 2017 to restrict immigration to the United States from seven majority-Muslim countries, including Yemen and Iraq, were quickly shot down by courts because they were unapologetically Muslim bans. Even though he couched his executive orders in the language of national security, the courts found his justification wanting vis-à-vis the Constitution's protection of freedom of religion. Trump's case was not helped by campaign promises he had made and comments by his surrogates, which spoke of this effort as a Muslim ban designed to appear as legal as possible. The attempted ban was self-sabotaging from the beginning. As analysts explained, the ban applied to countries whose citizens had not committed acts of terrorism against the United States and instead affected countries that were important partners for the United States in its counterterrorism efforts abroad, notably Afghanistan, Iraq, and Yemen. He was partially successful in his third attempt in September. This version of the ban included a few non-Muslim countries, including Venezuela and North Korea, but the ban still faces legal challenge.

Abroad, Trump's inflammatory language and attempted policies like the Muslim ban are perfectly suited for sound bites used in propaganda videos by groups like Islamic State or al-Qaeda. His vilifying of the entire Muslim world and his castigation of Islam as a terroristic religion justify the worldview of Salafist jihadists, who regard the West with suspicion and hostility, believing it to be opposed to Islam in general. Trump did the world no favors by recognizing Jerusalem as the capital of Israel. There was not the expected surge in violence immediately after his announcement, but American diplomatic stations across the world immediately issued alerts to American citizens about the heightened risk. Trump's move, aside from accomplishing little diplomatically, reinforces the jihadist depiction of the United States as a crusader state. In this sense, Trump not only validates terrorist propaganda and facilitates recruitment but also encourages the much-maligned "Clash of Civilizations" thesis first put out by Samuel Huntington in 1996, in which he wrote that religious identities were the source of all coming conflicts. Indeed, even if recruitment and radicalization do not increase from Trump's rhetoric, his distrust of Muslims may well affect relations with Middle Eastern allies who are crucial in the fight against terrorism. If, previously, Osama bin Laden in part justified his hatred of the United States because it stationed troops in Saudi Arabia, Middle Eastern governments might find themselves less willing to assist the United States in its counterterrorism efforts to avoid inspiring anger in their citizens.

Regarding Europe, this effect is purely secondary or tertiary, depending on how one chooses to analyze a potential breakup of the European Union or NATO, but it is worth discussing briefly, although it is mainly a topic outside the scope of this book. All the bad things that Donald Trump can do to encourage terrorism will affect the continent more directly because of its proximity to the Middle East. Right-wing populists have gained in the polls and according to several prominent surveys, the continent is experiencing anxiety towards immigrants from Muslim States.*

* Matthew Goodwin, Thomas Raines, and David Cutts, "What Do Europeans Think About Muslim Immigration," Chatham House, February 7, 2017, https://www.chathamhouse.org/expert/comment/what-do-europeans-think-about-muslim-immigration.

The United States, as the so-called leader of the free world, can shape the discourse of what is permissible rhetorically and policy-wise. The United States pursuing a ban targeting exclusively Muslims only gives fodder to populists in Europe, which will only aggravate relations with Muslims domestically. Even if no similar ban is passed, attempts like this will appear in propaganda, undeniably making Europeans bigger targets for attacks.

More worrisome is the notion of Donald Trump's encouraging the breakup of the European Union or NATO. The last American ambassador to the EU under President Obama suggested that Trump did indeed want the former, a concern that many European leaders share. In fact, the European Council president, Donald Tusk, actually listed the United States as a threat to the continent in February 2017. At other times, Trump has questioned the utility of NATO, arguing that most member states are not paying their dues and the United States ought to stop subsidizing their security. This matters for a few reasons. In practical terms, Europe is the first line of defense against Islamic terrorism emanating from the Middle East. Its proximity means it can control air, land, and sea routes that would-be terrorists targeting the United States can take. And given that Europe has been a staging ground for plots against North America before, greater European unity means that more resources can be dedicated toward monitoring and dismantling plots. The EU is also the route many foreign fighters take to arrive in Syria; it is well positioned to stem the flow.

More than that, the continent as a whole is a bulwark that supports American diplomatic efforts to end conflicts across the world. European leaders have played important diplomatic roles in attempting to force Assad out of power and to empower moderate Syrian rebels. They have also been critical in supporting American counterterrorism training missions in Afghanistan, Iraq, North Africa, Nigeria, and other places. These efforts are aggregated tremendously through the prism of NATO, which enables the United States to draw upon additional resources in times of need. As such, European allies have been critical linchpins in those moments when the United States has carried out large-scale counterterrorism missions, providing supporting or leading roles. In Libya, the effort to oust Qaddafi was spearheaded by the British and the French, and both countries continue seeking to stabilize the situation through the use of SOF. The French also were critical in pushing out al-Qaeda in the Islamic Maghreb from Mali after it managed to take over the northern half of the country, although this was not a NATO-led effort. And the United States cannot forget how NATO allies responded diligently to the attacks on 9/11, they themselves activating Article 5 to express solidarity with the country. In fact, they helped shoulder the burden in stabilizing Afghanistan after the United States began focusing on Iraq and have continued supporting stabilization efforts there for the past fifteen years. In other words, Trump's muscular foreign policy, which prioritizes American interests first, will enervate one of the key tools that has benefited the United States for many years and will undermine the country's ability to deter, contain, or fight terrorism in the world.

What is curious about the deleterious effect of the Trump phenomenon is that he might increase terrorism simply through politics and not through military action alone. This is the opposite problem that plagued President Bush during the Iraq War, where people argued that the invasion made it more likely the United States would be attacked while he simultaneously tried making a distinction between Islam and terrorism. As it stands right now, at a minimum, Trump has four years to change things structurally, but there are other centrifugal forces at play that can limit him. Domestically, the American foreign policy bureaucracy tends to be slow moving and hard to alter, unless there is major agreement with Congress and if the American judiciary finds his actions constitutional. Whether the Republican-led Congress will rubber-stamp Trump's proposed cuts to foreign aid or his policies stand up to judicial scrutiny is uncertain. Early indicators suggest this might not be the case, with early polls from his presidency showing high levels of disapproval, affecting the willingness of Republicans to bandwagon with him if it might cost them reelection. The judiciary seems to be resistant to Trump's more extreme policies as well, and there is increasing distrust by the institution as a whole after his numerous attacks against judges during his election and after he assumed the presidency.

Western Europe also seems resistant to Trump's policies. After Geert Wilders's loss in the Dutch parliamentary elections of March 2017, it is evident that there is a limited appeal to right-wing anti-EU populism that favors Trump. Afterward, Europe endured its biggest test during the French elections of April/May 2017. Again, the anti-populist forces won out, and Marine Le Pen saw herself losing the elections. While this victory is powerful, it should give the public cause of concern that around one-third of the French electorate cast its vote to Le Pen, suggesting her ideas have purchase in large portions of French society. The next big test was Germany. Angela Merkel soundly won reelection, but the AfD, a Eurosceptic far-right party, for the first time in its history won seats in the German parliament after receiving more than 12 percent of the vote. If these countries stave off extremist challenges and maintain a moderate path forward, then the core countries of the EU (Germany, Italy, France, Spain, among others) can limit the contagion of Trump's policies and rhetoric. Some countries in central and eastern Europe, such as Hungary, Poland, and the Czech Republic, are a different matter entirely. They have been part of the recent populist wave surging across Europe, but they do not wield much influence in the EU.

In summary, trying to predict the future of terrorism under Trump is difficult beyond stating that it carries the potential to make things easier for extremists to thrive. Unless there is some moderation in his policies, all proposals just seem to increase the probability that people will radicalize and attack. None of this is deterministic, of course, but it does change the perceived possibilities for would-be terrorists everywhere. Furthermore, the terrorist threat will continue unless his government finds a solution for ending the conflict in Syria, which seems to be the main driver for terrorism outside of the Middle East currently. Until then, what is most likely to happen is a continuation, and perhaps an increase, in terrorism and not a decline or end for the phenomenon.

ACKNOWLEDGMENTS

My section in this book was written under difficult conditions not unlike those facing Friedrich Schiller (if one is permitted for a moment to prepare great things with small) when he was working on *Wilhelm Tell* and *Demetrius*, which he never finished.

I would like particularly to thank my dear friend Bruce Hoffman, without whose continued encouragement this final piece would not have been possible. A work such as this could not have been completed without the contributions of several others, including Christopher Wall, my coauthor. Nicholas Vincent and Jordan Vincent both typed as I dictated, located authoritative sources, and assisted in the organization, composition, and structure of this work. Hijab Shah and my friend Heba El-Shazli helped translate Arabic passages into English and put them into their proper context. Irena Lasota and Jordan Vincent provided insightful feedback and reviewed the final manuscript. But also the following were of great help: Lauren Clemens, Jonathan Challgren, Sam Miner, Marissa Papatola, Melissa Goodall, Benjamin Aziza, Gladys Kamau, Chiara De Cuia, and Antonia Ward.

I know that not all of them agreed with every word of mine, but they still helped me, and I greatly benefited.

—WALTER LAQUEUR

For me, being able to contribute to this project has been one of the greatest honors of my life, and I want to thank Walter for giving me this opportunity. Over the years since I have been working with him, Walter and his wife, Susi, have shown me nothing but support and love. I would also like to thank my two mentors, Bruce Hoffman and Fernando Reinares, for their guidance, instruction, and friendship and for listening to early draft ideas for this project. I have learned so much from the two of them that the parts of this work that succeed I owe to their intellectual guidance. I'd also like to give a special thanks to our literary agent, Joe Spieler, for his vote of confidence in my ability and for helping me shepherd this project. Finally, I would like to thank all my close friends and family who provided emotional and intellectual support when I found myself lost in writing. Much of this was written during a period of duress and stress, and without your willingness to listen to me speak at length, I know I would not have finished this work.

—CHRISTOPHER WALL

INDEX